VICTOR

Breaking Free from a Victim-Based Society

JOHN H. HOVIS

© 2015 John H. Hovis
All rights reserved. No part of this book may be reproduced or transmitted in any form or by any information storage and retrieval system, without permission in writing from the publisher. Exceptions are made for brief excerpts used in published reviews. For permission requests, write or email to:

John H. Hovis
1917 Palomar Oaks Way, Suite 130
Carlsbad, CA 92008
johnhovis@victorliving.com

ISBN 978-0-9963230-0-0

Some names and identifying details have been change to protect the privacy of individuals.

All scriptures marked (NIV) are taken from the Holy Bible, New International Version®, NIV®. Copyright © 1973, 1978, 1984, 2011 by Biblica, Inc.™ and are used with permission of Zondervan. All rights reserved worldwide. www.zondervan.com The "NIV" and "New International Version" are trademarks registered in the United States Patent and Trademark Office by Biblica, Inc.™

All scriptures marked (THE MESSAGE) are quotations from THE MESSAGE. Copyright © Eugene H. Peterson 1993, 1994, 1995, 1996, 2000, 2001, 2002. Used with permission of Tyndale House Publishers, Inc.

All scriptures marked (NKJV) are taken from the New King James Version®. Copyright © 1982 by Thomas Nelson. Used with permission. All rights reserved.

All scriptures marked (NLT) are taken from The Holy Bible, New Living Translation Copyright © 1996, 2004, 2007, 2013 by Tyndale House Foundation. Used with permission of Tyndale House Publishers Inc. All rights reserved.

All scriptures marked (NASB) are taken from the New American Standard Bible, Copyright © 1960, 1962, 1963, 1968, 1971, 1972, 1973, 1975, 1977, 1995 by The Lockman Foundation. Used with permission. (www.Lockman.org)

Cover photograph by Jesslan Urquhart of Jesslan Lee Photography (jesslanleephotography.com). This image may not be reproduced or transmitted in any form or by any means without permission in writing from Jesslan Urquhart and John H. Hovis. For permissions, contact Jesslan at jesslan@jesslanleephotography.com.

Cover design by Janelle Hiroshige. No part of the cover can be reproduced or transmitted in any form or by any means without permission in writing from John H. Hovis. To contact Janelle email her at janelle.hiroshige@gmail.com.

Certain graphic embellishments contained within were produced by Lauren Thompson using the font Nymphont. Contact Lauren at nymphont.blogspot.com.

ACKNOWLEDGEMENTS

To My Father in Heaven, how could it be that you would love someone who has been so stuck in victim thinking for so long. Thanks for standing with me as I tried hard for over a half a century to earn the love you freely gave. I only hope the lessons I have learned on this journey are accurately communicated in this book. Thanks for "sitting in the dirt" with me as I wrestled with going your way. It has been such a wonderful journey! I wouldn't trade a single moment of it because you have been there all along. I am a victor because I am your beloved child!

To my wife, Barbara, you will never fully know what it has meant to have you as my wife. When I couldn't see God's presence, you were always there. Your support and belief in me has been unwavering and such a solid place for me to stand when things got rocky. Having you by my side proves to me that God is alive and well in our lives. Thank you for your love for all these years. I can't wait to see where our love takes us in the future.

To our children, Jesslan & Jay, thank you for bearing with me when victim thinking drove me to say and do things that might make you doubt the amazing people you are. Jesslan, you have always been and will always be a light in our lives. Your creativity and talents continue to amaze your mother and me. You have an amazing future ahead of you. Keep seeking God and following your heart. Jay, your Mom and I have always known you would do big things. Your drive and determination combined with the talents you have and are developing will pay off in ways that will astound us all. I am blessed to call you my children and value the friendship that has come as you both have set off on your adult lives.

Thank you, Manna Ko for the loving encouragement and the help in moving forward on this project. Thank you Shannon Saia (www.selfpublishingdoula.com) for your wonderful editing assistance and for being the doula that helped birth this book. Thanks to all those with whom I have had the chance to meet and "do life with" over the years. Our conversations are the backbone of all that is within.

I also want to thank my parents, Kenneth H. Hovis and Marrianne Garraffa. Your belief in your children is what has given Gregg and me such a powerful start in life. Thanks for believing in the victors we are in Christ. On a side note Mom, can you believe after all those pain staking and tear filled nights of writing papers in school that I would ever write a book? Miracles do happen!

Finally I want to thank you, the reader of this book. I hope you find the information you need to root out any victim thinking that might be in your life and in the lives of the people that are in your spheres of influence. Life is too short not to live it as the victors we were made to be. Thanks for being a part of that message so completely in my life.

Sincerely,

John H. Hovis

TABLE OF CONTENTS

PREFACE	i
Deciding to Take the Journey from Victim to Victor	
INTRODUCTION	1
Waking Up to a Victim-Based Society	
CHAPTER ONE	9
Role vs. Relationship	
CHAPTER TWO	26
The Role of the Church	
CHAPTER THREE	50
Our Standing with God	
CHAPTER FOUR	72
Religion vs. Relationship	
CHAPTER FIVE	93
Provision and Victimhood	
CHAPTER SIX	110
Prosperity and Victimhood	
CHAPTER SEVEN	135
Generosity	
CHAPTER EIGHT	156
When Bad Things Happen to Good People	
CHAPTER NINE	175
Brokenness	

CHAPTER TEN	196
Get To vs. Have To	
CHAPTER ELEVEN	214
Destiny	
CHAPTER TWELVE	228
Offense	
CHAPTER THIRTEEN	252
Bringing It All Together	
ABOUT THE AUTHOR	265
ADDITIONAL RESOURCES	267

PREFACE

Deciding to Take the Journey from Victim to Victor

Victim to Victor—sounds like another motivational message packaged into a book to help the "great unwashed" find their way from being in the place they are to the place they want to be. If you picked this book up because you need a pep talk or you want someone to tell you what to do to find success in your life, you have the wrong resource.

This book is about something more profound; something more lasting than just getting your attitude right so you are able to put yourself in the best position to gain happiness, or success, or more of the temporary things our culture seems to settle for these days.

For most of my life I have bought into the world of pep talks and quick answers to the questions about how to achieve success in my life. I've listened to the best of the motivational speakers. I have read the classic self help books. I have put into practice the goal setting and life planning techniques preached from pulpits secular and non-secular alike. I'm not saying these resources are of no use; within the right context they can be life-altering. The problem is trying to figure out

PREFACE

that context so these tools can be just that: tools to help me achieve an end.

But what is that end? What is the context of my life at *this* moment that defines how I will view the next one? If I can grapple with these important questions from the standpoint of a victor rather than a victim I have a better chance of successfully facing the many challenges that make me feel like I will never achieve my destiny.

As a follower of Jesus Christ, I have found that there is a fantastic industry of self-help books catering to Christian living. Just like their secular versions, these works are wonderful tools if taken in the right context. In fact, this book is the result of something I learned from one of these Christian self-help books—journaling.

I put this book together as a project to organize a bunch of what I thought were random thoughts that I had been journaling over the past several years. Over and over again, I kept seeing things in my life that were contrasts: good vs. evil, up vs. down, left vs. right. You'll see that contrast reflected in some of the chapter titles of this book.

One day it occurred to me to explore the contrast of victim vs. victor. In doing so, I found that many of the contrasts I had been thinking about were merely subsets of this overarching concept, what you might call the ultimate contrast. In other words, I saw that whether I lived my life as a victor or as a victim was predicated upon my understanding and application of a particular way of thinking about life. Let me give you an example.

I have always been taught that success would come my way with enough diligence and effort. The words of my mother still ring in my head today: "You can do anything you want if you put your mind to it." Through school and sports I had been trained that hard work does not go unrewarded, and I've experienced the reality of those rewards over and over again as a result of my sometimes self-sacrificing efforts.

Then one day something weird happened; something that really hadn't happened to me to such a great level in the past. All the hard work I had put into a particular project led to complete and dismal failure. In fact, I had worked so hard on this one particular project that

I became very ill; too ill to work for a pretty significant period of time. The foundational paradigm in my life which said that hard work equals success was shaken to the core.

Then failure happened again... and again... and again. I was victimized by the entire process. It was as though all those role models who had told me that hard work led to success had lied to me. What did they have against me to have so perversely misled me? Why me?

Without even knowing it, I was viewing life through the lens of being a victim. Doubt crept in. Over the years, this doubt was reinforced by other failures that seemed to debunk all the powerful and real lessons I had been taught in my life; lessons that had served me so well in the past.

Life wasn't all bad. I had successes after that string of failures, but they didn't seem as sweet. They weren't enough for me to be able to throw off the feeling that I would always be a victim of this or of that in the years to come.

Looking back from a different vantage point, I now see what I did. I was so intent on proving that I was a victor that I misused a valid concept (hard work equals success) in ways that made me believe I would always be a victim. I had tied success with being a victor so completely that when success didn't happen I couldn't see how I could ever live the life I thought a victor was supposed to live.

It wasn't that someone had victimized me by misleading me in a particular direction. It was that I just didn't believe I was a victor. I couldn't believe that I could be loved or accepted unless all my hard work turned into the success I was looking for, and if I wasn't a victor then I had to be a victim. I began believing I was a victim of my loved ones, a victim of life, a victim of the Church and, ultimately, a victim of God Himself.

Oh, yes—I should mention that this book is filled with a bunch of God stuff. If that offends you, I'm sorry. I have gotten to a point in my life where I believe I'm a victor, if for no other reason than because God loves me. All the other proofs of my being a victor that I have strived for over the years have failed me in one way or another. I'm starting to really believe that worldly proofs as to whether or not I am a victor will always let me down. They will never be enough to rid me of that nagging feeling that I will never measure up. If there is a God and that God is all-knowing and loves unconditionally, then shouldn't His love for me be proof enough that I measure up and that I am a victor?

Not only will you see a lot of God stuff mentioned in this book, but the "J" word is also going to be used over and over again; that's right—Jesus—one of the most controversial words in any language.

So, why Jesus? Why not Buddha, or Allah, or the God in Me? Simply stated, Jesus represents a religion that has the least amount of performance-based requirements to be acceptable to the Higher Being that that religion worships. All other religions require me to do things, in ever increasing ways, in order to be set right with my God. Christianity is the only religion where God came for me rather than waiting on me to get my life shaped up enough so that I could come to Him.

I have found that the concept of performance is at the root of whether I feel like a victim or a victor. If I perform up to the standards I have set for myself or that others have set for me, I feel like a victor. Fail to perform up to those ever-elusive standards, and I'm a victim. I have seen this same pattern repeated in religion after religion. I just can't stand being in a religion where performance makes a difference as to whether or not I'm a victor. Christianity, at its core, is the only religion I see that isn't performance-based and offers the least chance for me to fall into victim thinking with my God.

I am a victor in Jesus Christ. I didn't do anything to deserve His salvation. I can never do anything to repay Him. That's unconditional love. Jesus didn't do what He did for me in return for anything He could ever get from me. He did it just because of His love for the Father and the Father's love for His creation. Other religions require me to live up to some code and I will ultimately fail to do so. That makes me feel like a victim and causes me to take on a victim persona.

Following Jesus means that even though I will fail at times, I'm still a victor—there is no need for me to take on the lifestyle of a victim, no matter how bad life's circumstances may be.

Don't get me wrong; the Christian Church has messed up this concept of being a victor by adding do's and don'ts as much as any other religion in the world. Don't confuse the misapplied good intentions of the Christian Church with a relationship with Jesus Himself. I am a victor because of what Jesus did for me. There is nothing I need to do to be a victor other than to love the Father like Jesus does.

If you are not a believer in this Jesus thing, I hope you will still read on because, if nothing else, you might get a glimpse as to why the Church appears to be so screwed up at times. The Church has lived way too long in the shadow of victimhood that comes from requiring followers to live up to some level of performance. In that regard we are no different than the rest of the world, trying to DO in order to BE what we all long to be: loved, accepted, valued and cherished, now and forevermore.

I believe that performance is one of the main reasons why the Christian Church has turned off so many people over the centuries. Our hypocritical ways of dealing with the same stuff that those outside the Church deal with has made us ineffective and lacking in power when it comes to our knowledge of Jesus Christ. Churchgoers are just as prone to take on the damaging identity of a victim as non-Churchgoers. We are supposed to live like victors in Christ. Our misguided ways of dealing with this dichotomy (a victim who is supposed to be a victor) comes off in hypocritical and relationship-destroying ways. This is hurtful, and we have made victims of many people outside the Church. For that, I'm truly sorry.

I'm a living testament that eyes can be opened. I am an example of the fact that I can look like a victim but live like a victor. What I'm hoping is that I can help followers of Jesus Christ live the life of a victor no matter what their life looks like. Why? In hopes of letting the world see the true passion of the God I believe in. A passion that wants to unleash unlimited power into a dark world so that we can all live in freedom. Freedom from the pain of rejection. Freedom from the lasting sting of feeling worthless. Freedom from thinking that we are unlovable.

Let me make a promise to believers and nonbelievers alike. First for the nonbeliever: I'm not going to try and sell you on Christianity. Jesus isn't a product. This book isn't about conversion; it is about a conversation. Yes, there will be a lot of talk about God and Jesus. It is part of my journey so it is part of this book. What I promise you, the nonbeliever, is an honest expression of the ways I have taken bedrock principles, like hard work equals success, and twisted them in ways that have failed me and might be failing you as well. I think you might relate to those thoughts and might want to do as I have done, and investigate ways of living as a victor even when life circumstances seem to do a better job of making you feel like a victim. God is part of that picture for me. If it isn't for you, thanks for bearing with me as I describe my journey in this book.

For the believer, I promise this book will challenge you to the core. I believe that we inside the Church have been living a lie for way too long. We have used the things of God for our own well-being and haven't lived up to the ideals we have set for ourselves, let alone those we think God has set for us. We have caused enough damage in this world by trading our identities for something we are not. It is time we live life as victors, not victims. It is time to wake up to the fact that those principles that we have misconstrued as formulas that might lead us to a comfortable life just don't work the way we want them to, and this makes us feel like victims. No matter how much of a victor face we put on, the world smells the victim in us. It's time to be free of that stench and let the sweet fragrance of Jesus Christ be what attracts the world to God again.

So are you ready? It's time to move from victim to victor.

INTRODUCTION

Waking Up to a Victim-Based Society

We are facing an epidemic in our society. Everywhere you turn, there are victims. Victims of discrimination, victims of violence, victims of crime, victims of divorce, victims of this and victims of that. Am I out of touch, or does it seem like the percentage of the population today that can relate to being a victim is much higher than it was five or six decades ago? If so, are there really more bad things happening now than there were during the lives of our grandfathers and great-grandfathers? Knowing history as I do, I can tell you, I don't think so!

I'm not trying to be callous with this observation. I don't think we have evolved into a world of wimps or sissies. The reality is that this world is a hard place. Bad, and I mean really bad things happen to people every moment.

Take those three women in Cleveland who were held prisoner for over a decade. They were the victims of an evil man bent on having his own way no matter what the cost. And what about the families of the children killed in the various school shootings that have happened over the years? They were victims of deranged individuals who held such a poor belief in the sanctity of life that murdering innocent children didn't even seem to faze them. Then there's the loved ones of those people who showed up for work one day at the World Trade

Center Buildings in New York. They were victims of a senseless belief that those who don't hold to a particular view of God are not worthy of life.

I'm not in any way saying that it is bad to be called a victim when bad things happen to us. This book is not a slam against those who have faced terrible circumstances and found a way to survive. Those people are to be surrounded by society and their recovery is to be looked at as examples for us all to follow. The characteristic traits of people who get knocked down and somehow pull themselves back up again are the kinds of traits we need to be promoting. But what I am saying is that it appears to me that our society has shifted to a point where being a victim is seen as something admirable; something with perks and advantages; something that the mainstream wants to have without having to go through the terror of those women in Cleveland, or the pain of those parents of dead school children, or the horror that families felt as they saw those buildings crumble down on their loved ones on that clear, crisp September day in 2001.

No, being a victim hasn't changed over the decades. Bad things have happened to people throughout the ages and will continue to happen until the final chapter closes. There will always be victims of evil and demented thinking and misrepresentations of good in this world. What I feel is different about victimhood in today's society is that our perspective on what a victim is has shifted radically to celebrate the belief that we all are victims in one way or another.

THE DANGER OF VICTIM THINKING

There are some serious consequences to adopting the thinking that we all are victims. First of all, we devalue those who have been truly victimized by the evil in this world. If everyone is a victim of something then we are saying that those women who were traumatized for ten years in Cleveland are no more worthy of assistance, compassion and restoration than someone who has gotten a splinter from having an improperly sanded door installed in their new house. That's totally unacceptable, and leads to a further devaluing of life such that more and more Cleveland-type incidents might just be the result.

The second consequence to adopting an approach of universal victimhood in society is the tremendous assault to our psyche that living the life of a victim can create. This point is highlighted by the fact that there is actually a psychological condition that is being studied called Victim Syndrome[1].

Victim Syndrome can manifest itself in the thought (either perceived or real) that bad things always happen. When those feelings are left unchecked, the victims of Victim Syndrome can actually become victimizers themselves. In extreme cases, they might be guilty of unleashing anger and hurt upon others in their circles so as to help mask the feeling of loss of control caused by the bad things that happened in their own lives. All this is a result of the belief that they will ALWAYS be victims. Victimhood has become their very identity. This is incredibly bad for the individual and for society as a whole.

That's what I see is different about the world we live in today. Victims are everywhere. Not just the victims of serious actions, but people who seek reconciliation and restoration for even the most minor of offenses. We are on the verge of allowing victimhood to define who we are, and I believe this limits us in some powerful and significant ways that we will touch on later in this book.

Why is this happening? I have a couple of suggestions as to what has fueled this change in society.

First of all, freedom plays a big role in victimization becoming so universal. We are fortunate to live in a free society where choices abound. I believe that this freedom paves the way for an interesting thing to happen. As we begin to take the cost of our freedoms for granted, any perceived or actual limitations to what we want to do are seen as a personal assault resulting in victimhood. Here's an example.

---

[1] "Are You A Victim to Victim Syndrome?" a working paper by Manfred F.R. Kets de Vries http://www.insead.edu/facultyresearch/research/doc.cfm?did=50114?

Here in the San Diego area, a middle-aged man abducted a 16-year-old girl, killing her mother and brother. There was an Amber Alert issued as a result of this abduction. An Amber Alert is a state-wide broadcast of the details of the perpetrator when a minor is involved, in hopes the public can help resolve the situation as quickly as possible. Unfortunately, Amber Alerts happen way too frequently in our state. What was different this time was that the Amber Alert went out over the cell phone system in addition to other methods. I remember getting the bejeezus scared out of me when that alert came across my phone.

Since this was the first time an Amber Alert had been issued across the cell network I think they had some issues with how many times the alert went out and when the alert was broadcast. For some, the alert came in the middle of the night. I know it must have been a rude awakening for those whose phone made that terrible and frightening sound at one a.m.

Where this story really relates to what I'm talking about is the fact that there was an incredible buzz on social media the next day about how bad that alert was. In many cases, people actually felt they were victimized by the "powers that be" for having been awakened from their comfortable sleep. I understand the angst of being suddenly awakened by a god-awful noise coming from your phone, but victimized? Really? Can you, for a moment, compare your momentary discomfort of being jolted from your bed to that of a 16-year-old girl losing her mother and brother then being kidnapped and abused?

That's the beauty and the danger of freedom: it can be taken for granted. With freedom comes ease. With ease comes complacency. With complacency comes the feeling that anything that challenges that ease is an assault and that creates victims. That's the kind of victim I'm talking about in this book.

So, the incredibly easy freedom we experience in our lives is one reason for the universal victimization of our society today. I believe another is the reality that we have become and are becoming more and more of an instant-gratification-driven, self-centered society.

Did you know there is actually a disorder that describes this situation as well? NPD, Narcissistic Personality Disorder "is a disorder in which people have an inflated sense of their own importance and a deep need for admiration."[2]

Universal victimization isn't happening because we all have NPD. NPD is another example of the extreme of what can happen when we choose to let victimization become a significant part of our identity. Universal victimization is happening more and more because of the reality that we are becoming too comfortable with our own importance and stressing too greatly the need for being valued through admiration.

Those who suffer from NPD are ripe for universal victimization. How? Say, do, or project anything that can possibly be misconstrued as deflating the NPD sufferer's self-importance, or that in any way diminishes their admiration and voila: instant victim. In that sense, we all suffer from NPD to one degree or another. How do you feel if someone devalues you or you aren't the center of attention? That feeling is natural; but if that natural feeling takes you to a place where you think of yourself as being victimized over trivial matters, then you've crossed a line into victim thinking. Continue to cross this line over and over again and victimhood becomes entrenched in your identity.

Just look at how we are training the next generation of NPD sufferers. You don't have to go any further than children's sports to see what is happening. A professor of psychology at San Diego State University and co-author of the book *The Narcissism Epidemic: Living in the Age of Entitlement*, Jean Twenge, says it this way: "The concept of 'everyone is a winner' has become so commonplace these days that it's almost expected. You show up, you do terrible, you sit on the bench,

---

[2] "Is Today's Society Too Self Centered?" article on newstimes.com
http://www.newstimes.com/news/article/Is-today-s-society-too-self-centered-2450413.php
Monday January 12, 2009, Sandra Diamond Fox.

and everyone's trophy is the same size. No one keeps score, no one corrects mistakes..." [3]

There can't be any winners so as to make sure no one feels like a loser. No one really wants to make another person feel like a loser. What people fail to realize is that no one can make me feel like anything; I have to choose to feel that way. If I lost, I'm not a loser—I simply lost. It is very unlikely that I was a victim of poor judging or unfair circumstances, it might just be the simple fact that someone was better than me. That doesn't make me a loser, it makes me human. There will always be someone better than me in some regard, that's just the odds when living in a society with billions and billions of sample points called people.

AN ALGEBRA "LESSON"

I once was tutoring a friend's high school student in algebra. He had some learning disabilities that made attention to detail an issue. With algebra, detail is sometimes very necessary. He and I spent four or so hours one day reviewing the chapters that he had for an upcoming test. We agreed on some study techniques he might want to adopt and broke down the information covered into manageable, bite-sized pieces that he could tackle. Then we practiced problems using the techniques we discussed.

I left him with the direction to do what we had just done over and over again for each problem type for the next two days. I told him this would take time, time he had failed to invest earlier. He was going to have to sacrifice significant time now in order to get a decent grade on his upcoming text.

A week or so later I called to see how he did on his test. He got a D! Ouch. Maybe he was the victim of a bad math tutor? Though I

---

[3] "Is Today's Society Too Self Centered?" article on newstimes.com
http://www.newstimes.com/news/article/Is-today-s-society-too-self-centered-2450413.php
Monday January 12, 2009, Sandra Diamond Fox

may not be an expert in teaching algebra, I don't think this was the case.

When I talked to the boy's parents, they told me how stupid their son felt. Worse than that, he was beginning to think he was just a hopeless, stupid student. Full-blown victimization was setting in fast. I asked the parents if we could get together again so that I could talk to the boy. They agreed.

A couple of days later I asked him, "What happened?" He said, "I blew it. I just froze and couldn't finish the test." (A common issue I have seen with students with this kind of learning disability). I asked him, "How do you feel?" With a brave sincerity that you don't always see in teenage boys, he said, "I feel so stupid. I just can't get this stuff and I don't think I ever will."

I asked him one more question. "Did you work the techniques we talked about for each of the sections you had to study?" In other words, did you invest the time you needed to in order to get the information into your brain? His answer: "No."

At that point, I just smiled. I knew we were at a turning point. I said to this young man, "You are right to feel stupid. It was stupid of you not to do what we discussed." I think this caught him a little off guard. But I wasn't in the mood to hand out a ribbon to this young man for coming in last.

I went on to say, "Feeling stupid isn't necessarily a bad thing. What is bad is if we believe we are stupid. It was stupid of you to not do what we did in practice. Simply doing, over and over again, what we practiced is how you learn. You have to repeat what you know works for you in order to get this stuff. But if you think your identity is that of a stupid person simply because you did something stupid you are choosing to believe a lie. Now, if you continue to do that same stupid thing over and over again, then you run the risk of taking on the identity of a stupid person." He really took hold of that concept. On his next test he earned a B!

What I do does not define my identity. I'm not stupid because I did one stupid thing. I'm not a loser because I lost a race. I am stupid if I think I can choose to do nothing and get a good grade. I am a loser if I think I can just show up and compete with athletes who have trained more fully than I chose to do. I can always improve on my performance in anything I choose to if I'm willing to put in the work required to make a difference.

Universal victimization is happening because we have an incredible, easy freedom that enables us to take that freedom for granted and focus on ourselves in ways that make us feel that we are victims at every turn in the road. Universal victimization is making it possible for the characteristics of a victim to be incorporated into the very makeup of who we are. Not only is that bad for the individual, it is devastating to society.

Oh, but there's another way! There is the identity of a victor. Making the characteristics of a victor part of our identity is dependent on one thing: choice.

The fact is that we will always face challenges in this life—serious and deeply hurtful challenges that will victimize us in one way or another. What I'm presenting in this book is the possibility of being able to walk as a victor even when the problems that work to crush us make us look like victims every step of the way.

How do we get to this point? I believe that the first step is knowing who we are. Identity is the key to living a life of victory when the world is trying to get us to settle for being victims.

CHAPTER ONE

Role vs. Identity

Want to do something interesting and kind of fun? Walk up to someone and, out of the blue, ask them, "Who are you?" I guarantee their brain will be spinning.

This is such a challenging question for us all. Why? I believe it is because we really don't know who we are. Identity is such a big problem for us all in this world.

You may be ready to argue with me at this point. Maybe you are very secure with who you are right now. Bear with me and let me challenge your thinking for a moment.

You see, for the vast majority of us, we have chosen to link our identity to the things we do, the roles that we play. That's not necessarily a bad strategy. But what happens when our ability to live out a particularly key role with which we have been defining our identity goes in a direction that we didn't expect? That's when victim thinking can really take hold.

Let me give you a personal example. If you had asked me 15 to 20 years ago who I was, I would have answered that question by listing the three key roles in my life: I am a businessman, I am a husband, and I am a father. Just like you, there are many other roles that help to define what I thought was my identity at that time. But these three particular roles accurately described the most important characteristics of what I thought defined me not too long ago. Then trouble began.

The business I was starting just couldn't get any traction. Then failure came. Health issues quickly followed. I was stuck in a place of limbo. My wife's business supported us just fine, so our family really didn't have any financial worries. I was in a place, however, where I felt helpless to contribute to our family's finances, a "victim" to the cruel world in which we all have to compete.

This put me in a position where I started to doubt my effectiveness as a husband. Troubling thoughts started to creep into my subconscious. Thoughts like, "If I can't help provide for my family, what good am I to my wife?" Having been the "victim" of a divorce myself (my parents split up when I was 20 or so), I began to consider the possibility that my wife might, one day, want to leave me. Why? In my head I reasoned that if I wasn't living up to my identity as a businessman, how could I possibly live up to that other part of my identity as a husband? By my way of thinking, she would eventually get disillusioned and/or disappointed with me, and begin to wonder who this man was sleeping next to her. We would grow apart and BOOM—divorce.

Then the snowball really started rolling. Words in my head continued to condemn me. If I couldn't be of use to my wife, how could I ever expect to know how to father the two fantastic children with whom I had been blessed? I started to see shortfalls in the way I coached my children in sports, in how I helped them with homework, in how I passed on the lessons of life I had learned growing up. When they didn't live up to what I thought they should be doing, it reflected on my identity and I reacted in ways that were ultimately damaging to their little souls.

I no longer saw myself as a competent businessman, a capable husband or an effective father. The question, "Who Am I?" started to be the absolute worst question I could ever consider. My roles were failing me and my identity just wasn't something I could put my finger on. I felt lost. How could I possibly go on without knowing who I was? I was sinking into the identity of a victim and I couldn't find my way out.

That's the danger of allowing the roles we play to define our identity. Roles always change. We will find success in the roles we play and we will find failure as well. Roles should not define our identity. Show me someone whose identity is defined by what they do and I will show you someone who is now or soon will be stuck in victim thinking.

So, this begs the question: Who am I? Who are you? This is where the God stuff really kicks in for me.

The reality is that no matter what role we play, no matter how big that role is, no matter the lasting impact that role might have in this world, the roles that we look to for identity are temporary. My role as a businessman will end when I die; so will my role as a husband, a father and any of the other thousands of roles that I have considered in the past to shape my identity. You don't have to believe in a God to realize this.

This thought leaves me with an empty feeling inside that is best described by the question, "Is this (my roles) all that there is to my identity?" In other words, how can the tasks that I take on in life, which will end with my last breath, ever be enough to define the essence of who I am? That's where belief in a God becomes important to me.

I happen to believe that there is more to us than what we do in this life. A human being is way too complex a piece of machinery to just trudge through 85 or so years here on this rock and, poof, that's it.

Haven't you ever sensed deep down that you were made for something big—I mean really BIG!? I know that thought has been tempered by the naysayers in your life and by the horrible things that have happened to you over the years. But if you were to get quiet and listen, can't you still hear the faint strains of a voice that sounds remarkably like yours saying, "You matter!", or "You're better than this circumstance!", or "There has to be more than this!" I believe that voice you hear is not yours, but the voice of God Himself.

ROLE VS. IDENTITY

YOU ARE GOD'S CHILD

I have come to a place in my life where the roles I play just don't do it any more when it comes to defining my identity. I need something more. I need something that will last way past when I'm gone. For me, the only place that I have found an answer to that incredibly difficult question, "Who am I?" is the Bible.

1 John 3:1 says this:

> See how very much our Father loves us, for he calls us his children, and that is what we are! (NLT)

What's my identity? I am a child of God's. That's it. Nothing more, nothing less. I'm a beloved child of the Creator of all that we see, know and enjoy. Now, that's an identity! Best of all, that identity never ends. When this life is over I'm still His child. All the roles I play here on earth will end, but my identity as God's child never does. As simple as this concept is, it's an identity that carries with it something that all the earthly roles I might play will never have – longevity.

Too simple an explanation for you? I understand, but let the thought of being God's child roll around in your head a bit. Think what it really means to be a child of the King's. Isn't there the potential for unlimited power available to you? Aren't you highly esteemed, no matter how badly you mess things up, just because you are the King's child? Don't you think that there is a plan for you since you are His son or daughter? There are perks to being God's child. Benefits that we sometimes don't see or fully appreciate here on this side of eternity. Oh, if we could live a life with the mindset that we are a child of the King's!

I once was at a men's church retreat up in the mountains of Southern California. It was a Saturday morning and a few hundred men were gathered for a fantastic breakfast in the cool, crisp mountain air. Somehow food just tastes better in the mountains, and this morning was no exception.

As I was clearing my dishes, I ran into one of the kitchen staff, a man named Moses. Moses was a beautiful black man with a beaming smile that just drew you into him. He exuded a confidence that was something amazing to behold. I said to him, "Moses, thank you for a fantastic breakfast. You guys do such a wonderful job taking care of us." He beamed that amazing smile that seemed to bathe me in God's Love and said words I will never forget. Moses boomed out, "Nothing but the best for a son of the King!" That was the last I ever saw of Moses, but those words still bring me to a place of peace and rest no matter what my circumstance.

"Nothing but the best." Why? Because I am God's son. Moses didn't say "nothing but the best" because I'm a good businessman, husband or father. He also didn't say "nothing but the best" because I'm a "good" son of God's. He had no idea who I was in light of the roles I played or how well I thought I was living out being God's adopted child. He simply knew my identity – God's child – and because of that he was dedicated to do his best so that I could understand how much God's love is for me! Thank you Moses. You may never know what those words have meant to me.

It has been a lot of years since that chance encounter with Moses. I am finally beginning to believe that my identity is secure as God's child and now want to live that fact out to the fullest. Those words have changed my life. I'm hoping you begin to see how they can change your life as well.

Moses is a good example of why roles do a lousy job of defining who we are. From a role standpoint, Moses wasn't much to behold. A simple dishwasher in a tucked-away mountain retreat. Not much to brag about from the world's standpoint. Roles do us such disservice when it comes to identity. If roles are all Moses had, he might see himself a complete and utter failure, hopeless of ever being more than what society and circumstances had cast him into.

Unfortunately, most of the world sees Moses that way, as not much to behold. In fact, those of us who have a good handle on identity because the roles we look to for identity are working well for us at this moment might overlook Moses (on our best day) and even put him down (on our worst). How many Moses' have I discounted, discouraged and even denigrated because I didn't see their worth due to the lowly roles they were living out at that time in their lives? Roles work to put us in a place where we can think too highly of ourselves. Human nature is such that when we do this it is so easy to step over and even step on the Moses' of the world. Take a look at what Habakkuk says in The Bible:

> *Look at that man, bloated by self-importance— full of himself but soul-empty. But the person in right standing before God through loyal and steady believing is fully alive, really alive. Habakkuk 2:4* (THE MESSAGE)

"Bloated by self-importance... soul empty..." Roles, on their own, do that to us. When our roles are working well, we can't help but think more highly of ourselves than is good for us. The better our lives the more bloated we may become. We can begin to think that we are actually as good as others think we are. Know what makes a balloon big? Nothing but air. So it is with the soul of a bloated believer – filled with air, no substance, no foundation, dead in all the important ways.

Look at the opposite way to live spelled out in Habakkuk: "...the person in right standing before God...is fully alive, really alive."

That's what drew me into Moses. It wasn't just his smile. It was what his smile was conveying. He was alive, fully alive, like it says in Habakkuk. The confidence I saw in him wasn't that he was the best darn dishwasher in the world; it was that he was right before God. I am more and more confident that "right before God" means that we know who we are in His eyes. Life comes to us when we put down our roles and live "loyal and steady believing" that we are a child of the King's.

THE "ROLE" OF IDENTITY

So, does that mean that roles aren't important in our life? That couldn't be further from the truth. Roles play a critical "role" in our life. Here's a crucial statement I want you to ponder:

> The roles you play work to shape how your identity
> as God's child is used by God to fulfill the destiny
> that is the plan He has for you in this life.

Roles don't define our identity. Roles are empowered by our identity. Did you get that? Roles are *empowered* by our identity. Our identity is supposed to be the force behind any of the goodness, success or fulfillment we may achieve in living out our roles. Boy have I ever gotten that wrong many times in my life. How about you?

Humans seem to do things exactly opposite of the way God does them. We think that if we want to lead we have to take charge. God says to lead you need to follow, or serve (Matthew 20:25-28). We think that if we want to be first we have to do more and more to stay in front. God says to be first you will be last (Mark 10:44). We tend to do things to try and discover who we are. God wants us to live out who we are so that our doing will be effective in fulfilling His plan (1 Peter 2:9).

God uses our roles, in light of who we are, to fulfill His plan for our lives. That's where our destiny comes from. I can tell you right now I can't find in the Bible where it says God's plan is to make us rich, successful, powerful, influential, and/or comfortable in this life. I pray that those are roles you get to play in this short journey on earth. But if they are not, you are still loved by God and you are still a part of His plan for this world.

God's plan is so much bigger than how nicely our life turns out. His plan is to secure, for all eternity, a relationship with as many souls as possible. We are part of that plan. Our destiny will be seen as complete in as much as we let Him empower the roles we play through our identity as God's child.

I can assure you that my friend Moses, at that men's retreat, didn't grow up with the lofty goal of thinking that one day he would be a dishwasher (not a thing wrong with being a dishwasher, mind you). Don't you know Moses had dreams bigger than what his life turned out to be? So do you and I.

Think of all the twists and turns in Moses' life that led him to the place where his childhood dreams must have become so distant that one day he woke up to being a dishwasher. The reality is that as God's child, Moses' role that day as a dishwasher was empowered in such a way as to profoundly touch my life. Because of that chance encounter, empowered by God's presence, my life has been FOREVER changed! I fully believe this book would never have been possible had Moses not beamed that wonderful smile and infected me with life through those words he said to me. I am so glad that we serve such a personal and powerful God.

THE ROLE OF VICTIM

Earlier I mentioned the danger of allowing victimhood to take over our identity. The more we believe our identity is somehow related to the pains of life that have made us victims the greater the possibility that we, the victims, can become the victimizers. As dangerous as it is for the secular world to allow victimhood to define its identity, it is totally devastating for the Church.

I'm going to go out on a limb here and say something about the Church. I believe the reason the Church feels so ineffective in seeing change in our world today is because we have forgotten who we are. We have allowed society to co-opt our identity in such a way that the Heavenly power available to us has been diminished. Our continued practice of using roles to define who we are has mitigated our ability to tap into the Power of God available to His children. Remember, our identity empowers our roles. But we are stuck still trying to discover who we are by doing, doing, doing.

Just as the misapplication of roles has created an "identity crisis" in the Church, the same can be said for those of us victimized by bad things happening in our lives. The reality is that when bad things happen to us, when we are victimized by this world, it is nothing more than a role we are playing at that time in our lives. I know this sounds callous and short-sighted, but think about that for a moment. Roles are temporary. When we are dead and gone none of the roles we play will be a part of what is to come after death.

It's the same with being a victim. It is temporary. Those women in Cleveland WERE victims of that evil man. They aren't today! I'm not making light of the painful times they have ahead dealing with the horrible physical and mental damage inflicted on them. All victims have a long road to healing. The difference in the success of that healing process is identity – those who allow the role of victim to take over their identity do much worse in the healing process than those who choose to live the life of a victor, when it comes to overcoming the horrors life can throw at them. The fact is that when those women pass on from this life to the next, victimhood will no longer be a part of whatever that new life looks like. Being a victim is a role we play and all roles are temporary.

When those who choose to follow Jesus Christ allow any role to define their identity they end up forfeiting the power God has for them to impact that particular role in their life. For Christians, allowing the role of victim to influence their identity is particularly egregious.

You see, Jesus died to give us the right to be called children of God. That's what the entire Bible is all about. He didn't die to give us a role to play. He didn't die to make me a businessman, or a husband or a father. Neither did He die to make me a victim.

Jesus died to bring us into an eternal relationship with our Heavenly Father. That relationship starts today. He died to make us children of God, and *that* makes us VICTORS. Not victims. Because of the work of Christ we are children of God, and that makes us victors no matter what our circumstances look like.

Christians who have forgotten who they are or worse yet, who have allowed their roles to change their identity, have given up one of the most exciting and effective parts of their relationship with God. They have given up a connection through identity that is the very conduit of God's Power for this world. When we have taken on the role of victim as part of our identity we have, in many ways, forfeited the power of Christ's work in our lives.

I'm in no way saying that we have given up eternal life; that somehow our very salvation is coming into question. I'm saying that the John 10:10 "abundant" or "full life" promise is greatly compromised by our misunderstanding of identity. Christ's death is what makes us victors, not how successful we feel we are in the various roles in our lives. We are victors because of what He did for us, not because our circumstances are working out the way we want them to.

THE POWER OF A NAME

The reality is that the world wants us to forget who we are. Evil in this world has an amazingly effective strategy to help get us off course. It wants to change our names. Did you know that in the Bible your name was a pointer to how your identity as God's child would be seen in the world? For example, Abram's name meant "high father." God changed Abram's name to Abraham meaning "father of a multitude". Having your name changed in the Bible was a sign of a shift in how your identity as God's child would impact the world.

In the Book of Daniel we were introduced to a bunch of teenage boys who found themselves captives to an invading nation. Daniel and his friends Hananiah, Mishael and Azariah were called Sons of Judah. They were part of what was considered the strongest, most healthy, best-looking and well-taught young men in the nation. These four young men were taken back to King Nebuchadnezzar's homeland and treated as spoils of his victory over the nation Israel. The first thing Nebuchadnezzar did was rename Daniel and his friends.

Daniel was now Belteshazzar. Hananiah was now Shadrach. Mishael was now Meshach and Azariah, Abednego. I have read the story of Daniel and his friend's names being changed many times without ever thinking anything about the significance of the changes. But my eyes were opened when my pastor, Aaron Jayne, preached on this subject recently.

Pastor Aaron had us focus on what the names originally meant and what the capturing forces decided these young men would be called. The following table highlights the name change and the corresponding shift in how their roles could be played out through identity.

Original Name	Original Meaning	New Name	New Meaning
Daniel	God is My Judge	Belteshazzar	Bel (Nebuchadnezzar's favorite god) protect the king
Hananiah	God is Gracious	Shadrach	Command of Aku (moon god of Babylon) also tender – like a little girl
Mishael	Who is Like God	Meshach	Who is Aku – or guest of a king
Azariah	God has Helped	Abednego	Servant of Nebo – the Babylonian god of wisdom

The God-given role Daniel had in living out his life as God's child was to be a part of God showing the world that He (God Himself), and only He would be the judge of this world. Nebuchadnezzar saw it differently. He wanted to use the obvious power he saw in Daniel to "protect the king." Nebuchadnezzar changed Daniel's name as a way to make a request to a no-named god for protection of what Nebuchadnezzar had amassed over his lifetime. Same goes for Hananiah, Misael, and Azariah. The world worked to take their God-given role as described in their names and change that role to something that better fit the personal needs of those over them.

This is exactly what the world is trying to do with the roles you play. It wants to change the perception of your God-given identity so that you will lose the Heavenly power that comes with being His child. Daniel, Hananiah, Misael and Azariah never lost their true identity. They fought the world every day to maintain the reality of who God made them to be. Yes, their names were changed, but they never allowed society to co-opt their true identity. Their true identities empowered the roles they were to play so completely that society was ultimately changed from the top down. They were victors no matter what their circumstances looked like.

This became evident through something Shadrach, Meshach and Abednego said to the King on a particularly challenging day. The three young men were found guilty of defying the King's edict to worship a statue of Nebuchadnezzar. As a result, they were arrested, bound and condemned to die by being tossed into a blazing furnace. As they stood before the King they said these words:

> *If we are thrown into the blazing furnace, the God whom we serve is able to save us. He will rescue us from your power, Your Majesty.* <u>*But even if he doesn't,*</u> *we want to make it clear to you, Your Majesty, that we will never serve your gods or worship the gold statue you have set up. Daniel 3:17-18 (NIV)*

These young men weren't going to allow themselves to be defined by the victimization of this self-focused king. They were victors in God and fully believed that God could save them from the horrific death they were about to face. What really drives their victor mentality home to me is those five words: "But even if He doesn't…" Their circumstances weren't about to change the fact that these three were victors no matter how victimized they were about to be.

These three young men were likely to be dead in mere moments, but they were so sure of their identities that they knew they just couldn't lose. Either God would rescue them from the fire or they would quickly be in His presence. Win, win. Children of God know that they are victors no matter what their circumstance looks like. Victors just can't lose, even when the score seems to point out that they are behind from a worldly perspective.

There's a power in that kind of confidence that the world just can't match. The Church has suffered from the fact that we have misplaced the power found in our identity.

FEELING VS. KNOWING WHO WE ARE

Victorious living comes from knowing who we are. We are nothing more AND nothing less than His child. What we do as His child has nothing to do with identity. Our duties in this life are nothing more than opportunities to go on amazing journeys with our Father. Victors don't let the results of what they do impact the confidence that comes with being a child of the King.

Do you know who you are? One thing is for sure, you aren't a servant of God; you are His child. He isn't your master; He is your Dad! Victims serve God. Victors do what they see their Dad doing.

When Christians allow victimhood to define their identities they become timid and withdrawn. They lack the boldness to be a part of the amazing things God is doing in and around them. Fear dominates them. It's no wonder the world looks at Christians with the jaundiced eye of hypocrisy. We are the living sons and daughters of the King and we are hiding at the back of the room because of all our insecurities. Oh, if we only knew who we really are!

I came across a verse in Ezekiel that really spoke to me on the importance of why we need to know who we are. In Ezekiel 20:8-10 it says:

> *But they rebelled against me, wouldn't listen to a word I said. None got rid of the vile things they were addicted to. They held on to the no-gods of Egypt as if for dear life. I seriously considered inflicting my anger on them in force right there in Egypt. Then I thought better of it. <u>I acted out of who I was, not by how I felt.</u> And I acted in a way that would evoke honor, not blasphemy, from the nations around them, nations who had seen me reveal myself by promising to lead my people out of Egypt. And then I did it: I led them out of Egypt into the desert. (THE MESSAGE)*

God acted out of who He was, not how He felt. Roles make us live a roller coaster kind of life. One moment we <u>feel</u> we are on top of the world because things are going our way. The next minute we <u>feel</u>

we are sinking fast due to our roles not panning out the way we'd like. Wouldn't it be better to live the way God does, as described in this verse, and to act out of who we are? Acting out of a sense of how we feel is a terrible way to live. It causes damage to others and does nothing to help us in those times when things are not going the way we planned.

Identity makes it possible for us to choose how we are going to act. The same just can't be said when we are trying to act out of how we feel. When it comes to the Church, action based on identity brings honor, honor to us and to the God we love. When we try to act out of feelings, the results often make the Church look like a bunch of hypocrites. Identity issues are causing so much trouble in the world and in the Church as well.

All that can change. It has to. Today, you know who you are – a child of God's. Don't know what that looks like? Join the club and start the journey.

"ASK OF ME AND I'LL GIVE IT TO YOU"

Many years ago, I began a practice of taking January 1st as a prayer day. I did so at the beginning of the height of some serious depression I was experiencing in my life. Coincidence? I don't think so.

On that first day of my annual January 1st prayer time, I packed up my computer, which has my Bible on it, and headed off to my wife's office. I knew that the place would be deserted. I told my wife I'd be home sometime later that day – I was going to let God tell me when we were done with our prayer time. I really didn't know what to expect. This was the beginning of an amazing way I have started off every New Year for many years now.

I arrived at the office at 6 a.m., excited to see what God had in store. I played some worship music on the computer and just let God lead me on a journey that turned out to be the foundation for all I'm writing in this book. I spent a bunch of time just listening to the words in the worship songs that played for hours. I would be prompted to go to various verses from time to time. I took notes on what God seemed to be teaching me. I repented of sins. I put forth requests for situations in my life. I asked questions and got some answers. All and all, it was a very "productive" day.

At some point, I came across the 1 John verse I shared earlier in this chapter that speaks about God's great love for us being such that we could be called children of God. The issue of identity popped into my head for the first time from a Heavenly perspective. I immediately realized that I am so quick to trade my God-given identity for one that I find more useful in my life. I was confronted with the thought of how bad it must hurt God for me to be willing to trade my identity as His child for a temporary role that I might play. I felt the pain a father must feel when his child doesn't appreciate the life his father has made just for that child. I literally fell to my knees asking for forgiveness for causing such pain to my God.

As I knelt there, tears streaming down my face, I felt the familiar lightness of forgiveness. Oh, what a forgiving God He is. I love those moments of peace when something horrible has been forgiven by Him. As I knelt there, pondering my identity as God's child, and my tendency to trade it for a role I play, a thought began to materialize in my head. It was as though I was hearing God say to me, "Ask anything you want and I'll give it to you."

At first I did my best to push that thought from my head, but it wouldn't go away. Over and over again I heard, "Ask anything and I'll give it to you." The more it came the more convinced I was that God was saying that He would give me anything I asked for.

Can you imagine? I've hit the jackpot. God Himself saying He would give me anything I asked for? Wow! Does it get any better than that? God had my attention in a big way.

I got up off the floor. I realized that this was serious. After quickly eliminating what I knew were fleshly desires – a billion dollars, a couple of Ferraris, etc. – I got down to thinking this through in a serious and, what I wanted to be, Heavenly way.

Immediately a vision started to form in my head. I started to see a ministry develop. A healing ministry like no other. An amazingly detailed picture started to form in my mind of God's power being

ROLE VS. IDENTITY

brought to the hurting in ways that hasn't been seen since Jesus walked this earth. I have always believed in God's healing power. I have seen examples of His healing power flow through prayer times I have been involved with. I have even had people speak over me the belief that I was a "healer" and that healing power would be seen through God's work in my life. Could this be the opportunity to have all that come true directly from the Hand of God?

I started to formulate my request for that healing ministry to come through me in new and fresh ways. I carefully let that mind picture develop into words that I would put forth to God and I believed he would give it to me. After a few minutes, I felt I had the words "just right" and started to ask God for what had been formulating in my mind.

Just as I began to let the words roll out of my mouth, I realized I was doing it again. I was about to trade my true identity, that I had just discovered, for a "holy" role. I was about to trade my newly found, eternal identity as "child of God" for the temporary role of "healer." That crushed me to the core. I fell to my face sobbing; sobbing partly because I so wanted to feel the fulfillment that I knew would come with being that healer that I saw in my mind; and partly because I was about to hurt my Father all over again. I was about to trade my identity, for which He paid so much, for a job serving Him.

Sure, I was about to ask God for something good. After all, I resisted the temptation to ask God for a billion dollars or a Ferrari. How can it be wrong to ask for the world to be touched by the Power of God as it flowed through a specific ministry? The role I was about to ask for was a good role – a holy role. A tremendous amount of good would come from that role. People's lives would be changed. The Kingdom of God would be built. I wasn't asking for worldly stuff... or was I?

Immediately, I realized that I wanted a role of significance more than I wanted the security that comes with identity. Yes, I was asking for something that would change the world for God; but I was asking from a motive of great personal need. I just couldn't see how living as God's child without that significance would ever take away the emptiness I had been feeling for so long. I just couldn't trust God for what I thought I so desperately needed. I was about to trade my identity as God's child for a role that would make me feel a little better about myself. That's the danger of forgetting who we are; we will use the things of God to help ourselves in ways we might not even realize we are doing.

When I woke up to what I was about to do, I once again asked for forgiveness, and then heard that voice again: "Ask of me and I'll give it to you." I said to God, "Please let me live this life as Your child."

And, that's what He has given me. A journey with Him teaching what it is to be His child. I wish I could say it has been an easy journey filled with worldly blessings. That would be a lie. A lot of ups and downs have come since that initial January 1st prayer day. What you are reading in this book is a result of my request to live life as God's child. I'm no expert at the "how to" of living as His child. No one is. I'm just one of God's children who has had an encounter that has changed his life in some pretty radical ways.

Isn't it time to start that journey for yourself? I guarantee it will be an exciting ride. Lots of stuff will need to fall by the wayside, but what is lost is nothing more than burdens that we weren't meant to carry around in the perfect life God wants for us. Identity is the key to the process of moving from victim thinking to victor living. We are God's children and that makes us victors no matter what our lives look like.

Ask God what it means for you to live this life as His child. I guarantee it will make the challenges of this life more palatable knowing that they are nothing more than roles you are playing empowered by the fullness of the God of this Universe – Someone we have the right to call Daddy!

CHAPTER TWO

The Role of the Church

I want to emphasize an important point. I'm not into Church bashing. The Church is God's pride and joy. It is His gift to the world where we have the chance to see a clear picture of who He is. What you read in this chapter could be mistaken for some kind of problem I have against organized religion. It isn't. I'm just stating what I believe I'm seeing in the Church that limits us in living out our true identity as God's children.

Read any book on Church history and you will see mistake after mistake that we (the Church) have made over the centuries. Some of those mistakes have been profound and have put the Church in a negative light. What gives me great hope is that even though the Church has made so many mistakes, God has continued to work through those mistakes to bring His light into this world. In other words, no mistake the Church makes is too big for God to discount any one of us who are part of the Church.

Why does that give me confidence? Because I'm no better than the Church. I have made serious and significant mistakes and will continue to do so in the future. God's love, however, overcomes those mistakes; His love is so much bigger than the screw-ups I might make in His Name.

He loves His children just like He loves His Church – after all we are His Church. He calls us "The Bride of Christ." I think He takes

His love for us seriously and not only overlooks our various wanderings from His path, but uses them to confound the evil in this world that thinks our mistakes can somehow derail God's Plan for salvation.

So, with this disclaimer in mind, let's do a quick review of what we have discussed so far in this book.

We have already come face to face with the fact that Christ died to give us a relationship with God that is real and extremely personal. We saw from 1 John 3 that God's love for us made it possible for us to be called His children. Christ died to make us children of God and this makes us victors. Christ didn't die to give us a role, He died to give us an identity that begins today and lasts forever.

We have also covered the fact that all roles we play are temporary. Most of them last for a short while in our lives and are gone. All of them will be gone when we die and go home to be with God forever. The same goes when bad things happen to us and we are victims of this evil world. This, too, is a role we are playing. It is a temporary assignment that, one day, will be gone.

Christ didn't die to give us a role – He died to give us an identity. I can't say this enough. I need to be constantly reminded so that I don't settle for accepting a role as part of my identity. Victimhood isn't my identity – child of God is my identity, and that makes me a victor no matter what my circumstances look like.

Got it? OK. Then let's press on and learn how the Church can help us or hinder us in this knowledge.

LIVING AS A VICTOR VS. VICTORIOUS LIVING

The problem with the word victor is that our minds immediately move to the word victory. We believe that if we are victors than we must be victorious, right? It is way too easy for us to interchange these two words. The fact is that they are very different in their meanings and in how they operate in our lives. Let's evaluate that for a bit.

If you ever wanted to read a chapter in the Bible that oozes the idea of victorious living you have to read Psalm 37. Take a look at it here with me. I've chosen to highlight some of the verses in bold and others I've underlined. We will consider what the highlighting means later in this chapter.

Psalm 37, A Psalm of David: (NIV)
[1] <u>Don't worry</u> about the wicked <u>or envy</u> those who do wrong.
[2] For like grass, **they (the wicked – those that are against you) soon fade away.** *Like spring flowers,* **they soon wither.**
[3] <u>Trust in the</u> <u>LORD</u> <u>and</u> <u>do good</u>. Then you will **live safely in the land and prosper.**
[4] <u>Take delight in the</u> <u>LORD</u>, and he will **give you your heart's desires.**
[5] <u>Commit everything you do to the</u> <u>LORD</u>. <u>Trust him</u>, and **he will help you.**
[6] **He will make your innocence radiate like the dawn,** *and the* **justice of your cause will shine like the noonday sun.**
[7] <u>Be still in the presence of the</u> <u>LORD</u>, and <u>wait patiently for him</u> to act. Don't <u>worry</u> about evil people who prosper <u>or fret</u> about their wicked schemes.
[8] <u>Stop being angry</u>! <u>Turn from your rage</u>! <u>Do not lose your temper</u>— it only leads to harm.
[9] For **the wicked will be destroyed,** *but those <u>who trust in the</u> <u>LORD</u> will* **possess the land.**
[10] Soon the **wicked will disappear.** *Though you look for them,* **they will be gone.'**
[11] The **lowly will possess the land and will live in peace and prosperity.**
[12] The wicked plot against the godly; they snarl at them in defiance.
[13] But the Lord just laughs, for he sees **their day of judgment coming.**
[14] The wicked draw their swords and string their bows to kill the poor and the oppressed, to slaughter those who do right.
[15] But their swords will stab their own hearts, and their bows will be broken.
[16] It is better to be godly and have little than to be evil and rich.

17 For **the strength of the wicked will be shattered**, *but the* LORD *takes care of the godly.*
18 Day by day **the LORD takes care** *of the innocent*, and **they will receive an inheritance that lasts forever.**
19 **They will not be disgraced in hard times;** *even in famine* **they will have more than enough.**
20 But **the wicked will die.** *The* LORD's *enemies are like flowers in a field —* **they (the Lord's enemies) will disappear like smoke.**
21 The wicked borrow and never repay, but the godly are generous givers.
22 Those the LORD blesses will **possess the land**, but those he curses will die.
23 **The LORD directs the steps** *of the godly.* **He delights** *in every detail of their lives.*
24 **Though they stumble, they will never fall,** *for the* LORD *holds them by the hand.*
25 Once I was young, and now I am old. Yet I have **never** seen the godly **abandoned or their children begging for bread.**
26 The godly always **give generous** loans to others, and **their children are a blessing.**
27 Turn from evil and do good, and you **will live in the land forever.**
28 For the LORD loves justice, and **he will never abandon** the godly. He will **keep them safe forever, but the children of the wicked will die.**
29 The godly **will possess the land** and will **live there forever.**
30 The godly **offer good counsel; they teach right from wrong.**
31 They have made God's law their own, so they **will never slip from his path.**
32 The wicked wait in ambush for the godly, looking for an excuse to kill them.
33 But **the LORD will not let the wicked succeed** or **let the godly be condemned** when they are put on trial.
34 Put your hope in the LORD. Travel steadily along his path. **He will honor you by giving you the land. You will see the wicked destroyed.**

THE ROLE OF THE CHURCH

> *³⁵ I have seen wicked and ruthless people flourishing like a tree in its native soil.*
> *³⁶ But when I looked again, they were gone! Though I searched for them, I could not find them!*
> *³⁷ <u>Look at those who are honest and good</u>, for a* **wonderful future** *awaits those who <u>love peace</u>.*
> *³⁸ But* **the rebellious will be destroyed; they have no future.**
> *³⁹ The* **LORD rescues** *the <u>godly</u>;* **he is their fortress in times of trouble.**
> *⁴⁰ The* **LORD helps them** *(the godly),* **rescuing them** *from the wicked. He* **saves them,** *and they* **find shelter in him.**

WOW! That's the kind of life I want. The epitome of victorious living, Right? The good guys always win and the bad guys always lose. Take a look at the amazing promises the psalmist is making in the verses above. The promises stated in this striking chapter of the Bible are highlighted in bold above. Let's review the promises found in Psalm 37.

For the bad:
1. The wicked (rebellious, evil, plotters against good) will be gone (disappear, wiped out, destroyed, crushed, no future, no power, no success, condemned, die, put to death, fail, face judgment, no strength, future generations will not be there), never to bother the good again.

For the good:
1. You will be helped, taken care of.
2. You will live in (possess) your land, forever, and will prosper and live in peace.
3. You will be given the desires of your heart.
4. He will make your cause shine and be radiant. You will be honored.
5. You will receive an eternal inheritance.
6. You will have more than enough. You (nor your children) will never need to beg for more. You will have so much

that you will be able to give generously. You will have no disgrace.
7. You will never fail. You have a wonderful future ahead of you. Your steps will be directed.
8. You will never be abandoned, never condemned.
9. Your children are a blessing.
10. You will be kept safe. You will never slip from His path. You will be rescued. You will be saved.
11. You will be good counselors and teachers of right and wrong.
12. God is your fortress in times of trouble. He is your shelter.

Powerful descriptions of victorious living spelled out in God's Word to us. But there's a problem with these promises. Do you see the same problem I do? Let me elaborate.

How many of us are living this kind of life? Do you have any troubles impacting you right now? Will you ever have troubles in the future? Are you lacking anything (job, money, health, etc.)? Are all the desires of your heart coming into focus in your life? Do you feel any disgrace, any lack any honor? Do you have any failure in your life (lost job, etc.)? Are your children walking the good walk with God? Do you feel lost, wandering around in this life? Do you feel totally taken care of or are the troubles of this world weighing you down?

I can't imagine a single person, no matter how good their circumstances are right now, being able to confirm all these promises in their life. It just isn't human not to have some doubts, or failures, or troubles, or misgivings about this life as a result of the circumstances that we all face or will face in the future. Troubles are part of this world; it's just a fact of reality. We will always find it such that circumstances will make us a victim from time to time.

But how can that be? God's Holy Word is as plain as the nose on your face. Psalm 37 says that we are promised victorious living. Those promises are spelled out very directly in the verses we just read. There seems to be a contradiction between what we experience and what the

Bible says. Left unchecked that contradiction can grow into doubt and disbelief that can make victim thinking a reality. Worse than that, those doubts can grow so large that we might actually turn away from God all together.

What a great opportunity for the Church to step in and speak truth in light of what seems to be an obvious contradiction. But instead of speaking the truth in ways that dispel the contradiction that seems be there between what Psalm 37 is saying and what we ALL see as reality in our lives, the Church seems to be speaking in ways that work to compound the seeming contradiction.

Some of us in the Church openly equate being a victor with having a victorious life here on earth. In other words, some of us are saying that you aren't a victor unless most, if not all, the promises being spelled out in Psalm 37 are happening in your life. Some of us have taken the concept of a "blessed life" to mean that our troubles will be taken away as we learn how to approach our Father in powerful times of prayer and communion with Him. At the very least, the Church has allowed us to believe that if we somehow get ourselves "right" with God then victory, like that in Psalm 37, is ours for the taking.

In my opinion, both of these views just aren't supported as I read scripture. Victory isn't guaranteed in the Bible for any of us victors here on earth, nor is our lacking in victory a sign that we have to get ourselves right in God's eyes. These two views certainly aren't supported by the vast majority of the characters we read about in the Bible.

Part of the problem I see in the Church today is that we have equated being a victor with experiencing victory. Who is it that graces the stages of Churches when guest speakers come to our Sunday worship times? If your Church is like mine, the people who are guest speakers are testifying to the miracles they have seen in their lives. They are victors and they can prove it by the level of victory they have seen directly from The Hand of God. Think about it. How many guest speakers stand up and say, "I know God heals but I haven't experienced a healing in my life and that is very depressing to me right now?"

Now, I'm not saying that it is bad to hear the testimony of those who have a story to share about receiving such a wonderful gift from God. What I'm pointing out is that we, the Church, have a tendency to equate victory with being a victor.

The reality that the Church has failed to point out is that those of us waiting on our victorious time are just as much a victor as the person who has received a miracle from God. We are still victors even though our miracle hasn't caught the attention of the Church, who seems to want to "market" Jesus by using His Power as a key benefit to a relationship with Him.

By failing to pay attention to the vast majority of us who can't claim victorious living to the extent of those who have powerful testimonies to share, the Church is subconsciously promoting the fact that it takes victorious living to prove that you are a victor in Christ. This is just not the case, and it is making those of us not experiencing victorious living doubt our place with God. Our very identity is in jeopardy and the power that comes from that identity is being jeopardized as a result.

Remember, we are all victors because of Christ's work. It isn't the reality of victory in our lives that makes us a victor. The unwitting promotion of victorious living on the stages of Churches each Sunday morning contributes heavily to the fact that many Christians secretly feel they are somehow victims in this walk with God.

GOD THE VICTIMIZER

You see, I believe that most of us at one time or another have felt like we are a victim of God! (I know what you are thinking, "Get away from this guy, lightning is about to strike!") There are so many of us who have prayed and prayed and prayed but our delivery has failed to materialize. Either there is something wrong with us or something wrong with God. Both conclusions couldn't be further from the truth. That's where we end up as we continue to connect being a victor with always experiencing victorious living. I believe that this opens the door

THE ROLE OF THE CHURCH

to victim thinking as we wait for God to show up in ways we are quick to define and sometimes demand.

Think about it this way: how many people do you personally know who might, deep down inside, relate to somehow being a victim of God because of the dire circumstances they face right now? In other words, how many people do you know who have been praying for something powerfully important in their lives only to be in a "holding pattern" with God? I bet it is many, many times more than those you personally know who have received a miraculous delivery from God.

Hear me loud and clear on this one: I'm not arguing as to whether God is moving powerfully enough in our world or not. He does and is! Contrary to the popular teachings of some prominent pastors, God's Power is still alive and active in mysterious and miraculous ways today. I'm just saying that the Church has to get away from consciously or subconsciously promoting the connection between our identity that makes us victors and victorious living as the proof of our victor status.

What I'm concerned about is that we are missing a crucial fact in our lives as followers of Christ that sets us up to live a life of victimhood rather than the victors we are in Him. The bottom line of this book is so simple. Victory doesn't make us a victor just as the lack of victory shouldn't make us a victim. The sooner we get this into our daily walk the more powerfully we are going to be able to impact this world for and through Christ. Hard thoughts to grasp when the trials of life seem to batter us like waves on the seashore.

THE HALL OF FAITH

Part of the reason we are seeing such a connection with being a victim inside the Church is that the Church has a tendency to promote victory as being the result of living a life as a victor. This just doesn't pan out in the Bible.

There's a chapter in the Bible that has been nicknamed the "Hall of Faith." Hebrews 11 begins by giving an amazing definition of what faith really means and then goes on to list people God saw as having that kind of faith. This chapter is like the "Hall of Fame" for a particular sport. Chapter 11 is where you can really see that victory doesn't always mean victorious living from the worldly viewpoint. Let's take a look at some of the superstars of faith named in Hebrews 11 and see how victorious their lives as victors really were.

Take, for example, Abel, Noah, Abraham, Sarah, Isaac, Jacob, and Joseph. Were they victors? How about Moses? Was he a victor? How about Rahab, Gideon, Barak, Samson, Jephthah, David or Samuel? God thought enough of them to devote significant portions of scripture to these people and had their names placed in the "Hall of Faith" of the Bible. That fact alone makes me believe that these people should be considered victors in our eyes. They certainly were so in God's.

Now consider this. Were these people victorious? Abel was murdered by his own brother! Why? The sacrifice brought by Abel was pleasing in God's eyes, more pleasing than that brought by his brother Cane. In a fit of jealousy, Cane killed his brother. For pleasing God, Abel is killed. Is that victorious living?

How about Abraham? Here's a guy who has serious personal and, dare I say it, psychological issues. He's forced out by his family to wander the desert, abandoned by his nephew for the best land, and finds himself childless, even when God tells him he will be the father of many nations. He is the victim of some pretty serious life challenges.

Yes, big things work out for Abraham; but look at the wake of dysfunction he spread as he applied what I see as victim thinking in his life. He abandoned his wife, not once but twice, to the king of a land that he was traveling through to save his own neck. Think his wife, Sarah, felt like a victim or a victor by those actions? How about his teenage son, Isaac? Consider the level of victim thinking he must have dealt with after he saw his Dad ready to kill him as a sacrifice to God on some cold dark mountaintop.

Then there is Ishmael (Isaac's half-brother). As a young man, he and his mother are driven out into the desert (by Abraham and his wife Sarah) to fend for themselves. Ishmael is the "father" of the Arab people. Isaac is the "father" of the people of Israel. Think there was some hatred felt by Ishmael towards Isaac? Victim thinking as seen by the actions of people listed in the Hall of Faith has caused a hatred between two groups of people that continues in the Middle East even today. The peace of the entire world is threatened as a result of the actions that came from the victim thinking of two brothers many thousands of years ago.

It doesn't stop there. Isaac is a chip off the old block and abandons his wife Rebecca to a king in a land he is passing through (like father, like son). Could it be victim thinking that made Rebecca convince her favorite son, Jacob, to trick his father (Isaac) into getting the blessing that culturally belonged to his older, twin brother Esau?

Victim thinking made Jacob run for his life because of his deceitful actions against his older brother. Jacob had a son, Joseph, that is so hated for his arrogance that his brothers sell him into slavery, abandoning him into the hands of people they would never have associated with themselves. Victimization caused by victim thinking. And every step of the way, God is there redeeming all the messed up actions of these "Hall of Famers" in ways I don't completely understand.

So much dysfunction. So much pain and suffering. So much room for victimhood. There is no doubt that God shows up in big ways for each of these people. Miracles happen, hearts are changed and God's power is seen. The fact is that God uses the seeming dysfunction, and the misguided actions resulting from that dysfunction, to show His power in in ways that can only be described as "Biblical."

On the surface of it all, would you say the lives of the people mentioned above are a picture of living the fruit of a victorious life? Would you want your life to look like theirs? I would venture to say you wouldn't. Neither would I. I wish it stopped there in the Bible. Victorious living is a challenge even in Jesus' life.

JESUS AS VICTOR

Would you say Jesus was victorious in all He did? Well, from the worldly standpoint, the answer would be a big and resounding NO!

He prayed to His Father for mercy and His Father said it was better for Him to die a terrible death than for that cup to pass in another way. Jesus died at the young age of 33, just three years into His ministry. Does that sound like victory to you? From a worldly standpoint, Jesus was just like the rest of the major players in the Bible. They all could be classified as victims of one thing or another, maybe even as victims of God's Plan itself.

That's the point of this book. Being a victor isn't about being victorious in this world. Abel, Noah, Abraham, Sarah, Isaac, Jacob, Joseph, David, Samuel, and particularly Jesus were all victors. They weren't victims. They were victors. Their lives didn't always turn out victorious, but victory isn't what makes us victors.

The fact that each of these biblical characters had a real, tangible and dynamic relationship with God is what made them victors. It isn't how well their lives turned out or how well they lived their lives. It isn't even about whether God's plan was ever seen in their lives. This point is emphasized by a haunting scripture found at the very end of Hebrews 11:

> *All these people earned a good reputation because of their faith, yet none of them received all that God had promised. Hebrews 11:39 (NIV)*

None of these Biblical characters received all that God promised. What makes these characters victors is that they chose to believe in the God who made the promises and they didn't let their circumstances (whether they received those promises or not) define their status as victims or victors. They let their walk with Him be the only proof they needed to live the life of a victor in this world as they held on to the hope that they would experience victory for all eternity.

Can you begin to see the futility of chasing victorious living as proof of being a victor? If these real people of the Bible didn't get all God promised then what makes those of us in the Church think that we deserve more? What makes you and I think we somehow deserve better that what Jesus Himself experienced?

Each of the people mentioned in Hebrews 11 chose to follow God even when the outcome of that choice made it look, from the world's perspective, that they were going to be victims of this or victims of that. Jesus chose this path as well, and that is what made Him the perfect example of faith for us all to follow.

He didn't see dying for our sins as a sign of failing. He didn't consider Himself a victim of this world or of God the Father for carrying out God's plan of salvation for us all. Quite the opposite; Jesus was able to live as a victor even when victory was not in the cards from the world's perspective. How could He do this? I believe scripture gives us such a simple and profound answer:

> *Jesus knew that the Father had put all things under his power, and that he had come from God and was returning to God; so he got up from the meal, took off his outer clothing, and wrapped a towel around his waist. After that, he poured water into a basin and began to wash his disciples' feet, drying them with the towel that was wrapped around him. John 13:3-5 (NIV)*

Here we see the architect of the universe, Jesus, taking on the role of a servant. The hands of the same person who put into place the very earth we live on are now stooped so low as to wash the dirty feet of a bunch of nobodies. It doesn't get much less victorious than that from the world's perspective.

How could Jesus humble Himself to live a life that was filled with worldly proof that He was not victorious? I see two things that make this possible from the John 13 reading. One, He knew where He came from (therefore He knew who He was). And two, He knew where He was going (He had an eternal perspective that trumped the things of this world).

Jesus knew who He was and where He was going after this life. He came from God and He knew He was returning to God. What this world thought of that fact didn't matter to Jesus. Because Jesus knew He was a victor no matter how much this world victimized Him.

Victim thinking just wasn't part of Jesus' consciousness and the world was changed by the power of God through Him as a result.

Jesus' firm grasp on identity along with an eternal perspective made Him a victor in this life and victorious for all eternity. Want to know a secret that Satan doesn't want you to know? You, too, have the same power Jesus has to live as a victor no matter what this world throws at you. You have the same authority to claim the life of a victor even when living victoriously seems just out of reach. You have the same choice Jesus did, to live life as a victim because victory isn't part of your reality right this moment, or to live life as a victor knowing that the victory is God's.

Not an easy decision. Jesus literally sweat blood when He came to the crossroads of this decision in His life while praying in the Garden of Gethsemane. You and I will also strain for all we are worth to try and live a life of victory when we are standing in the reality of victimhood in our lives. It is human nature to do so. But oh, how the Heavens rejoice when we choose to be what God made us to be, a victor!

What I hope this book does for you is make it easier to recognize the many times in this life when that same choice is staring you square in the face. Of course, we are just human and will likely remain in victimhood from time to time. That's totally okay with God, in my opinion. What isn't okay is us staying there, squandering the power that comes with choosing to live the life of a victor when the world wants us to remain powerless as a victim.

THE ROLE OF THE CHURCH

Back to the Church for a moment. How has the Church gotten it wrong in light of the victim to victor discussion? We continue to spend way too much time promoting victorious living rather than reinforcing our identity that makes us victors. We use way too many sermons teaching how to be victorious in this world rather than focusing on the fact that we all are victors no matter what our

THE ROLE OF THE CHURCH

circumstances look like. For way too long we have ignored the fact that those sitting in our congregations who haven't experienced victorious living are still victors because of the saving work of Jesus Christ.

We in the Church look at a man's circumstances in order to judge how much of a victor that man is. This is wrong, and it makes those of us who don't measure up to a certain elusive standard of victory feel like victims. The lack of victorious examples in our life right at this moment make us feel like second class citizens, somehow forgotten by God and often ignored by the Church. We struggle to eke out whatever connection to God that we can while fighting the overwhelming feeling of shame that results when we realize, for whatever reason, that we just can't be like all those others the Church promotes as being victors, who look to have it all together in their lives.

If all this is true as I believe it is, why is the Church guilty of acting this way? The really hard and uncomfortable answer is that it is because you and I demand that the Church do this. We demand to know how to live victorious lives. We are the ones seeking any way possible to guarantee that our lives will be okay. We have adopted a belief that pain in our lives just cannot be tolerated. Why not learn how to call on the unlimited power of the God that saved us to get rid of all pain in our lives?

We, the Church attendees, have placed on the Church the responsibility of not only teaching us how to save our lives (through Jesus) but how to save our wellbeing (by learning how to be victorious). It just isn't acceptable to us that a God of Love could allow pain to be part of a victor's life. The pressure we put on the Church has made it possible for the Church to focus on the wrong characteristics when it comes to who we are and this has limited our effectiveness in society today.

We have driven the Church to tickle our ears with formulas and easy ways to get the attention of God in order to rescue us from the trials this world tosses at us. We want to see testimonies of victorious living, we don't want to hear about people fighting and not receiving victory. We can't stand the thought that God would allow our comfortable lives to be challenged by evil in this world, even if that challenge will bring more glory to God in the long run.

We have allowed the Church to get off track and to actually limit the power we can have and should be experiencing in a day-by-day walk with our Father in Heaven. I believe all this has happened because we have forgotten who we are: saved by Christ, children of God and therefore victors no matter what our lives look like.

DELIGHT IN THE LORD

Here's how we can get things so mixed up. Let's go back to Psalm 37. Earlier, I showed you all the amazing promises of victory found in this chapter by highlighting them in bold. Now, let's focus on the underlined parts of this chapter (you may want to go back and reread Psalm 37 as annotated in this book). Here's a synopsis of the items I underlined in Psalm 37:

1. Don't worry or fret.
2. Be godly.
3. Don't envy.
4. Trust In God – put your hope in Him – stay on His path.
5. Do Good – turn from evil.
6. Commit everything to God.
7. Be still in God's Presence.
8. Wait on God.
9. Don't be angry – turn from rage – don't lose your temper.
10. Be found innocent – love justice – make God's law your own – be honest and good.

Notice anything similar about these statements? They are statements of action. Do's and don'ts clearly specified in the Word. They seem to have a connection to the promises highlighted in bold. It is easy to believe that what Psalm 37 is saying is that if we do these underlined things then we will receive the promises in bold. Let's take

THE ROLE OF THE CHURCH

a closer look at that possibility by studying one of the verses from chapter 37 of Psalms. Take a look at verse four with me again.

> *Take delight in the* LORD, *and he will* **give you your heart's desires.** *(Psalms 37:4 NIV)*

As I read this verse it appears to be saying that if I delight in the Lord I will receive the desires of my heart. I want the desires of my heart to come about – don't you? I have some BIG desires. I bet you do as well. So, on the surface, it appears that all we need to do is to get busy and start delighting in the Lord then all the desires of our heart will be ours. That's what the Word says, isn't it?

I'm an engineer by training. I have been taught that things work by formula. I have trained myself to be a pattern recognition machine. If "A" happens and "B" is the result, then anytime "A" is recognized then "B" must be just around the corner.

As part of the introduction of this book I described a formula I had been raised with that says "hard work equals success." I outlined how I had spent decades misapplying this truth in an effort to gain the things I needed to feel good about myself. I also described how when this formula seemed to fail me it was devastating in my life.

I have also attempted to apply formulas to my relationship with my wife. That didn't work out too well. Same goes with my relationship with my kids. The results stank! The only one that seems to respond well to my formulas is my dog! God isn't a dog, neither is He my wife or my child. He is my Father, and formulas don't work with Him either.

But that doesn't stop me from trying to find formulas to help me get what I WANT out of God in this life. That's what a formula in relationship to God is all about. It's a statement of demand that goes something like this: "God, if I do this, then You HAVE to do that." Not a very workable, long-term relationship-builder with humans, I have learned the hard way. This is a totally devastating method of relationship building with God.

Back to verse 4. If I want the desires of my heart it seems that the Bible is saying that I need to delight myself in the Lord. Problem is, I don't have a clue what "delighting myself in God" even means. Okay – time to do a little Bible study.

This is exactly what I did when I came across this verse a number of years ago. At that time I was facing the reality that the desires of my heart just weren't happening. This reality was driving me into deeper and more frequent bouts of depression. When I read this verse I thought I had been given the winning lottery ticket. If I could just discover what God meant by delighting myself in Him, then He would HAVE TO give me the desires of my heart. I had God in a corner and I wasn't about to let up!

I had been taught over the years how to dig into God's Word with resources like concordances, commentaries, Biblical dictionaries and an entire list of tools developed by other "engineers" and formula-thinkers like myself trying to back God into a corner. I decided to look at what I determined were the three key words of this verse: delight, desires and give. If they meant what I knew them to mean then, "God, I've gotcha."

First, let's look at the word "give." Important word. Does it actually mean to give like a present, or does it have some deeper meaning that I need to be aware of?

The word "give" comes from a root word in the Hebrew language "nathan" (pronounced na-than). Here's the Strong's definitions of this word:

1. to give, put, set
    a. to give, bestow, grant, permit, ascribe, employ, devote, consecrate, dedicate, pay wages, sell, exchange, lend, commit, entrust, give over, deliver up, yield, occasion, produce, requite to, report, mention, utter, stretch out, extend
    b. to put, set, put on, put upon, set, appoint, assign, designate
    c. to make, constitute

That's excellent. The word in Psalms 37 verse 4 "give" really means to give. In fact, it is more profound than that. It also means to "give" in a sense that if I do one thing than I am to be given something in return. Where did I get that? Take a look at the various definitions used in item "a" above. To "give" is synonymous with the action of selling something. If I pay a price then I get what I paid for. It is also synonymous with exchanging, or the paying of wages. I exchange my efforts for a payment. This is really looking good! A formula is starting to materialize and I'm getting excited.

Now let's take a look at the word "desire." This word comes from a Hebrew word, "mish'alah" (pronounced as it is spelled). This word is pretty direct. It means "request, petition or desire." It comes from the root word "sha'al" which means to ask for or to beg for. Sha'al can also have the meaning "to be given on request."

Can't get much better than that. So far, what the Bible says is looking pretty good for my cause. It is literally saying that my petitions (desires or requests) have to be paid out to me as wages (I've earned them by doing something) and they are due upon my request.

Now comes the hardest word of the bunch, "delight yourself." This is the "do" portion of the verse. This is the action that, if done correctly, should result in the "getting" of what I so want to receive. If I can just figure out what this means then I will be able to know how to do what I need to do so that I will be able to live a life of victory (receive the desires of my heart).

The word "delight" in Psalm 37:4 comes from the Hebrew word "anag" (again, pronounced like it is spelled). Anag means to be "soft, delicate, dainty, pliable" and, in one concordance, "flexible." Nothing like I thought it would mean. How does this apply to this verse? Let's put all the definitions together to see if it makes any sense.

> Original Wording: Take delight in the LORD, and He will give you your heart's desires.
>
> Studied Wording: Be (soft, delicate, dainty, pliable, flexible) with the Lord, and He will (bestow, grant, pay, give, entrust, give over...) the (desires, requests) of your heart.

Here's where the Holy Spirit comes into play when reading the Bible. I took time to lay the studied wording of this verse before God in prayer. I asked God, what does this mean? Only through the power of God can the Scripture be truly understood for our lives.

As I asked God to teach me what this meant, an answer began to develop in my mind. Suddenly the verse became so clear to me. This wasn't a formula on how to get God to give me what I wanted. It was a method of changing my life so that the Power of God could really be seen in all my circumstances.

I felt like God was saying to me, "Be flexible with me. Don't be demanding to get your way. Your way might not be the best for our relationship or for my Glory to be seen in this world. Walk with me and you will get the desires of your heart because you will want what I desire more than those things you desire." Immediately the verse Jesus stated from the Garden of Gethsemane came to mind:

> *Abba, Father," he said, "everything is possible for you. Take this cup from me. Yet not what I will, but what you will. Mark 14:36 (THE MESSAGE)*

It was best for Jesus to face a horrible death at the hands of all us sinners and rejection of the Father so that we all could be saved. The victim side of Jesus was seeking the personal desire of safety, comfort and victory by asking, "Is there any other way?" The victor side of Jesus was flexible with God and wanted God's desires more than His own, saying, "Not My will, but Yours be done."

The Holy Spirit was teaching me something profound by looking deeper into the meaning of Psalm 37:4. Though the exact words I felt God was saying to interpret this verse for me personally can't be found specifically in any translation of the Bible, everything mentioned in this "new" meaning of Psalm 37 God gave me is totally biblical. The Holy Spirit was interpreting this verse for me in ways that really changed my thinking. God wants the best for me – His desires are for my best.

THE GUARANTEE OF PERSPECTIVE

Sometimes His best for me doesn't look too good from the earth's perspective. I need to be flexible with God. Not demanding when it comes to my way, but willing to approach God with a soft heart so that my heart can be touched, healed and changed in ways that make me see my identity even more clearly than before. When I clearly see my identity, circumstances will have less of an impact on how I view the challenges this world will throw at me. His Power will be seen in even greater ways through me as a victor because of my identity rather than me demanding victory because I believe the Bible says I will receive it.

That's what Psalm 37:4 was saying to me. It's not that I found a formula that would enable me to get my way. It's more that my ways are changing into God's ways. By remaining open to Him, I am beginning to learn that we all can experience His presence in ways that make living like a victor something that isn't tied to seeing victory all the time.

What this "new" meaning of Psalm 37:4 did for me was to shift my perspective. You see every promise mentioned in Psalm 37 is one hundred percent true when viewed from God's perspective. Every one of the promises spelled out in this chapter of the Bible **are guaranteed** in Heaven. Victorious living cannot be expected all the time here on earth (as the earth defines victorious living). In Heaven, however, it's a totally different story. Victory is our Lord's, and we are guaranteed victorious living in Heaven because we are His children.

This is a key point we have to grasp in order to keep victim thinking from taking control of our lives. God's promises are viewed from Heaven looking to earth, not the other way around. We tend to see Biblical promises and demand that they be fulfilled in our lifetime. By what authority do we have the right to make such a demand?

Victors believe God always delivers on His promises, but realize God has all eternity to make His promises come about. Victors live in the reality that this short span here on earth isn't all there is. Learning to view this life from a Heavenly perspective is what enables victors to live victoriously even when this world wants to label them as victims because of all the bad that has happened in their lives.

Studying God's Word allowed me to go on a journey with God that changed my expectations when it comes to the promises I read in the Bible. I expect and believe that these promises are guaranteed in Heaven. I'm grateful when they happen here on earth but I cannot be "mad at God" for long when they don't. I'm still a victor whether I get these promised victories in my lifetime or not. I'm a victor, not because of victories but because of God's great love for me, His child.

This is a game changer, people. Church, it's time to grasp this thought and make it the focus of all we do and say.

That's the perspective change we all need to have so that we can help the Church get back on track teaching that we are all victors and spending less resources wasting time trying to teach us all how to have victory.

THE JOURNEY TO DELIVERANCE

Moving from victim thinking to victor living is a journey that we must take with God. When talking about this journey, one pastor put it this way. In the Old Testament, God saved His people from slavery by bringing them out of Egypt. Now God is in the business of getting Egypt out of His people. There are things in all our lives that God needs to help get out of us in order for us to live the life of a victor He wants for us.

Each and every one of us who has put our trust in Christ has been rescued from the slavery of sin. Just like the nation Israel some 4,000 years ago, we have seen the waters parted and we have walked into a relationship with God that is our promised land. Now God is hard at work getting the sinful nature out of us – getting Egypt out of His people.

You can't live in slavery for most of your life and be expected to know instantly how to live a free life when freedom comes. Convicts, after being released from a long prison sentence, find it hard to

THE ROLE OF THE CHURCH

acclimate to the non-structured life freedom affords. Many times this lack of adjustment drives these ex-cons into doing things that get them put back in captivity again. Same goes for those of us who have been freed from the slavery of sin. When freedom comes we have to go on the journey with God to help us discover what it means to live the free life.

God has already saved us from the slavery of sin through Jesus Christ. He has saved us, but we are still in the process of being sanctified. Though we are victors because of the finished work of Jesus, we still have vestiges of victimhood flowing through our veins. It is completely up to God to be the driving force behind the process of getting Egypt (victim thinking) out of us. Philippians 2:13 says, *"For God is working in you, giving you the desire and the power to do what pleases him." (NIV)*

God's plan is for the cup of deliverance to be something we have in our lives. The cup of deliverance is what is needed to get the old ways out of us so that we can live in the power of being God's Child—the life of a victor. It's God that gives power and desire to do the work that has to be done for the cup of deliverance to get Egypt out of us. We can't will it to happen. It has to come from God. Even the basic desire to be changed has to come from Him.

Victims work to be better from a place of guilt, saying "I don't measure up." Victors work from a place of desire that God puts in their hearts. Guilt from not measuring up isn't a motive. Christ made it so that we don't have to live in shame because of the guilt we feel over sin in our lives.

The Church needs to be more involved in sharing the vision that we are victors and spend less time worrying about what victory looks like. We are in a wonderful position to be different than society over this one issue. The rest of the world seems to want to allow their identity to be morphed by the circumstances that happen to them. Christians have the unique opportunity to live out a different way; the way of the victor.

We have to be careful in living this way because we might come off as believing ourselves to be "better than others." Victors' confidence doesn't come from being better. Their confidence doesn't come from their success. Heavenly confidence comes from relationship with God. Isn't that what the Church is supposed to be teaching? This life isn't about convincing God to give us a good life. It is about allowing this life (the roles we play) to be empowered by our identity to make a difference in how God's kingdom is brought into our circles of influence.

The Church has an amazing opportunity to show the world a better way. There is great peace that comes with being a victor. The world is missing that peace and is hungry for it. Instead of teaching the Body of Christ tips and techniques to make our lives better wouldn't it be more productive to teach how to live in the powerful freedom of being God's child?

Wake up, Church. It's time to choose. Are we going to continue to set ourselves up to be powerless victims by imitating the rest of the world and constantly striving for victory? Or are we going to do as Jesus did? He lived life as a victor – allowing God's victory to be seen when, where and how God chooses to allow that victory to be experienced. The same is possible for us. It's time to live in the power of who we are. Come on Church, it's time to start living like victors!

CHAPTER THREE

Our Standing with God

A new identity can be a really difficult thing to deal with. Hollywood has produced countless movies about poor, average, run-of-the-mill people who were catapulted to places of riches, power and prominence. It is both comical and unnerving to see the difficulties that are created by this sudden shift in identity. The same goes for those of us who are just coming to grips with our true identity – that of a child of God's.

What does this look like? How do we live this out? For those of us who were raised in a religious system that makes God look big and unapproachable, we are scared to think about the freedoms that might be ours as a child of the King's. Then there are those of us whose earthly fathers weren't much of an example of love and compassion. We might be viewing the possibility of being a child of the Heavenly Father in the light of being the child of a fallen and failed earthly father. Lots of confused thoughts and wrong thinking can cloud our view of how to live this life with an identity that guarantees our standing before God.

The key to being able to live a life in the "new normal," as God's child, is to come to grips with our standing before God. We have to get to a place where we can look into God's eyes and see our reflection clearly. We need to see ourselves as God sees us. Not knowing our standing before God leaves the door open to victim thinking. We need to do all we can to close that door so that circumstances of this life don't impact our victorious approach to living this life.

To illustrate this point, let me give you a short quiz. How do you think that God views your performance as His child at this moment, right now in your life? Give yourself a grade of one to ten, with "one" being an absolute failure at being God's child and a "ten" indicating you are living perfectly as God's child. Take a moment and think about how God might rate you.

What was your number? On my best day I think God would see my life as a six when it comes to being His child. How could I rate myself higher since I'm just learning what it means to live as God's child? On my worst day, that's an entirely different story. I have had way too many days where "one" doesn't even come close to how badly I have failed at being His child.

But the fact is that through Jesus Christ, God sees each and every one of us as a resounding and perfect TEN! Shocking isn't it? On your very worst day, God sees you as perfect; not because of how good you are but because of Jesus' sacrifice for you. Obviously we aren't perfect; but He sees us through the completed work of Jesus Christ. God doesn't take into account the incomplete way our lives are playing out right now. If He did, we would all be in a world of hurt. God sees us as a ten because He sees us through the sacrifice Jesus made for us. That's why we can live like victors even when it looks like we will be nothing but victims our entire life.

It's back to perspective. God sees us from a Heavenly perspective; from Heaven looking down. As His child we are adored and loved beyond human understanding, even when we are in a place of messing up more than we care to admit. We are seen as not needing anything to perfect that love He has for us.

THE MEANING OF "HOLY"

In the Bible you will see the word "holy" used time and time again. One of the verses that always jumps out at me when I think of the word "holy" is 1 Peter 1:16. It says, *"Be holy, because I am holy."* (NIV) Holiness plays an important role in our standing with God.

Because the word holy in this verse is connected to God we sometimes think that holiness is something we achieve by doing things. If I pray more… if I give more… if I attend church more… if I sacrifice more… then I might be more holy. This is exactly what Satan wants us to think. He wants us to believe that we need to DO more to be holy. Busyness is one of Satan's best tools at distracting God's people from tapping into the power God wants His children to experience. "Doing" is the enemy of "being" when it comes to holiness.

Have you ever considered what the word holy means? Holy is simply defined as "to be set apart." It isn't an action and shouldn't be applied in our lives as a verb. It is a statement of being. There is nothing we can DO to be holy, except to make Jesus part of our daily lives. We are holy because He is holy. That's what the 1 Peter verse is saying.

Of course there is doing in this life, but the motivation for doing is so different from what most of us believe and apply in our lives. Take a look at the verse below. When we understand that doing has absolutely no impact on being holy we have a better chance at not letting the results of our daily doing trap us into victim thinking. The verse says:

> *But just as He who called you is holy, so be holy in all you do. 1 Peter 1:15 (NIV)*

Peter, the man who wrote both of these passages on holiness, was the king of "doing" in the Bible. I've heard pastors describe Peter as a "ready, FIRE, aim" kind of guy. Peter's mouth ran a little faster than his brain at times and that characteristic landed him into some interesting circumstances. I find it particularly impacting that God chose Peter to make the point that it isn't "doing" that makes you holy. It is holiness that makes your "doing" have the power to change the world.

In this verse God is saying that He is set apart from this world. Though He created it, the world doesn't define the fullness of who God is. Because of God's great love, we too are holy; we aren't holy because of what we do, but because of who we are (identity again). From this perspective, the fact that we are set apart means that we can do all things with the power our Father gives us. Furthermore, our standing with Him doesn't depend on the results of the things we do. Just as the world doesn't define the fullness of God, success or failure at a particular role in life doesn't define who we are either.

This is the basis of how victims in the world can live like victors. Doing, and the results of doing, shouldn't have the kind of impact in our lives that drive us to victim thinking. Victims allow the results of their doing to define them. The success or failure of a task impacts their identity. Victors "do" and the results of their doing doesn't change their thinking when it comes to who they are or their standing with God. Victors are holy because God is holy, and that's it!

Salvation is what makes us holy. It's what sets us apart. Our holiness has no connection whatsoever to our performance. We are holy because of the Blood of Jesus. This is why we have the authority to live the life of a victor no matter our circumstances. God doesn't punish us for messing up, nor is He trying to teach us a lesson when bad things happen in our lives. That approach to life is the epitome of victim thinking. Jesus has done it all. It is finished. We are holy as well as victors simply because we are God's children.

GOD'S ECONOMY

I have just finished reading the story of Job in the Bible. You probably remember the plight of Job and his walk with God. Satan takes notice of Job and comes before God and says that if all Job's blessings were taken away from him, Job would curse God's Name. God says to Satan, "That could never happen." Then all hell breaks loose. In one day Job's children, wealth and health are taken from him.

For more than thirty chapters of The Book of Job we listen to one diatribe after another. Job is put in the unenviable position of having to defend his integrity against his "friends" who are convinced that it is because of Job's sin that all this badness is happening in the first place. To these self-imposed defenders of misunderstood holiness, all Job has to do is admit to his wrongdoing and everything will once again be as it should. The Book of Job is a sad expression of what religion does to individuals when it applies important concepts from the wrong perspective.

Both Job and his friends were far from the truth of what holiness actually is. To Job's friends, it wasn't conceivable that God would allow such horrible things to happen to an innocent, holy man. After all, Job's friends' good life was a blessing from God rewarding them for walking so perfectly with Him – right?

It must be something bad that Job had hidden in his life that caused all this bad stuff to happen. Job's friends lived in the hope that good things happen to good people and bad things can only be a part of the lives of people who have sin hidden in their hearts. They desperately needed to believe that good only happens to the holy and cursed are the unholy. Nice formula, but we have already seen how formulas don't seem to work with God.

It is terribly easy to believe the same about our lives. Think about it yourself. Deep down inside, don't you believe that victors deserve victory and victims are to be doomed to failure? In God's economy and on this side of Heaven, this just isn't always the case. Victory and defeat will be part of the holy's life just as it will be part of the lives of the unholy. Oh, but the day when we are called home, how things will change!

I have said it several times now, but I will repeat it again: In Heaven we will never face failure or defeat. Victory is ours! Here on earth, the same can't always be said. Those stuck holding onto the premise that the holy deserve only blessing or good are doomed to see victim thinking dominating their lives and impacting their identity. Such was the case with Job and Job's friends.

I hope you are beginning to see how our connecting blessing with how we apply holiness in our lives simply isn't from God. Bad stuff will happen to good people in this world. Job's friends just couldn't come to grips with that. After all, if bad stuff happens to good people then they might be in line for bad things as well. That was not an acceptable picture of the god (notice the small "g") Job's friends decided to serve. Which god do you serve? Do you serve the God of the Universe that has done all the work to make you His child? Or do you serve the god of this world who wants you to constantly be seeking blessing and to be tormented when failure comes?

You see, Job's friends had taken it upon themselves to grade Job's walk as God's child based on the warped thinking they had about blessing and the holiness of God. They saw the bad in Job's life as a sign that God viewed Job as a "one" or less in his performance as His child. Job's standing before God must have been compromised by something Job had done that disqualified him from being called holy.

Thinking that we are less than perfect in the eyes of God is so damaging to our ability to live as victors in this world. Having our friends try to guilt us into believing we are less than perfect is just about more than a person can stand. Time and time again, Job lashes out in his own defense. He is so passionate in his response that we see certain statements come to light that describe a view of God that is just as inaccurate as the one being dumped on him by his friends.

Job starts to see God in a light of indifference towards his plight. Understandably, Job sees his life as a victim and gets mighty close to calling God the victimizer as a result of all the bad that has befallen him. Though he never crosses the line and curses God, he comes close to the line and is about to set himself up for trading the benefit of being a victor as God's child for the failed identity of a victim. Then God shows up in a powerful way in Job's life.

JOB'S LESSON

I can't tell you how many sermons I have heard that I feel get it all wrong when it comes to what the story of Job is about. Preachers stand in the pulpit and espouse that God allowed all this horrible stuff to come into Job's life because God wanted to teach Job a lesson about who He (God) really is. Don't get me wrong, Job encounters

God and the result of that encounter is a significant and lasting change in his view of God in powerful and unmistakable ways.

But it is my strong belief that it is wrong to say God intended to knock Job down so that He could be built back up. That's a warped view of the sanctification process we all are on. That view has to be changed in the Church.

How can I state with so much conviction that God's plan or intention wasn't to teach Job a lesson? Let me state it another way; how can I be so confident in God's view of Job as being a perfect "ten" when all evidence pointed to him being something less than that? Because it is in the Bible.

Take a look at the very beginning of The Book of Job:

> *¹ In the land of Uz there lived a man whose name was Job. <u>This man was blameless and upright</u>; he feared God and shunned evil. ² He had seven sons and three daughters, ³ and he owned seven thousand sheep, three thousand camels, five hundred yoke of oxen and five hundred donkeys, and had a large number of servants. <u>He was the greatest man</u> among all the people of the East.*
> *⁴ His sons used to hold feasts in their homes on their birthdays, and they would invite their three sisters to eat and drink with them. ⁵ When a period of feasting had run its course, Job would make arrangements for them to be purified. Early in the morning he would sacrifice a burnt offering for each of them, thinking, "Perhaps my children have sinned and cursed God in their hearts." This was Job's regular custom.*
> *⁶ One day the angels came to present themselves before the LORD, and Satan also came with them. ⁷ The LORD said to Satan, "Where have you come from?"*
> *Satan answered the LORD, "From roaming throughout the earth, going back and forth on it."*
> *⁸ Then the LORD said to Satan, "Have you considered my servant Job? <u>There is no one on earth like him; he is blameless and upright, a man who fears God and shuns evil.</u>"*
> *⁹ "Does Job fear God for nothing?" Satan replied. ¹⁰ "Have you not put a hedge around him and his household and everything he has? You have blessed*

*the work of his hands, so that his flocks and herds are spread throughout the land. *¹¹* But now stretch out your hand and strike everything he has, and he will surely curse you to your face."*

¹² The LORD *said to Satan, "Very well, then, everything he has is in your power, but on the man himself do not lay a finger." Then Satan went out from the presence of the* LORD. *Job 1:1-12 (NIV)*

God says it twice in the first few paragraphs of the story of Job. I underlined it above. God said that Job is blameless, upright and great. There is not one like him on earth! Does this sound like the description of someone who is to be graded anything less than a perfect "ten" in God's eyes?

What part of blameless leads you to believe there is something that God needs to change in Job's life? How in the world do we get to the point of thinking that God wants to teach Job a lesson so badly that He needs to completely wreck Job's life to do so?

See how that kind of thinking sets us all up for believing that we are somehow less in the eyes of God? See how that kind of thinking makes us think the bad stuff that happens in this world is somehow an attack on our identity? Our standing before God has to be fully understood, believed and applied on a daily basis or we are doomed to judge ourselves or someone else in the wrong light and cause a serious identity crisis in this world.

We need to begin to read and apply scripture in our lives from the foundation of our true standing before God. Scripture comes alive when we live the life of a victor. Why? Because as God's children we are secure before Him. We are holy because He is holy.

The God I serve isn't in the business of waiting for me to make a mistake so that He can use that mistake to make me better. That isn't sanctification; that's what I call evil. God is in the business of loving His children. He knows we aren't perfect but we have been chosen and that sets us apart from the world in ways that we will learn the more we "ARE" holy rather than trying to "DO" holy.

Job was in no way walking with God in what anyone could call a perfect way. None of us are. God seemed to be more than okay with that fact in Job's life. So it is in our lives as well.

How do I know that? It's in His own words: "Blameless and upright…No one like him (Job) in all the world…" These aren't the words a person uses to describe someone who needs to be set straight. These are the words of a Father beaming over a son whom He sees as a delight.

I know it is hard to understand and accept, but this is how God sees you as well. God sees you as holy, perfect, blameless, no one like you in the whole world. That's the standing you have with Him. That's what it means to be a child of God's.

Job's standing was the same before the tragedies befell him as it was after his life was restored. Job is, was and always will be holy because God is holy. Job's devotion to God is what made him holy, not how much sin was driven out of Job's life by all the bad that came against him. Job was a victor when he was living the victorious life, and he was a victor when all the victory was gone. Every word stated above is just as true for you. I hope you feel the freedom in that as deeply as I do.

For those of you living a Job-like life and going through bad times right now, don't listen to Job's friends telling you that the sooner you learn the lesson God has for you in this part of the journey the sooner you'll get out of this mess. This is a miscommunication from people who don't understand who God is and don't understand how they are viewed as perfect by a perfect God. Your holiness is assured by a Holy God. You are set apart for powerful and revealing glimpses of God's Hand in your life.

Though the world is working to make you feel like a victim, don't let the words of those who just don't understand tempt you to trade your identity as God's perfect child for anything less. Of course you will learn lessons about who God is as a result of going through bad times with God leading the way. That's only natural. But the trials you are facing aren't a result of a lack of holiness in your life. It is because you are holy that the world wants to see you fail. The world wants to drag you down to a point where being set apart doesn't mean a thing in your life. You have the power to stop this.

I wish that meant you have the power over circumstances in life, but that just isn't the case. Bad stuff is going to happen. Sometimes the temporary role we play in our lives is that of a victim. What we have to hold onto is the fact that our God sees us as "blameless" and "like no other" just like He saw His son Job. We are that way, not because of our actions but because of our acceptance of the work Jesus did to allow God to forgive ALL our sins—those we have done, those we do now, and those we will do in the future.

Isn't it time to start living like we are blameless? Satan is trying so desperately to get us off track by considering circumstances as proof that we can't trust our God given identity. He wants us to believe that bad circumstances are signs that our lives need some more work before we can be considered blameless. Victims get caught in this trap of deception. Victors have found their way out by simply believing their identity is what sets them apart.

RIGHTEOUSNESS

The good news is that we aren't alone in this battle. God has sent His Holy Spirit to help us in this cause. Did you know that the Holy Spirit's main job is to convict, counsel and promote the fact that we are righteous because of the holiness that comes from being called and saved by a Holy God? I hate to say it, but even this fact has been limited by our wrong thinking when it comes to our standing before God.

How many times have you heard the statement, "The Holy Spirit convicts us of our sins?" How can this be? If this is the case then the Bible saying that Jesus died to pay for our sins isn't true. If Jesus died for all our sins, why do we need a helper from Heaven pointing out sins in our life?

I believe that we have once again misinterpreted scripture to make God's role in our life be something it just isn't. Again, this is a ploy by Satan to get us off track, to let doubts creep into the reality of who we are through Jesus Christ, and to encourage us to pick up the mantle of being a victim. Let's focus on the Holy Spirit's work as it relates to righteousness and how this impacts our standing before God.

The word righteous is a word that is used a lot in Christian circles. It is one of those "Christian-ese" terms that many of us really don't know what it fully means. If you take a secular dictionary and look up "righteous," here's an example of what you will find:

> right·eous adj.[4]
> 1. Morally upright; without guilt or sin: a righteous parishioner.
> 2. In accordance with virtue or morality: a righteous judgment.
> 3. Morally justifiable: righteous anger.

Strong and convicting words. Who of us can say that we are without guilt or sin? We just can't, but we have to get into our heads that this is how God sees us through the work of Jesus Christ. We are without sin, not because we don't sin, but because Christ has paid for ALL of our sins. If we have no sin, then why do we have guilt? If there is no guilt, then there should be no shame. Shame can't coexist with being a child of God's because they are polar opposite identities. Either you have one and forfeit the other, or you claim one and deny the other. It's our choice, and the Holy Spirit's job is to help us see the power of making the right(eous) choice.

The fact that God sees us as righteous doesn't mean that we don't need to repent of our sins. We are constantly going off track and we need to be in a place where we realize that our sinful nature is something that goes against having a powerful relationship with God. Repenting for those times we know we are willfully disobeying God is a powerful way to throw off the guilt that comes with sin.

On the other hand, we are not to take on the attitude that God forgives us of everything as a license to go out and sin all we want. We are to realize that we are sinners saved by grace and that God sees us as perfect even when our actions don't always confirm this truth.

---

[4] From The Free Dictionary - http://www.thefreedictionary.com/righteous

GOD'S RIGHTEOUSNESS IS <u>OUR</u> RIGHTEOUSNESS

Our standing before God requires us to walk a fine line with Him. On one hand we aren't to think so highly of our standing that we take advantage of God and others in our sin. I have seen victimizers do this in ways that have created victims all throughout the Church and society as well. On the other side, we aren't to think so lowly of ourselves that we reject the Holy Spirit's promptings about our righteousness before God.

Just like holiness, righteousness comes from God. It isn't based on something that we can do to earn more of it. We have to rely on the fact that through Jesus we are made righteous. Also, like holiness, those who don't understand how righteousness manifests itself in the life of a victor are doomed to rigorous and futile striving. At some point you are guaranteed to fail when you rely on your own efforts to stand righteous before God.

Over the long run, that failure sets you up for thinking like a victim. Why? Because eventually even your best efforts at doing the right thing will fail you and the temptation will be to believe that your identity is somehow impacted by the sins that might sneak into your life. When we rely on our own efforts to be righteous instead of allowing the Holy Spirit to convict us of our righteousness we come face to face with the feeling of condemnation. Long-term condemnation is the foundation of victim thinking.

Have you ever done something stupid and heard a voice in your head say, "You are such a stupid person!" That's the voice of condemnation speaking. Most times we just blow that voice off and move on. But left there long enough, that voice can work its way into our souls such that we can begin to believe that our identity is something less than what God made it to be. Anything that impacts our identity greatly limits our effectiveness in walking with God.

CONDEMNATION AND CONVICTION

It is human nature to doubt our ability to measure up in this world from time to time. Even the most confident person, I believe, has issues that bring worry into play. Victim thinkers worry about how they will be able to keep it all going as it is when and if their good fortune comes to an end. Those worries aren't allowed to see the light of day often or for long. But they are there, I'm quite sure of that fact.

That's what condemnation is all about. That feeling that we just don't quite cut it; that we deserve all the bad the world has to offer. Condemnation is an identity crusher.

What I love about being a Christian is the fact that God doesn't burden us with the responsibility of having to "do" in order to be right with Him. All we have to "do" is believe that God has done it all for us through Jesus Christ. We are holy, righteous children of God because of Jesus, and that makes us victors!

Take a look at the following two verses:

> *For He made Him who knew no sin to be sin for us, that we might become the righteousness of God in Him. 2 Corinthians 5:21 (NKJV)*

> *There is therefore now no condemnation to those who are in Christ Jesus, who do not walk according to the flesh, but according to the Spirit. Romans 8:1 (NKJV)*

These two scriptures sum up what the Bible says about our standing with God. These verses say nothing about us doing anything in order to be righteous. When we allow things into our lives that aren't righteous there is no condemnation because of Christ. He has already done all we need to let go of any sense of condemnation that comes our way.

I don't know of any other religion where personal performance is so clearly negated by the Love of God. That's what the Holy Spirit is charged with doing in our lives; convicting or, it might be more accurate to say, convincing us that we are righteous. I said it earlier, but I feel the need to say it again. He doesn't need to convict us of our sins – they have all been paid for. The major work of the Holy Spirit is to convince us that we are right with God.

So where do we get the incorrect notion that the Holy Spirit's job is to convict us of sin? I believe it comes from the misreading of the following verse. In John it says:

> *And when he comes, he will convict the world of its sin, and of God's righteousness, and of the coming judgment. The world's sin is that it refuses to believe in me. Righteousness is available because I go to the Father, and you will see me no more. Judgment will come because the ruler of this world has already been judged. John 16:8-11 (NKJV)*

The Holy Spirit's job isn't to convict believers of sin. The Holy Spirit convicts "the world" (those who don't know Jesus) of sin. The only "sin" the Holy Spirit convicts of is the sin of not knowing Jesus as Savior. Why is not knowing Jesus a sin? Simply stated, God knows how futile it is to try and be holy and righteous, even in a secular way, without the power of being God's child.

God knows that on our own we are destined to fail and that failure can have a detrimental impact on our ability to live the full life He wants for us now and for all eternity. The reality of this statement breaks God's heart for us. The Holy Spirit does all He can to help us see a better way through Jesus. With that relationship secure, we have the opportunity to live the abundant life God wants for us no matter what our circumstances.

For the believer the conviction is about righteousness, not about sin. If Jesus died for our sins, once and for all (like it says in the Bible), then there is no need for God to be there badgering the believer about sin in their lives. This is important as we work to grasp our standing with God. Without knowing our standing with Him, our identity is in jeopardy and we can end up in a place where we will always be guessing about who we are in God's eyes.

Unfortunately, way too many Christians think righteousness, just like holiness, is up to them. We often work so hard to lead a righteous life. We serve. We read. We pray. We fellowship. We do all these things to be a righteous follower of Christ. Sadly, working to be righteous puts us in an amazing position of living a victim filled life.

The reality is that our efforts to be righteous will always, always fall short. There are times when we will find ourselves in a position of failing. Our righteousness is never as good as God's righteousness for our lives. As we find ourselves in a position where our efforts fall short of living as a righteous person the door is wide open for Satan to whisper to our heart that we are no good! As we experience the feelings of our inadequacy over and over again through our failure to earn our own righteousness, we settle into a victim lifestyle. But if we give in to the reality that God's righteousness is ours fully through the gift of Jesus Christ, we find ourselves in a place of incredible freedom. This freedom makes it possible to live the victorious life God paid such a high price for.

Victim thinkers are trapped in a vicious cycle of trying to live up to impossible standards. Victors are free, living in the fullness of the reality that even on their worst day God sees them as perfect through Jesus Christ.

THE ULTIMATE FREEDOM

I said it earlier: I believe that Christians have lost touch with their identity. Without knowing our standing before God we are doomed to waste time in this life trying to figure out who we are. Satan loves us being stuck in that mode. He also loves the various side effects that result when Christians fail to recognize who they are.

I believe Christians don't have to suffer the same kinds of sadness, panic and depression that the rest of the world struggles with. Many Christians, myself included, have fought these kinds of mental attacks all their lives. For me, I can clearly tell you that not having an appropriate understanding of my identity took me to dark places from which I found it difficult to recover. At one point, in fact, I was in such a dark place that no amount of God seemed to be able to get into my consciousness. That was a pretty hopeless time in my life. Thank God for the miracle of the medical community and for medication that literally saved my life.

I believe a significant portion of the blame as to why I faced the kinds of mental illness that I have in the past was a direct result of a lifetime of fighting to try and understand and prove my standing before God and man. After correcting my chemical imbalance, I can now comprehend my standing with God, and frankly I could care less about my standing with man. That's a significant change in my thinking, in my attitude, and in the day-by-day joy I now experience.

Mental illness is not the only potential result of a failed view of our image. I believe the epidemic of addictions that we deal with in life have a direct connection to our continued attempts at trying to cope with the deep pain that accompanies the feeling of not measuring up.

Coping mechanisms can be the foundation for addictions that come to rule our life. It doesn't always have to be drugs or alcohol that we turn to for relief of the pain inside, and our coping mechanisms don't necessarily have to be seen as bad things to the outside world. Sex, work, family, food, church, sports, cars, games, thrills, etc. can all be considered coping mechanisms that may turn into addictions as we use them to cover the pain of not knowing who we are and not buying into our standing before God.

You just have to believe me when I tell you that the draw of the sinful things I turned to in order to cope with the pain inside of me has been greatly reduced as a result of focusing on the concepts that I'm writing about in this book. This isn't a quick fix by any means. I believe that understanding our place before God can be the start of some personal healing in your life. That healing might help you, too, break the bonds in your life that have taken hold as a result of your attempts to cope with the cloud of shame you sometimes feel around you.

It's no wonder we need God to remind us that we are okay in His eyes. So much of this world works against us in ways that make us look and feel defeated. That is a direct attack on our identity and when we give in to that attack we begin to apply victim thinking. Our standing before God is such a powerful reminder of who we are. This is what the Holy Spirit is trying to get us to believe.

CASCADE OF LOVE

As a believer in Christ you are...

1. Lavishly loved by God
2. A child of God's
3. Holy – in spite of your actions
4. Viewed as perfect from God' perspective – no matter your circumstance
5. Righteous – no need to be convicted of sin
6. Not condemned
7. A victor, not a victim

Do you believe this cascade of statements? There are days I do and some days I just can't seem to grasp the fullness of these truths. Those days that I do grasp this reality, things (even the bad things) just seem to be much lighter. The same cares and concerns that are there every day just don't weigh me down like they do on days when I can't grasp these points. On those days that I fail to grasp this cascade of truths I'm doomed to endlessly chasing my tail, trying to prove to the world and to myself that I measure up.

Take a look at what Zac Poonen says about living the life of a victor through Christ:

> *This is now the unshakeable foundation of my life: GOD LOVES ME JUST AS HE LOVES JESUS. It's not because you don't fast and pray sufficiently that you are not entering into the victorious life. Victory comes, not through self-effort but through faith. Faith in what, you may ask? Faith in God's perfect love for you. Many believers live under the condemnation of Satan who keeps telling them, 'You are not fasting enough. You are not praying enough. You are not witnessing enough. You are not studying the Bible enough,' etc. They are constantly being whipped up by such thoughts into an endless round of activity and into a multitude of dead works. Do you realize that all your self-discipline, fasting, praying, tithing and witnessing are dead works, if they do not originate in love for God?*

And they cannot originate in love unless you are secure in God's love first.[5]

See how the wrong understanding of who we are and what our standing is before God can impact our ability to live the John 10:10, abundant kind of life? We can't live under condemnation. Condemnation is like that person in your life who spoke bad things about you all the time. Eventually you begin to believe their lies, and their words become self-fulfilling prophecies for you. When we believe we are condemned we begin to see all the things around us that seem to be adding to that condemnation.

We can't live under the self-imposed thought that we can do more to earn holiness or to make our lives righteous. Eventually we will get things wrong, and holiness and righteousness go out the window. We quickly end up back in a place of self-doubt that is exemplified by the feeling that God has abandoned us for someone more capable than ourselves. The more we try to prove we are holy or righteous the less love seems to be part of our life. We fail to love ourselves and to love others, and we get worse and worse at seeing God's love in and around our lives.

If any of these words are ringing true to you it is because the Holy Spirit is working desperately to try and break through your self-imposed structure, theology and standards to tell you the truth. You are okay with God! Your standing is assured. You have nothing to fight for – it has been freely given. Stop arguing with the Holy Spirit and start listening to the truth that He is trying to get across in these pages. Freedom is yours if you just stop arguing with God and give into His great Love for you!

THE FREEDOM ARGUMENT

Unfortunately, humans seem to love to argue. Ever notice in the Bible how much arguing Jesus had to do with those who really should have

---

[5] Taken from article entitled, "Being Secure In The Love Of God," April 2003. Used by permission of Zach Poonen. Publisher's website: www.cfcindia.com

known who He was? If anyone was in a position to have seen Jesus coming it should have been the religious establishment of that day. They were the educated ones. They were the ones who knew about the coming of the Messiah.

Sadly, their own expectations, desires, and need to protect their way of life blocked their ability to see the truth that was staring them in the face. This ultimately led to their downfall and opened the door to unspeakable persecution by those around them who hated the fact that Israel **IS** the chosen people of God. They lost the ability to see that they were victors and lived lives as victims. How sad!

Let me be quick to point out that the same thing has happened in my life and is happening now in the lives of millions of people who call themselves followers of Jesus. Our expectations, desires and need to protect our way of life continues to get in the way of the truth that is staring us in the face. Our standing before God is secure no matter what our life looks like.

Jesus said it this way:

> *If you hold to my teaching, you are really my disciples. Then you will know the truth, and the truth will set you free. John 8:31-32 (NIV)*

Freedom—that was the issue at stake for the Pharisees during Jesus' time. It is what is at stake for you and for me today. How free do you feel right this minute? If you are like me, the answer to that question depends on how well you perceive your life to be going at that moment. Give me a bad day—say a hiccup in my income stream, or a bad report from the doctor, or a call from school regarding a wayward child... These and similar things remind me that my life can feel like it is hanging on by a thread. Whether it is actually hanging by a thread or just feels that way really doesn't matter. This feeling can make me doubt whether I have access to any level of freedom in my life or not.

Feeling free because life is going well is a temporary freedom, since this world will always have something bad to serve up to us if we live long enough. The truth Jesus is offering is found in the answer to these questions. Are we going to choose our way of life, our desires and/or our expectations, all of which lead to bondage? Or, are we going to choose Jesus and freedom?

Upon hearing Jesus' challenge for freedom in John 8:32, the religious leaders answered:

> *We are Abraham's descendants and have never been slaves of anyone. How can you say that we shall be set free? John 8:33 (NIV)*

Wait just a minute. Did the Pharisees forget that they were in bondage when they made this statement? At the very time they spoke these words to Jesus they were subjects of Roman rule for goodness sake —slaves in the most profound of ways, telling Jesus that they are free.

Did they really believe that they had NEVER been slaves? Did they forget about Pharaoh during Moses' time? What about Nebuchadnezzar during the time of Daniel? Did they really think they were free while living in such times of oppressive captivity? When I read their response to Jesus' call for freedom in John 8:32-33, I think, "Were those people really that dense back then?"

Oh, if it were that simple. The fact is, I am just as dense as I want to believe the Pharisees were. To top it off, I'm surrounded by a multitude of dense Christians who find it easier to deceive themselves and to argue with Jesus about freedom than to live out the freedom He has already given to us. We often find ourselves spouting off just as many absurd statements as the Pharisees as we try to justify our belief that the comfortable life we have right now is enough freedom for us.

In response to their (and our) absurd justification, Jesus says:

> *Very truly I tell you, everyone who sins is a slave to sin. Now a slave has no permanent place in the family, but <u>a son belongs to it forever</u>. So if the Son sets you free, you will be free indeed. I know that you are Abraham's descendants. Yet you are looking for a way to kill me, because you have no room for my word.*

OUR STANDING WITH GOD

John 8:34-37(NIV)

If the Son sets me free, I will be free indeed! What a powerful and hope-filled statement. Why is it I choose so often to reject the promised life of freedom Jesus is talking about? Why do we choose a freedom that is less than that based on the truth Jesus wants us to live out in our lives?

I'm starving for freedom. I hunger for the Church to live in the power that is the kind of freedom Jesus promises in John 8. I'm tired of seeing Christians victimized by the circumstances of this world and becoming so beat down that they settle into lives of quiet desperation. I hate seeing that reality in my life, and I passionately want to be surrounded by a body that yearns to live the life of freedom promised by our savior. That freedom is filled with power: power to change this world; power to build God's Kingdom; power to run the race and finish strong like Paul speaks of in the Bible.

Simply stated, I want to live like a victor. Not a victor as the world defines it. That kind of victor feeling is fleeting. It is so temporary. I want to be a victor the way Jesus was and is a victor. The problem is that I am way too quick to believe the lie that I am a victim. Reality is that you, too, may be quick to believe that lie!

Our standing before God is what makes it possible for us to derail those bondage-laden feelings of victimhood when they show up in our lives. Living under the love of God requires us to let the Holy Spirit convince us that we are okay before Him. There is nothing we need to do to get more love from Him. There is nothing we can do to lessen the love He has for us. Do you believe those two statements? If not, I join the Holy Spirit in saying, "You are wrong!"

The key to ridding your life of victim thinking is to believe that Christ did it all. Your job is to grow in your love for Christ and learn what a relationship looks like with the God that created you. That's what our next chapter is about—relationship. I pray that as you read the upcoming chapters, that you will begin to let the Holy Spirit whisper the words your soul so longs to hear, "You Are MY Beloved!"

Victory is yours. Circumstances don't define that victory, God's love for you does. When bad times strike, let the Holy Spirit pour on you the healing balm of love as He opens your eyes to the power of freedom that's there for you, a child of the King's!

CHAPTER FOUR

Religion vs. Relationship

I believe God despises religion. How's that for a bold statement? Again, I'm not Church bashing with a statement like this. I'm simply stating how I believe I saw Jesus handle the leaders of the religious establishment when He walked this earth. On the surface it appeared that He wasn't very nice to them. Maybe He had a good reason to act that way.

RELIGION DRIVES PEOPLE AWAY FROM GOD

At the time Jesus was alive, the religious leaders were not only in charge of the Church, they also ruled the people. The government of Israel at that time was a Theocracy: there was no separation of Church and State. The priests ruled both the secular and the non-secular governments. The Pharisees and Sadducees were the two main "parties" of their governmental system. Just like our government today, these two parties fought with each other over the powers that were available to them, but united when they had to in order to maintain the prestige and prominence of their office.

Not only were the people subject to the jockeying of religious leaders for position in their community, the Jews alive when Jesus walked the earth were under the rule of a foreign nation to boot. Rome controlled vast stretches of the world, including Israel. In order to maintain their control over such large chunks of the world, they had to enlist the help of key leaders in the community to keep the people in their place.

Rome basically let the carefully chosen leaders of each nation they conquered remain in power if they promised to keep things under control in their land. This gave the ruling class tremendous powers that, in some cases, led them to do things that served themselves at the expense of the people they were supposed to be representing. Their allegiance was to Rome first and everything else second. Sound familiar? God help our country.

Jesus came into this world at a time when the very people who were supposed to be helping the masses find God were instead ruling in a way that did just the opposite. The untold number of rules they imposed on the people along with burdensome, never-ending taxes worked to push the people further and further from their God.

The Pharisees were notorious for taking the Law of Moses (ten simple commandments) and turning them into books and books of rules and regulations that made it almost impossible to live under the law. For example, God told Moses that His people should commit one day as a Sabbath, a day of rest. On that day no work was to be done. The Pharisees took it upon themselves to define what work was. Pages and pages of rules were written to define the word "work" so that the Sabbath could be honored. They even went as far as to define how far one could walk before it was considered work—one step further than their man-made definition of work and the people had sinned before God.

The more rules the people were burdened with, the greater the possibility for the people to see God as uncaring and unapproachable. The religious leaders were driving people away from their God rather than drawing them near.

Same goes for their finances. Israel always had what was called a temple tax. This was a tax imposed in Moses' time to help fund the expenses required to perform the various tasks defined as part of temple worship. Over the years, this tax grew to help support more and more people associated with running the government, including the religious leaders of the time. A good idea gone bad, as those in charge began to realize how easy it was to support their lifestyles at the expense of those they were supposed to be serving and representing. Again, sound familiar?

When Rome took over, the tax situation became overbearing. Now the religious leaders, backed by Roman authority, could use the tax to do things that God never intended the people to support. Most of the religious leaders lived lavish lifestyles all funded by the hard work of the people. In addition to the local taxes, Rome required their own tax structure. With all these rules and financial burdens, you can see how the average person living during Jesus' time might see no way out when it came to living their simple life.

Jesus hated the fact that the religious leaders had become so corrupt. It tainted religion itself. He couldn't stand the hypocritical application of rules and regulations by the religious leaders. Not all the religious leaders of the day were like this, but enough were, such that Jesus publicly ridiculed the ruling class. In the Bible, you will find Jesus calling them serpents, vipers, murderers, fools, losers, and probably some things that couldn't be printed in God's Holy Word. Jesus hated what religion had become because it made it so hard for the people to see what God wanted most from His creation: relationship.

GOD WANTS A RELATIONSHIP WITH YOU

God hasn't done all He has done in this world for us to create and maintain an organized religion. God hungers for and is passionate about relationship with us. He walked through the garden with Adam and Eve in the "cool of the day." They communed together and this gave God great joy. As society grew, man saw the need for more and more structure to somehow help us better understand what should be a growing relationship with God. It's sad to say, but structure is where people seem to always get it wrong.

With structure comes roles. With roles come positions of authority. With authority comes power, and as it has been said: power corrupts; absolute power corrupts absolutely. Leave any structured organization long enough and the power/corruption connection will play a significant role in the performance of that organization. The same can be said for churches of any kind then and today.

Why does structure and the power/corruption connection seem to always restrict an organization? I go back to what we have been discussing all along. It comes down to identity. With roles, positions of authority and power come the opportunity for some kind of corruption as we forget who we are. Better stated, we cause damage (the results of corruption) when we allow roles, positions of authority and power to *define* who we are.

When we allow our standing in this world to define who we are we will always find ourselves in situations where we have to defend our position or authority. The leader who feels his/her identity is tied up in leadership will always be defending against becoming a victim of anything that might threaten their position. Corruption is nothing more than a natural means of self-defense. Unfortunately, this attempt to protect the leader's identity from being challenged by circumstance makes it so that their actions can actually victimize the very people they are charged with leading.

This is what God hates about religion. He hates how our implementation of religion can be so self-serving. How is it that we can choose to use religion to make a name for ourselves; a name that God wants to give us in the first place?

God loves that people want to gather to worship Him. It is when leaders of a religion use control and power to help maintain their position that things get dicey. Control and power can damage the people's view of what a relationship with God is to be all about. That's something God just can't stand. Oh, how I look forward to the day when religion and relationship can be united and mean the same thing. Unfortunately for most of us who have experienced the ugly underbelly of religion, today is not that day.

That's why I wanted to write this chapter. We simply cannot live the life of a victor without understanding the difference between religion and relationship. Religions are filled with people who apply victim thinking. That thinking filters down from the top. Leaders who are even minutely focused on their position more than they are on their relationship with the God who put them there in the first place, are doomed to succumb to victim thinking. As a result, their identities will be negatively impacted. That shift in identity is handed down to individual congregation members that these leaders are charged with caring for. It's a terrible cycle that is repeated every single day in churches of all shapes, sizes and beliefs around the world.

Some of you might recognize what I'm talking about because it's happening in your religious community right now. Others might be thinking that I'm talking about a specific religious group or denomination when I differentiate between religion and relationship. Hear me loud and clear: what I'm saying in this chapter is true for all groups who have some kind of structure when it comes to trying to figure out how to worship our God. There is not one religious group guiltier of failing to promote relationship over religion than another. Nor is there one religious group getting it more right than another. We all have vast room for improvement. We also all have shining examples of leaders in various religions who get the fact that it is about relationship. It was the same in Jesus' day as well.

So when I speak of religion in the remainder of this book I'm talking about a structured way of relating to God that is based on man's understanding of how to achieve the relationship God wants. Religion that I consider negative and counterproductive is something that values and promotes rules and regulations over the actual relationship God wants us to have in the first place.

WHAT'S WRONG WITH STRUCTURE?

People tied to a structure that focuses on rules and regulations to relate to God are doomed to be placed in victimized positions. Why? Rules and regulations require standards. Anytime there are standards, people will see the need to make themselves keepers of the standards, and this creates a level of, dare I say, slavery. This simply goes against all God did for us. Jesus died to set us free, not to create a system that promotes any level of bondage!

Jesus spent a lot of time talking about the downfalls of religion implemented in man-serving ways. So did the Apostle Paul. In Galatians, Paul wrote the following:

> *Those heretical teachers go to great lengths to flatter you, but their motives are rotten. They want to shut you out of the free world of God's grace so that you will always depend on them for approval and direction, making them feel important. Galatians 4:17 (THE MESSAGE)*

Man, left to his own devices, will always move in a direction that benefits himself. Whether through flattery or dominance, those who have forgotten the power of their identity in Christ seek followers who will be dependent on them rather than free to follow God completely. These kinds of leaders need to feel important. Why? They have forgotten how important they are in God's eyes and need to do all they can through their own efforts to make a name for themselves. This is victim thinking to the max, and victim thinking causes victimization, a terrible cycle that continues to show itself in organizations of all types, including the Church.

Religion wants you to conform. It institutes rules and regulations to turn the act of conforming into a system; something that can be propagated and measured in clearly defined ways. When you get people to conform you can control them better. Uniformity is the hallmark of those preaching religion. Rome loved uniformity; it's how they controlled vast swaths of the world in their day. Religion can be just as much about control as conquering nations can be when religious leaders forget who they are. Relationship, on the other hand, leaves room for difference and diversity.

Check out this verse from Colossians. It really hits the nail on the head when it comes to what religion tries to do when control and uniformity become the goal.

> *So, then, if with Christ you've put all that pretentious and infantile religion behind you, why do you let yourselves be bullied by it? 'Don't touch this! Don't taste that! Don't go near this!' Do you*

think things that are here today and gone tomorrow are worth that kind of attention? Such things sound impressive if said in a deep enough voice. They even give the illusion of being pious and humble and ascetic. But they're just another way of showing off, making yourselves look important. Colossians 2:20-23 (THE MESSAGE)

Paul is trying to get those of us who have accepted Christ as our Savior to realize that we don't need religion, as described in its worst forms. We need relationship. That relationship is secured in what Christ did for us: He made us God's children. This is what makes us victors. The "do's and don'ts" of religion are a means of stepping backwards, not moving forward. The illusions of holiness that leaders pass on to followers are quickly shattered by the slightest hitch in the results of the plan that religion-based leaders put into action. With God, it is all about relationship. The foundation for this relationship is identity.

Deep down inside of us all, there is a hunger to be known. We work so hard to satisfy this hunger by doing things that make us look good to the outside world and make us feel good inside. Oh, how temporary this is! This kind of satisfaction is such a jealous mistress in our lives. It is never satisfied!

We want to be known so that we might have a shot at knowing ourselves. Again, it is all about identity. We deeply want to know who we are and to be accepted in that knowledge.

Far too often we take on a bunch of rules and regulations in an effort to fit in so that we will be accepted in who we are. That's the way of religion. Religion doesn't let us be known because it is too worried about maintaining its own identity to let our identity be seen and appreciated. When it comes to identity, relationship is the only way to the freedom that God intended for us in the first place.

Religions get really confused when positions are tied to identities. Let me paint a picture of how this might look in a local place of worship. Though the specifics of how an organization might look will vary, what I am about to describe can be the case no matter what your brand of religion.

HOW RELIGIONS GET IT WRONG

Let's take a fairly typical Protestant brand of religion and pick on them for a while. Those who aren't part of this style of leadership structure remember, you can be just as guilty of religious behavior as what I'm about to present below. See if you recognize any of the characteristics of this story.

Let's look more deeply into that beautiful little church on the corner of 1st and Main in your town. This church is probably led by a pastor who feels he has been called to lead a group of people to a deeper realization of who Christ is in their lives. Like most pastors, he has sacrificed much to follow this calling and has put his family's personal well-being on the line to be a part of what God is doing in and through his life. He is a man to be honored for such a sacrifice.

So far, so good. There is nothing "religious" about what I have presented so far. But we are on the verge of allowing religion to take hold.

This pastor, who is living out his "destiny" to reflect the love of Christ, was probably hired and is overseen by a group of elders or leaders. The Bible lays out clear leadership structures for local churches and even goes as far as to give guidelines as to who would be good overseers.

This local church has been very careful to follow the Bible's lead on how to organize their leadership. In our example, this group of men and women who oversee this local body has a feeling of calling on their lives as well. They take their jobs of protecting their local church seriously and for good reason. There are a lot of forces out there trying to destroy the local church. Now things start to get a bit shaky on the "religious" front.

The leaders are held in high esteem by the local congregation. Uh-oh, identity issues are about to arise. The leaders feel the pressure of this esteem and don't want to do anything that might jeopardize their standing among the people. This is the point where their true identity as children of God's is starting to morph into something that will greatly limit their ability to lead in relationship rather than leading as a religion.

The congregation trusts these leaders to make the kinds of godly decisions that will enable their church to be a shining example of what Christian living is supposed to look like. After all, the congregation wants the rest of the town to be impressed by the fact that they attend this particular strong and inspiring church. The congregation's identity issues are now clouding their motives for attending church in the first place. For some, church is more of a social club where it is good to be seen rather than a place where relationship is the key.

The congregation expects the leaders to hire pastors who will help them to be the best people they can be so that they can live their comfortable lives without God finding fault in what they do. Their efforts aren't always focused on trying to be holy. Sometimes all their efforts are aimed at trying to keep God from finding fault in their lives. Religion can often be about appeasing God so that He will not bring some kind of punishment down on them. Now we are getting into places where religion has more than taken hold. When the personal interests of an individual come before God's plan for them, identity gets awfully confused, and power is wasted in ways that greatly limit our impact in this world.

This pressure from the people to make sure they attend a church that will be recognized as being in good standing with God and with the community can force the leadership to make decisions that look good in the world's eyes rather than decisions that match up with God's plan. Fundamentally, the term "good standing" is something that is so wide open to interpretation that when a group of people are involved misunderstanding and conflict can't help but arise. The bottom line to good standing is the innate desire to be seen as part of something good. It is the desire to have your identity validated by something you do, including going to church.

So the leadership of this local church feels the pressure of "good standing," and in defense of their identity they want to make sure they can cover enough bases so as to please the greatest number of people attending the church. The leaders are struggling to make sure they are able to prove that the decision of the people to put them in positions of leadership in the first place was a good decision. They want the people to continue to see them as competent and effective leaders, as people who can be trusted to make good things happen.

The leaders turn to church experts, consultants and leaders of other successful churches to help them devise standards and measurable results in their church to make sure they are heading in the right direction. They want to be able to prove to their congregation, and to themselves, that they are right in the middle of what they believe to be God's will. They fall into the trap of thinking that numbers always prove that they are doing the will of God. They believe that the growing size of the congregation is proof of God's pleasure in what they are doing. Identity has now been changed to something worldly, and the Heavenly power of living as God's child has been more than compromised for this church.

The poor pastor is caught in the middle of all this mess. His job depends on being able to make sure everyone's identity is upheld. His very identity is tied to how well he can pull off the balancing act between doing what the congregation demands the leaders to do for them and the call God has placed on his life in the first place.

More and more, the pastor relies on measurable results to gauge his level of success at meeting God's call. The pressures of the job of being a pastor outweigh the lightness of walking with God in a direction He has put on this pastor's heart. The pastor's identity is now dependent on how well he does his "job." Calling has now all but been abandoned.

The congregation needs to feel they are seen in the best light both inside and outside the church. The church leadership needs to be confirmed in their leadership abilities by making sure the standards that were established to prove they are in God's will are adhered to. The pastor needs to prove that his calling is, in fact, true by making sure he does all he can to meet the standards of success this church requires.

So the pastor focuses his teaching on areas where change can be most recognized and easily measured. He institutes programs to teach people certain biblical strengths so that they will be good little soldiers in the Lord's army. More and more control is instituted. Conformity to the system is rewarded. Uniformity is celebrated.

Sooner, rather than later, this local church becomes a closed system of worship. Strangers, particularly "strange" strangers who might disrupt the uniformity of the church, are nicely "handled" in a way that helps them quickly realize that this place is not for them. The church might have growth, but that growth is typically from people, like themselves, who want the kind of uniformity that best suits their personality and collective goals.

Every step of the way in our little example the local church is buffeted by the power struggles that result when we have forgotten who we are. I believe Jesus Himself faced this kind of potential for identity crisis. Take a look at what it says in the following passage:

> *After the two days he left for Galilee. Now, Jesus knew well from experience that a prophet is not respected in the place where he grew up. So when he arrived in Galilee, the Galileans welcomed him, but only because they were impressed with what he had done in Jerusalem during the Passover Feast, not that they really had a clue about who he was or what he was up to. They were impressed only by what he had done. The beginning of victimhood is not knowing Him. John 4:43-45 (THE MESSAGE)*

Why is it that prophets aren't respected where they grew up? It's because the people there remember them as messed up and messy children, not as the person of God they have grown into. The locals can't get past the worldly identity they remember to see that the prophet is empowered by his true identity as a child of God. Such was the case with Jesus as well. But why was He accepted in other places? Because of the things He had done. They didn't know who Jesus was, they had only heard what He had done. Religion is such that we are only as good as our last performance.

This is the pressure we put on pastors and Church leaders. We want action. We want results. We want whatever it takes to make us all look good. This is the worst religion has to offer. It kills relationships both horizontally (with people) and vertically (with God). Actions, and the results of those actions, offer lousy proof of who we are. They put us in a position of always having to perform in order to prove who we are. That's why I think God hates religion. It has the ability to make us doubt who we are in His eyes.

Is this what Jesus had in mind when He said, "Go and make disciples?" I hardly think so. This fictional picture of what the local church can look like is happening in every single type of religious organization in the world today to some degree or another. I'm sorry if that statement offends you, but it's true. Identity is being built on things we do rather than on what Christ made us to be. This causes the worst in any organization, particularly religious organizations.

HOW IDENTITY INTERFERES WITH RELATIONSHIP

Don't for a minute think that any of you are immune to this condition. I'm the worst offender of them all. Let me give you a real life example.

I have been part of a church for over twenty years now, Coastline Church in Carlsbad, CA. I love this beautiful church. It was founded by a bunch of godly men and women who came out of some challenging circumstances in another local church. Many of the leaders of this church have turned out to be lifelong friends; more than that, they are family. We have gone through a lot together.

Over the years, most of the original founders of this church have left. Some on good terms, others on not so good terms. But somehow this little church keeps getting blessed with godly and amazing people to lead us, week in and week out.

Today our church is pastored by Aaron Jayne. Aaron is a dynamic man, full of so much drive and energy. Aaron came to Coastline Church at a time of some pretty incredible and difficult changes. Although Aaron has done some amazing works for God since he was nineteen years old (check out The Dream Center in Los Angeles), Coastline was Aaron's first opportunity to pastor a local church.

One day Aaron came to me and asked me to be Coastline's Prayer Pastor. What an honor to be asked to fill such an important role. As honored as I was, my first thought was, no way! Why? I knew that I have an annoying tendency to let roles shape my identity, and taking on such a critical role for my beloved church might be more temptation than I could handle. I simply didn't want to let my identity be impacted by anything I did inside the church.

After a bunch of prayer, I decided to talk more with Aaron about what I thought I could and couldn't do as Prayer Pastor. After our discussion, I felt the go-ahead from God to take on this role.

A funny thing happened just a few days after I accepted this position. We had a Thursday evening prayer and worship service. Aaron had announced my position to the congregation the weekend before, so this was my first opportunity to be in a place of "official leadership" at a church-sanctioned prayer function. All day before the event I felt a familiar uneasiness. I couldn't put my finger on why I was feeling the butterflies like I was. At one point in the day I had to just stop and get quiet so I could see if God was trying to show me something. Sure enough, He was.

It became clear to me that He didn't want me to compromise my identity as His child in any way. The uneasiness I was feeling was a growing pressure I was putting on myself. Deep down, I felt I needed to do something that evening to prove that Aaron's trust in me to be Prayer Pastor was correctly placed. I wanted (maybe needed) God to move through me so that everyone there would see that Aaron was a wise man in choosing such a "godly and capable" person as me to fill this position. That's totally sick!

See how a religious spirit can come from that kind of thinking? See how I could become corrupt letting that kind of thinking lead my way? See how I could set myself up for victim thinking and possibly put myself in a place of victimizing others to protect myself and or my position? What a mess we cause when we let our true identity be compromised by anything temporary like a position, even a church position.

I remember saying to myself that I refused to do anything that evening without the feeling that God had given me permission to do so. A peace came over me that confirmed that I had made the right decision. The butterflies were gone and I was free to enjoy the time of worship and prayer that evening.

My wife and I arrived at church and I was immediately greeted by Aaron. He pointed out to me where the open microphone would be and encouraged me to speak anytime I wanted to. During the worship music Aaron once again came to me giving me permission to speak anything I felt needed to be said. I know all Aaron was trying to do was to make sure I was comfortable with speaking at this event if I wanted to. Satan, on the other hand, was trying to do something very different. He was trying to tempt me to take the bait and let my need for approval overshadow the power I have in my identity. I smiled and told Aaron I would step up if God gave me something to share.

About half an hour into the service I got one of those "words" from God that kind of knocks your socks off. It was amazing. Right on the mark for the group that evening. I felt that familiar sensation of dizziness and lightness that comes to me when I feel the presence of God so clearly. I just knew this was from God and I was about to jump up and share it before the group when I stopped and did something that I so often forget to do. I asked God, "Do you want me to share this thought right this moment?" Though I knew clearly that this word was for our church, I felt the overwhelming sense that God was saying, "No!"

Normally that kind of answer would have confused me to no end. Why would God speak such a clear word if He didn't want it shared with those it was so obviously for? Fortunately I had already dealt with identity, and the importance of a word from God wasn't going to change who I was, whether I gave that word or not.

What a powerful place to be. A place of freedom that doesn't rely on what we do to feed who we are. I was free to continue enjoying the evening. Later on that night, God opened my eyes to something that

He gave me permission to share. I was prepared to share from a place of who I was, not from a place of trying to prove I was something that I wanted to be.

The difference between religion and relationship is identity. Religion uses roles to empower the identity we want or think we need in an effort to make the best happen for the Church. Relationship allows identity to empower the roles we have in the Church so that God's Plan can be more fully put into place.

Any time we allow the roles we are given to shape our identity then the need for success comes into play. If our roles are working well we feel good about who we are. God forbid the results of our roles should be less than what we (or others) expect. This causes us to doubt who we are and maybe even get to the point of doubting God Himself. People who have their identity wrapped up in roles they play will fall into victim thinking. Religion is such that it is so easy to let roles define who we are. This can open the door to victim thinking throughout the congregation.

STOP STRIVING

In religion we worry about the results because results reflect on our identity. We do good, so therefore we must *be* good. Failure means there must be something wrong with us. This is victim thinking.

Relationship doesn't have to worry about results for the same identity-driven reasons religion does. Of course, those seeking relationship want things to turn out right. If they don't, it doesn't change the fact we are victors because we are God's children. Victors realize that relationship is what God wants, not results.

Victims think that results are what make it possible to have good relationships. What a terrible way to live life. Religion, in its worst form, is fostering this kind of living. Maybe that's the reason organized religion has been so lackluster in its ability to bring real and lasting change in today's world.

In the Psalms there is an interesting verse that so clearly defines the difference between religion and relationship. It says:

Be still and know that I am God… Psalms 46:10 (NIV)

A friend of mine once studied this verse very carefully and was struck at the meaning of "be still." It means to stop striving. Striving is one of those words that, when looked at carefully, isn't all that pretty of an action to have in our lives. Striving basically means to do what it takes to get something to happen. Striving is very different than just trying. Striving has a sense of desperation that just doesn't have to be there to know God or to be known by Him. Striving isn't bad in all circumstances, but it is a killer in relationship.

Striving is what religion does to try and prove that those caught up in religious activities know God. But that's not what this verse (and many more) says. God wants us to stop striving to know Him.

I can also argue that He wants us to stop striving to be known as well. The Holy Spirit wants us to rest in God. As we strive we fall victim to the guilt of failure. No matter how grand our efforts we will eventually fall short in striving to know Him or to be known by Him. It's in those times that victim thinking once again rears its ugly head.

Lack of striving doesn't mean lack of action. It just means we do all we feel we need to do but leave the results up to God. People who rest secure in their knowledge of God and God's knowledge of them are victors. They are the ones who know that the results of their busy lives don't challenge who they are. They don't have to strive to know God. Their knowledge of Him is exactly what it should be, nothing more and nothing less. Victors also know that their knowledge of God will grow as life progresses. It's just a natural thing that those in the relationship will get to know each other all the more.

As we strive we do work *for* God. As we rest we work *with* God. Working with God creates a confidence that makes us victors even when the world falls apart around us. Religion is full of striving. Works abound. Relationship, exemplified by a peace in action, is the best example of what the Bible calls "rest." Want to be a victor and know God? Stop striving!

I believe that striving is one of the hardest things for us to give up. Striving leads us to use words like "servant" and "master" when we describe our relationship with God. Yes we do serve God and He is our master, but do you really believe, that as His children, we are servants? Do any of you parents call your children servants?

We are God's children, not His servants. He is our Father, not our Master. Yes, we serve an all-powerful God, a God who is to be feared, but that same feared God is our Father. Striving comes into play when we think of God as our Boss. Striving is also a part of our lives when we misrepresent God the Father by putting on Him the failed ways our earthly fathers tried to love us.

God did not create us to be some kind of hired hand. Nor did He create us to work to try and earn His love. Both these views make the negative side of religion come alive and kill the possibility of a real and active relationship with the God that made us.

Those who are caught in victim thinking see worshiping God as a religious duty. This kind of religion portrays God as a being that demands perfection through our own efforts. For the religious, striving is the only way to ever please this God, since we just can't seem to "be" enough in our own eyes to ever rise to His standards.

Every failure we experience drives home the fact that we just don't measure up. Slowly our victimization leads to an isolation where relationship has a hard time ever being seen as a possible alternative. It feels good to just try to uphold the requirements of religion since at least sometimes we get some of them right. But deep down inside, victim thinkers know that their own efforts will never be enough, and this scares them to death.

Victors see God as a Person. Their view of Him grows to a point where they actually believe God might just love them no matter what their life looks like. They have crossed that line where they realize their own actions are useless and have surrendered to the finished work of Jesus when it comes to approaching this God that made them.

Victors get to spend the rest of their lives discovering what relationship really means. They make plenty of mistakes along the way but victors have given up on striving because they have tasted the reality that "being" outdoes "doing" when it comes to drawing near to this God.

Victors aren't inactive. They just realize that their activities have no relation to how they appear to God. This understanding of God's love keeps them in a place of contentment that seems to last even when the bad times come. Victors aren't perfect from the world's standpoint either, but victors believe that they are blameless in God's eyes and that is enough for them.

GOD HATES RELIGION

What I'm talking about again is freedom. Religion leads to bondage. Relationship with God is all about freedom. The apostle Paul wrote a book in the Bible that screams freedom. The Book of Galatians is an amazing read. It is even more eye opening when you read it from Eugene Peterson's *The Message*, a paraphrase of the entire Bible. Check out what Paul is saying about those who try to use "doing" to find relationship with God.

> *So those now who live by faith are blessed along with Abraham, who lived by faith—this is no new doctrine! And that means that anyone who tries to live by his own effort, independent of God, is doomed to failure. Scripture backs this up: "Utterly cursed is every person who fails to carry out every detail written in the Book of the law." The obvious impossibility of carrying out such a moral program should make it plain that no one can sustain a relationship with God that way. The person who lives in right relationship with God does it by embracing what God arranges for him. Doing things for God is the opposite of entering into what God does for you. Galatians 3:9-11 (THE MESSAGE)*

Utterly cursed—that's what we are when we try to relate to God through our actions. Utterly cursed are those who religiously put rules and regulations on others in a veiled attempt to get them closer to God. They are doomed to failure. That failure will ultimately make both leaders and followers feel like victims, and victim thinking will rule the day.

I love the last line of the Galatians passage above: "Doing things for God is the opposite of entering into what God does for you." If you want to radically change how you do religion, put this verse into practice. Stop doing and not doing because you are told so and start looking for what God is doing and join in with Him.

When are we going to realize that God doesn't need us to do a single thing? He doesn't need us to be holy. He doesn't need our lives to reflect Him to this world. Do you seriously think that you are so important to the plan of God that if you fail you will make God fail? If so, you serve a weak and shortsighted God.

My God doesn't need me, HE WANTS ME! Wow! That's a game-changer.

That's the basis of relationship: a mutual desire to be connected in some way with each other. He doesn't want to be with us because we bring something to the table that He is missing. He wants to be with us because He loves us. We find it hard to believe that kind of love and think we have to do something about our imperfection in order to deserve and reap the benefits of that love.

But love isn't about finding or attaining perfection. It is about seeing perfection through God's eyes. If we expect our earthly relationships to be built and grown on a foundation of measuring up to some level of expectation we will always find that relationship will fail us. We will find ourselves victims of that relationship we thought so highly of in the past. Perfection in a relationship will kill the love that can grow from it. So it is with our relationship with God. If we are caught in the religious mode of doing to try and achieve some level of proficiency in order to gain His Love we will always feel slighted by God; victimized by the lofty ideals religion holds out as being necessary to draw near to Him.

Rule-keeping doesn't work with earthly relationships for long. It doesn't work with trying to keep a relationship with God alive either. Look what Paul wrote about keeping rules in the passage below:

> *The person who believes God, is set right by God—and that's the real life. Rule-keeping does not naturally evolve into living by faith, but only*

perpetuates itself in more and more rule-keeping, a fact observed in Scripture: The one who does these things [rule-keeping] continues to live by them. Galatians 3:11-12 (THE MESSAGE)

Religion approaches God in a "form and function" manner. This always leads to a conditional kind of give and take in relationship. Religion says, "If you do this, God will do that (and the other way around)."

Religion approaches God in a businesslike manner. Immersed in religion, we live with God as a tenant. We are a hired hand hoping to get it right so that we might get a small bit of His pleasure lavished on our life. This is a downtrodden way to live. It is the victim's method of passing through this life trying to hold onto what little control we can to get by. This is the kind of life that is filled with opportunity for the victim to become the victimizer.

Victors have learned that the victim thinking way of life doesn't work. They have found that religion without relationship isn't something that they can live with. Relationship isn't a form and function, business kind of approach with God. It is family kind of approach.

This approach is built on character, and God sees our character as perfect through Jesus Christ. This makes His love perfectly unconditional. Victors aren't tenants or hired hands; they are God's children. He isn't their boss, God is a victor's Dad. This makes victors more apt to show the same kind of unconditional love to others in this world as God is so willing to show them. Victors are less likely to create victims in their wake because they just don't have to compete for God's love in ways that damage others around them.

Why do I think God hates religion? It is because religion, in its worst form, makes us victims. God didn't do all He has done for us to make victim thinking part of our lives. Jesus came to make us victors.

What parent doesn't think they have the best kid around? In God's eyes, we are perfect. God is our Father and His love for us is what religion should be all about. Not rules and regulations. Not striving. Nothing that makes us ever think that we are less than the victors God knows us to be should ever get in the way of relationship in the name of religion.

Next time you come up against religion in any organization you are a part of (secular or non-secular alike), choose relationship. That's where the kids of the King hang out. It is in relationship that we find our place and our power in this world.

CHAPTER FIVE

Provision & Victimhood

Ever been challenged in being able to provide for yourself or your family? Most of us have been in this position in one way or another. Maybe we haven't been challenged to the point of living moment-by-moment like some do around the world, but there are few things that can cut us to the core more than that feeling that we just don't measure up in the area of provision.

Provision is definitively connected to victimhood. When we are in a place where provision isn't an issue, we feel like a victor. Nothing seems to get us down. But when the hard times hit and provision is something at which we have to work doubly hard, victim thinking can sneak its way into our lives and play havoc with our ability to see things clearly.

It never ceases to amaze me that when times of difficult provision hit it feels like everything I attempt to do just doesn't quite happen like I thought it would. Everywhere I turn I get slammed with the feeling, "You just don't measure up." Provision plays a powerful role in all our lives.

Since 1989, my wife, Barbara, has been the breadwinner of our family. Barbara and I both attended the same college, Drexel University in Philadelphia, PA. She graduated with a business degree and I obtained a degree in engineering. After college I hit the ground running with a very well-paying job while she started a business in the personal financial planning field.

Those first few years were a real battle for Barbara in the area of provision. For me, provision seemed to be a piece of cake. But after a few years, the reality of the difference in income potential between working for someone versus working for yourself began to come into play. By the end of the 1980s, Barbara was making much more than me, so much so that I came to work for her company.

Those early years working together were so much fun. We spent many, many hours together building a wonderful business. We both have great memories of those long, hard days working side by side. Then kids came into the picture.

Now we had a major decision to make. Both of us felt that raising our children shouldn't be left up to anyone other than us. Though we had help in the house, we decided that one of us needed to be predominantly a stay-at-home parent. Due to the fact that the business we had built was structured around Barbara and her partner it was obvious that I would run things from home.

Looking back on that decision I don't regret a single thing, but it didn't come without much personal difficulty. There were times when the fact that I wasn't the provider for my family really hit me hard in ways, that looking back from where I am today, played into my victim thinking. It didn't help matters that the Bible seems to stipulate that a major role of the man in a marriage is that of provider. Toss on top of that the fact that I actually had well-meaning people from church directly question me as to whether I was doing the right thing by staying home with our kids, and I think you might be able to see how victim thinking was able to get a foothold in my life in the area of provision.

Even though Barbara and I felt that God was leading the way and blessing our decision for her to be the "provider" of our family, I couldn't help but feel less of a man as a result. Can you guess why? You got it, identity. Hate to sound like a broken record, but I was allowing my role to influence my identity and that allowed victim thinking to take over. And take over did it ever!

As our children got older and started to challenge us, as children will do, I began to feel that I was failing at being a father as well. A couple of issues came into our marriage that made me doubt whether Barbara and I could even make it together as husband and wife. Then our church hit challenging times, and I didn't seem to be able to influence it to the degree that I thought I should be able to, in order to bring about change. Friendships seemed to fail me as well. Victim event after victim event seemed to plague me everywhere I turned.

With every challenge came that gnawing feeling that the problem was ME! I just couldn't seem to get anything right. Knowing what I know now, I realize that I was firmly in the grips of victim thinking. More and more I found myself in the throes of depression. Just like everyone, I would have the occasional down day, but my down days began to come with an alarming frequency that I just couldn't seem to control. Finally, on July 27th, 2010, whatever the chemical is that helps to regulate mood simply stopped working in my life.

For the next several months it was all I could do just to get out of bed. I actually remember sitting on the couch thinking this is as good as it is going to be—I guess I'm going to have to figure out how to live like this for the next 20 or 30 years of my life. I had a terrible case of victim thinking that I just couldn't seem to find my way out of.

I can't blame the depression I was experiencing directly on my not being a provider for my family, but I can draw a pretty straight line from those decisions we made decades ago to where I ended up in 2010.

Does that mean that we made wrong decisions back then? Absolutely not! Would I change anything I did back then? I don't know that I can think of a single thing I would change other than trying to apply what I'm writing in this book in my life. I can't help but believe that had I known my identity as a Child of God then as fully as I do now, I might not have ended up in the same situation. Of course, I also wouldn't have had the kinds of experiences that made it possible to pen the thoughts in this book, either.

As has been said many times already, this world has an amazing ability to knock us down from time to time. That's particularly the case with provision, which is such a challenging area for men and women alike, especially when provision is linked to identity. For those who believe in a Judeo/Christian God, God the Provider can add an entirely new layer of confusion when it comes to provision and its ability to impact our identity.

GOD AS PROVIDER

God of the Bible has many names spelled out in the text. In the original language the various names of God literally roll off the tongue. Names like Jehovah Rapha meaning, "the Lord our Healer" and Jehovah Shalom, "the Lord is Peace." If you were to do a search on the web for "the names of God" you would find many links to places that list hundreds of names and/or characteristics of God. Of all the names of God in the Bible, the one I have heard Christians lean on the most is Jehovah-Jireh (pronounced Jira). This beautiful name means, "The Lord will provide."

There are many, many scriptures in the Bible that attest to God being the focus of our provision. Stories abound of God showing up at just the right moment with just the right thing to help biblical characters get out of the crazy situations this world placed them into. Speak to Christians and you will find that they, too, have experienced this same provision, time after time, in their own lives.

I have no problem with believing in God as the provider. Where I find that we get into trouble is when our expectations of what that provision looks like isn't exactly met in the timely manner we have set forth before God. When it looks like God isn't providing how and when we want, victim thinking is quick to take hold in our lives.

I can't tell you how many Christians I have counseled that have doubts running through their heads and hearts about God because certain situations have failed to work out when it comes to how they have been praying for God's intervention in their lives. Thoughts like, "I don't know if God loves me" and, "I must have some sin in my life that is keeping God from hearing my prayers" make it possible for children of the King to think that they have been abandoned by their Father.

This warped view of what provision from God must look like has made the name Jehovah-Jireh something of a lie in the eyes of the victim thinker. What I have found with the Bible is that if one part of what it says seems to be failing you then it won't be long before you find more and more "contradictions" in the Word that make it possible to believe God will continue to fail you. Victim thinking starts when our expectations aren't met in ways that we demand.

I have a friend who is an amazing man of God. I'd be lying to say that my friend's life is perfect or that his expression of God's love to the world has been all nice and clean; it hasn't been. My friend has had some serious challenges in his life that have buffeted him from side to side at times. But all through the storms, he has stood close to God.

I told my friend during a particularly turbulent time in his life that he was one of the most messed up Christians I had ever met. Yet, on that very day, he heard something from God that was so dead on in my life that I can't begin to tell you how important it was for my walk with my Heavenly Father. Isn't that the way of God—using "cracked pots" (like you and me) to bring the light of revelation into the world?

My friend has always been one of those people who has experienced God showing up at just the right time with just the right amount of provision over and over again in his life. I think that is why his walk with God has been so filled with amazing intersections of the miraculous; my friend believes God provides because He always has!

This friend is one of those Christians who has always leaned heavily into the Jehovah-Jireh name of God. Then there came a time in his life when God's provision didn't match up with what the natural world said was needed. At times, income wasn't there for house and car payments. Possessions were lost. Relationships were strained to the breaking point. There were times when I heard my friend say things about his walk with God that I now know was steeped in victim thinking.

My friend's expectations of Jehovah-Jireh made God's provision seem meaningless and misguided when he was trapped in victim thinking. Yet to his credit, he stood with God all through this turbulent time and God continues to provide things that make my friend a wealthy man whether his bank account reflects this fact or not.

I met this friend for coffee not too long ago. Our paths hadn't crossed in over a year, and it was good to sit and meet with him. Though many of the specific circumstances that had put this man in a place of doubting God's provision hadn't changed, his attitude had made a dramatic shift from victim to victor. While we were talking, he asked me if I wanted to hear something amazing God had been teaching him. Knowing how this man hears from God, I was excited to know what God had been saying.

He began to tell me how God had been opening his eyes to what God's name, Jehovah-Jireh, really means. He pointed out that the common meaning of Jireh is accurately described as provision, but God had been showing him a deeper meaning as to what the provision really is. My friend was waking up to the amazing revelation that provision in God's eyes is so much more than just giving us what we think our needs are.

His studies had shown that Jireh has an element to its meaning that has to do with "to see and to be seen." Wouldn't you know it—Jireh is really about identity. Interesting coincidence isn't it? This friend who has walked a life with God the provider was seeing a new meaning to provision and sharing it with me, who has been walking with God over the issue of identity. Fascinating that this new meaning of provider my friend was sharing had something to do with a combination of how God has shown Himself as real to each of us over the years.

In its simplest state, Jehovah Jireh means "God will provide", however, that provision comes through opportunities for us to see Him, and in ways He will be seen in our very own circumstances. Now that's a very different take on provision than what many of us in the Church have thought when it comes to provision from God.

I have heard the story of a certain man of God who took it upon himself to house orphans and street children hundreds of years ago. This man wasn't a man of means. He didn't have the money to feed all the children he had taken in. Day after day, he would sit his "family" down at the dinner table, set for a meal, with no food on the stove. They would hold hands and thank God for their non-existent meal. As the story goes, not long after they would say, "Amen", they would hear a knock on the door and there would be someone with food in hand who felt "led" to bring them a dinner. Talk about Jehovah-Jireh, God will (and did) provide for this man's needs.

What I wonder about is those days when there wasn't a knock on the door? Would the words of thanks be as powerful and as filled with hope if the table had remained empty? We just don't know until we cross that bridge.

GOD, PROVISION AND THE VICTIM MENTALITY

We will eventually find ourselves in a victim mentality if we box God into being our cosmic grocery store. If this is the extent of our faith, we will eventually be disappointed when God's provision turns out to be something other than what we expected it to be.

A victor is one who lives in a place where all he expects is to see God. He doesn't put all his hope in the expectation that God will provide his next meal, a healing, a good worship service, a revealing word... A victor is grateful when those things come from the hand of God, but doesn't expect them in a way that jeopardizes his relationship with God if they don't appear. A victim is made when the expectations of provision aren't realized in the way or according to the timing expected, even when that expectation requires a trust in God's hand to provide.

God is desperate for us to see His Face. A victor isn't looking for God's "handouts," he's looking to see into the "soul" of the Father so that the victor will better understand who he is as seen through the eyes of God Himself. It's great to have our needs provided for as we walk out this life ministering in the spirit of God. But Jehovah Jireh is so much more than a warehouse of supplies there for those who have been called according to His purposes. Jehovah Jireh is the promise that God's presence can and will always be there. His presence will be something we can count on, lean into, and be led by. His presence may not always fill our stomachs or our bank accounts, but it is real and can be counted on in the life of a child of God's.

The next time that issue of provision that you prayed for so fervently, that thing you called out for Jehovah Jireh to provide, doesn't come at the right time or fails to materialize at all, remember that it is very likely that God, in His infinite wisdom, saw it better for Him to be seen by you in not receiving that important thing in your life. You didn't fail Him. He didn't fail you. You aren't a victim of a Father who needed to discipline His child or the victim of a loveless Father using you like a pawn in some cosmic game of chess. Victim thinking draws us away from that Father. Even when the provision you so needed to happen doesn't, you are a victor, ripe for the presence of the Father to be seen and for His presence to be shown to those around you.

The realization of what Jehovah-Jireh really means in the area of provision is profound, and has to be the foundation of victor living if we are to fight off the feelings of victimhood in this world of crazy events. Provision is all about identity. It's about the reality and truth of God's identity in our lives and the reality and truth of our identity in God's eyes. If we allow circumstances to take our eyes off of who God is and who we are, victim thinking will lead us down some long and dark paths.

EXPECTATIONS: THE KILLER OF FAITH

Here's a key truth for you to keep close to your heart: expectations are the killer of faith. If my expectation of God, or anyone else for that matter, is not met, then I'm going to believe less about that person or God. We are in great company when it comes to this fact.

Jesus had an interesting cousin named John. John was just a few months older than Jesus. God used this man for a very important task during Jesus' time. The entire story of John's birth is nothing short of a miracle itself. You can check it out for yourself in Luke Chapter 1.

John's life purpose was to announce the coming of Jesus. He was taught from a very early age that he would see the miracle of the coming of a Messiah (savior) and his "job" would be to point people to Him. John had a ministry in the desert that included baptizing people in the ways of God.

One day Jesus Himself came to John and said that He needed to be baptized. John refused at first because he knew Jesus was from God. He was perfect in every way and was in no need of baptism. John told Jesus that he, not Jesus, was the one who needed to be baptized; in other words, John knew he needed Jesus in order to come under the full authority of God. Jesus persisted, however, and John baptized Him.

As Jesus was coming out of the water the Holy Spirit came on Jesus. A voice from Heaven heard by Jesus AND John said:

This is my son in whom I am well pleased. Matthew 3:17 (NKJV).

Though simple on the surface, this was an incredible statement to make for two reasons. The first reason this is so important is that Jesus hadn't done a single thing with His life as of yet. God was saying, "I'm pleased with My Son because He is My Son," not "I'm pleased with My Son because of what He has done."

This statement from God is important for you and for me as well. He is pleased with us (being His children) because of our identity, not because of what we do with that identity. Hold on to this fact – it is where victor thinking has the power to overwhelm victimhood in our lives.

The second reason this is such an important statement is that the voice from Heaven he heard was the foundation from which John knew without a doubt that Jesus was the one. The fulfillment of John's life was reached when John heard that Jesus was God's Son directly from the mouth of God. Sadly, the world has ways of making such definitive statements pale to the horrors that get thrown our way.

It wasn't too long after this amazing moment that John found himself in prison. In fact, he would soon be beheaded by a lust-filled Roman ruler. As John sat in that dark prison, he asked his disciples to go to Jesus with this unbelievable question:

PROVISION & VICTIMHOOD

> *Are you the one we were expecting or should we be looking for someone else? Matthew 11:3 (NIV)*

How did John go from hearing God's own voice saying Jesus was the one to doubting that He really was The Messiah? In my opinion it was through misplaced expectation that such a radical shift in perspective could happen.

You see, John thought the Messiah (Jesus) was coming as a conqueror. He believed Jesus was coming to defeat the evil Roman Empire that held Israel in bondage. John's expectation was that Jesus was the Savior of his particular circumstances. If Jesus was there to defeat Rome, surely He could spare John from the despot that held his life in his hands.

But God saw the role "Savior" as something so much larger than just bringing Israel out of Roman rule. Savior was even bigger than saving John's life. God's plan was to save us all! John's expectations of what Jesus' "job" was in this world almost made him miss the reality of God's presence in John's life, even after hearing God's words for himself.

If wrong expectations could get John off track after literally hearing from God Himself, think about how easily we can be derailed by wrong expectations. Expectation is the killer of faith in God and faith in our fellow man. Expectation is what sets us up for victim thinking. It ruins our ability to see God in our lives and to live our lives as God sees us. It kills our ability to believe in ourselves and the power of God that flows through us.

What I have learned is to expect God to be seen in my life. The only provision I can allow myself to have any expectation of when it comes to God is the provision of His presence. What that presence looks like has to be left up to God. If I hold out any expectations of what God's presence is supposed to look like in my life, particularly in the area of provision, I will ultimately be disappointed—that's the beginning of victim thinking. I wish I could say I'm good at living such that I'm satisfied with however He chooses to show Himself in my life. Truth is, oftentimes I'm not. But this way of thinking has gone a long way to help me live as a victor no matter what kind of horrible circumstances I face when it comes to provision.

Just like John we sometimes get so taken off guard by the challenges of this world that we can forget the power of God that has been part of our lives in the past. When we have expectations for God to provide and we define exactly what that provision is to look like, we have now put God into a place of submitting to our desires, and He simply won't stay in that place for long.

THE GREATNESS OF GOD

I can remember a time, not too long ago, when I was in a season of amazing provision from God. Everything just seemed to be clicking. Ever feel that way? I sure do wish that feeling was there more in my life than it is.

One morning, during a quiet time with God, I was worshiping Him and found myself thanking God for how GOOD He was. Isn't it so easy to thank God for His "goodness" when things are going our way? Am I as willing to thank God for His goodness when things are going badly? Ouch—too close to home! As I basked in the glory of thanksgiving for God's goodness that particular morning, a thought came into my head that I attribute directly to God Himself. This was a profound thought when it comes to provision. Let me explain.

God is good no matter how much goodness we have in our lives. I have mentioned before that Satan's main goal is to get us to doubt God's goodness. He (Satan) does this by enabling this world to be such that bad stuff can and will happen in our lives.

When we are surrounded by good things, we can take God for granted. We can begin to think that it is God's responsibility to be good to us. Complacency can put us in a place where we might be tempted to think that our view of God's provision is to be expected. When our idea of what provision is doesn't materialize exactly as we expected, we can be crushed as a result. Victim thinking is something that can come when we rely on God's goodness to be "proven" by the goodies we have in our lives.

What God said to me on that morning when I was thanking Him for the abundance I was experiencing was don't forget how GREAT He is. It is so easy to forget that He is the sovereign God of this universe. The Jehovah-Jireh (God will provide) God who is so easy to worship when His provision matches up with my expectations. He is the same great God when His provision is something that I never expected. His greatness is to overshadow my view of His goodness all the time. God wanted me to remember this important point so that I wouldn't switch into victim thinking at the first sight of trouble in the area of provision.

The Greatness of God is all about one thing. God is God...we are not. He knows best. His way of doing things might be totally different than ours. In fact, He might find that our discomfort is better for His plan of salvation for this world than our demand for a good life. That's the greatness we have to remember when Satan orchestrates things in our life that might call God's goodness into question.

If we are truly His Children, then God's plan for us is to make us exactly what we need to be so that His Plan for this world will come to complete fruition. Provision viewed from God's perspective is the only way a victor can expect to see God's goodness when the good things of this life seem to elude them.

AT THE END OF YOUR ROPE

Still doubt God's ways aren't the same as our ways? Consider the Beatitudes in Matthew 5. This sermon, given by Jesus, is considered by many theologians the most profound sermon ever presented in all of history. It begins with this simple verse:

> *Blessed are the poor in spirit, for theirs is the kingdom of heaven.*
> Matthew 5:3 (NIV)

The Message transliteration puts this verse in a context that is mind-blowing to most of us today. It says:

You're blessed when you're at the end of your rope. With less of you there is more of God and his rule. Matthew 5:3 (THE MESSAGE)

You are blessed when you are at the end of your rope. Have you ever been at the end of your rope? I bet the last word you would use to describe that time in your life is "blessed."

God's economy is so different than ours. We feel blessed when things are going well. Why would God want it taught that we are blessed when things are going badly? Because that's when we seem to be more open to seeking and finding Him. "With less of you there is more of God and His rule."

I have said it over and over again in this book, God is all about relationship. It isn't that He doesn't want to provide for us. It is often that provision makes us comfortable and when we are comfortable we are more apt to forget Him altogether. Look what it says in the Book of Hosea:

When I fed them, they were satisfied; when they were satisfied, they became proud; then they forgot me. Hosea 13:6 (NIV)

This is an interesting pattern that must be recognized in order for the victim thinker to move toward victor living. Provision can lead to satisfaction. Satisfaction can lead to pride. Pride leads to forgetting God altogether. Victims fail to recognize this pattern and fall into its trap all the time.

I'm in no way saying that God doesn't want to provide for our every need. He does in ways we don't even recognize. What I'm saying is that we have to stop blaming God's apparent lack of goodness when we don't get what we need when we need it. It might just be that the fact that we didn't receive what we needed was because it was so much more important in God's plan for salvation for us to feel the pain of less stuff so that the world could feel the pleasure of more of Him.

I also don't want you to get the idea that God would keep something good from us just because He wants us to know Him better. How many of you would put your children out into the cold just to teach them to appreciate the warmth you provide? If you did that you might find your children taken away from you by Child Protective Services. That's nothing less than child abuse.

So it is with God. I just can't see that He would ever consider harming us by withholding provision to teach us a lesson about loving Him more. That's just sick in the human realm and unacceptable to my view of what I hope the Heavenly realm looks like.

FRESH BAKED BREAD

Tim Keller is an amazing pastor located in NYC. A friend of mine told me he heard a sermon by Tim on the Lord's Prayer that was simply radical. Most of us know bits and pieces of the Lord's Prayer from our younger days attending church services. One of the lines goes something like this, "Give us this day our daily bread…" That's the epitome of God's provision. Just enough to get by; not too much and not too little.

Our expectation is so different than God's reality of provision. We expect God to give us exactly what we want. The truth is that you and I could get by with so much less than what we have been given? We have come to believe that our daily bread is so much more than what God knows that we need.

I have heard pastor after pastor preach that this verse on daily bread is about teaching us to do with exactly enough. That God wants us to know He is our provider but that He will only provide what we need, not always what we want. Not a bad interpretation, but it so misses the mark when you consider what Tim Keller said about this verse.

Tim put it this way. He said that we are so busy gathering up extra bread just in case God doesn't provide for tomorrow's allotment that we miss the beauty of what God is trying to get across in this verse. Tim poses this question: Which would you rather have, stale and hard nine-day-old bread you slaved to gather yourself, or a freshly baked loaf of bread God gives you each day?

You see, this verse is about God giving you the best. It's not about God withholding from you to teach you to settle for less. God's best for you and for me is to have freshly baked bread. Can't you almost smell that loaf of bread baking in the oven right now? Why don't we trust Him enough to give us the best instead of killing ourselves to try and storehouse more in case God doesn't come through?

We look at the bread situation as God holding back to teach us how to appreciate what He provides. God sees it as giving His children the absolute best He could possibly provide. That's the kind of provision a good AND a great God provides. Our attitude needs to change to see that what God is doing is the best for us, even when His best falls way short of our expectations. Max Lucado puts it this way:

> *Faith is not the belief that God will do what you want. It is the belief that God will do what is right.*[6]

Victims get caught up in wants at the exclusion of what is right. Their faith takes them down paths where they believe they have to work really hard to get right with God so that they will get what they want – the provision that God promises.

When God doesn't seem to come through from time to time, this leads victims to times of deep despair in ways that can have far-reaching impact in their lives. They are left with the doubt that God might not be willing, or worse yet, able to provide for them. The issue of "getting" overwhelms victims to the point where life can feel like a living hell. Look what Jesus said about the issue of getting and how victimhood is the result of that focus:

> *What I'm trying to do here is get you to relax, not be so preoccupied with getting so you can respond to God's giving. People who don't know God and the way he works fuss over these things, but you know both God and how he works. Steep yourself in God-reality, God-initiative, God-provisions. You'll find all your everyday human concerns will be met. Don't be afraid of missing out. You're my*

---

[6] Taken from *He Still Moves Stones* by Max Lucado Copyright © 1993, 1999 by Max Lucado. Used with permission of Thomas Nelson. www.thomasnelson.com. All rights reserved.

> *dearest friends! The Father wants to give you the very kingdom itself." Luke 12:29-32 (THE MESSAGE)*

The very kingdom itself; that's what God wants to give you and me. Just relax. Stop chasing your tail for provision. It doesn't help to fret and worry about tomorrow. Yes, we need to use our brains to plan and work accordingly but no amount of worry will guarantee God providing exactly what you think you need. He knows you too well to let you fall for that trick of Satan's.

We are called to respond to His giving. What is it that He has given you today that is clearly from His hands? What does He want you to do with that? Answering those questions puts a victim in a place where he might be able to throw off victim thinking and move into a place where he can live life as a victor. This doesn't guarantee all your worldly needs will be met, but it does mean you will be in a better place to see, feel and experience God's presence in your life.

"I AM" LEADS TO VICTORY

I often meet with an amazing woman who has struggled with many of the same questions and physical/emotional problems that I have dealt with in my life. She has this beautiful way of seeing God in ways that I truly admire. One day we were talking and she said that she would like to get the "I" out of our LIFE with regards to obeying God.

As she was saying this I immediately remembered the movie *"The Prince of Egypt."* This incredible animation tells the story of Moses from the Bible. It was a favorite of my kids when they were young. Although I haven't seen this movie for years, the thought of the burning bush scene still brings tears to my eyes.

In this scene Moses comes across a bush on fire in a cave. Although the bush is fully engulfed it seems to sustain no damage. Moses is intrigued and draws near the bush. As he approaches, a voice—the voice of God—whispers Moses' name from the flames. At one point Moses asks, "Who are you?" God answers with a power and confidence that still moves me just thinking of it, "I AM that I Am!" As strange an answer as it seems to be, when you think about it, these two simple words, "I AM" encompass everything God is and might be in our lives.

As this friend and I were talking, it hit me that we are to replace the "I" in LIFE with the "I Am". When people encounter the "I" in life they get something less than what is possible when they encounter the "I AM". "I," if left to itself, always leads to self-centeredness. Self-centeredness leads to a demanding spirit that will ultimately leave victimization in its wake.

"I AM" leads to openness, freedom, acceptance, generosity and love that goes so far beyond what you and I will ever be able to provide on our own. "I" can't help but be the victim: Why did this happen to me? What did I do to deserve this? Why am I not good enough to get what I need from my God? "I AM" leads to victory, since we are walking in a place of power with Christ in us.

Want to live the life of a victor that God intends for us? Get rid of the "I" in your life and replace it with the "I AM." God does provide. He is the Great I AM. Nothing gets past His knowing, especially the needs of His children.

Victors are people who can rest in the knowledge that even when provision doesn't seem to be happening the way we think it should, our Heavenly Father has our best interests in mind. Don't let Satan lure you into a place where victim thinking can come into your life. He will try to attack you by making things happen in your life with the hope you will believe that God's goodness isn't for you. When the goodies of life don't seem to be coming your way, remember that the Greatness of God IS your provision. It is His Greatness that has made you a victor, and nothing this world can deliver up against you can change that fact.

CHAPTER SIX

Prosperity & Victimhood

In our last chapter we dealt with a "pro" word that seems to be amazingly adept at setting set us up for victim thinking. Provision is one of those concepts that can make or break us if we don't have the right perspective on what provision really means. In this chapter we need to consider another "pro" word that can be even more damaging to the psyche of fragile humans. Prosperity is one of those concepts that really challenges us all from time to time.

What's the difference between provision and prosperity in light of the topic we are covering in this book? The way I've been looking at this is that provision is something that challenges us from day to day and can change like the wind. We can have provision today and feel like a victor, lose it tomorrow and be victimized.

Prosperity is something that impacts us over a lifetime. The deep and long-lasting attitudes that can result surrounding the issues of prosperity can allow victim thinking to slowly and permanently take over our entire being.

From a victim to victor perspective, I equate the kinds of damage we sustain from victim thinking over the issue of provision to being shocked by an open wire. It hurts immediately and causes clear and evident wounds. Those wounds (victim thinking) can be treated and overcome if we choose to recognize they exist.

The damage done by victim thinking when it comes to prosperity is more like what happens to the frog cooking in a kettle. The frog's ability to adapt to temperature changes doesn't allow it to recognize it is being boiled to death until it is too late. The victimization aspects of prosperity come in slowly, sometimes over a lifetime. The results are harder to recognize and sometimes much more difficult to treat. That's why I wanted to take time to investigate the challenges of both provision and prosperity separately as we move from living as a victim to being the victors that we were made to be.

THE DREAM OF PROSPERITY

Prosperity is something that we all have dreamed about. For most of us, that dream has tarnished with each passing year as we come to realize that we may not ever achieve that dream.

When I was 27 years old I believed that I would be worth $30 million by the time I was 40. This was a real and profound dream of mine. It was something that I took seriously. I actually expected I would be in a position to do all I could to make that dream happen.

As I sit and write this book, more than a decade and a half has passed since that magic number of 40. I am nowhere near achieving the goal that I saw so clearly almost thirty years ago. Part of the pain and suffering I have personally endured both physically and mentally since I turned 40 has come from the fact that I have had to face the ever-growing possibility that this dream of prosperity from my youth will never be achieved.

Something deep down inside suffered a near death blow that can be summed up with this question: "If the big dream of being worth $30 million by the time I was 40 didn't materialize, can I ever trust that any dream will come true?" Hear the familiar tones of victim thinking in that question?

Where provision can make us slip into and out of victim thinking on a daily, even on a moment-by-moment basis as the resources we use to provide for our needs come and go, the lack of our definition of prosperity is like a cancer that slowly takes over in the deepest reaches of our being. Sometimes the impact of not achieving our idea of what prosperity is in our lives makes that cancer hard, if not impossible, to detect, let alone treat. The "symptoms" of victim thinking that result from lack of prosperity can be hard to recognize and easily brushed off early on. Left to linger, though, those symptoms take root and grow into something that, often times, can never be completely removed from our lives.

The good news is that the victim thinking that results because of our lack of what we believe prosperity looks like aren't fatal like that undetected cancer can be. We aren't doomed to just lie there in the kettle like that poor frog whose own physical makeup is letting him down in this important survival moment. We have the ability to change from victim to victor even when the tentacles of victim thinking have been allowed to grow deep and wide in our lives.

We can choose to change. It may take time and concerted effort, but it can happen.

I still feel the pains from the realization that my 40th year has come and gone without me having achieved the goal of prosperity that I saw so vividly was from God. Moments of doubt, fueled by victim thinking, still grab me. I continue to fight off the feeling that no dream can be trusted. Welcome to the recovery required to shake the deep and long-lasting effects of victim thinking that surround a lack of prosperity.

My belief in dreams is returning, but not because I am achieving all my new dreams. No, my belief in dreams is returning because I believe I'm a victor whether my dreams come true or not. It makes it so much easier for the power of victim thinking to be reduced in one's life when we realize who we really are.

PROSPERITY: HOW MUCH IS ENOUGH?

What victors need to realize is that prosperity really isn't about money. Did you get that? The damage that lack of prosperity causes isn't necessarily a result of us living in squalor. Living conditions are always an issue of provision and that can change at a moment's notice.

You see, as I sit here today, I don't have that $30 million that I dreamed about when I was 27 years old, however, I am considered abundantly and ridiculously rich by 99% of the world's population. Though my net worth is but a tiny fraction of that BIG dream I had in my younger days, I am living a comfortable lifestyle and can be viewed as wildly prosperous by most people on this planet.

The damage that I have seen as a result of my lack of what I viewed as prosperity isn't about whether I have enough money to live; I have more than enough. My view of prosperity and the resulting damage it has caused in my life has come about by my having assigned an arbitrary definition to prosperity. But all of that is changing because of how I view prosperity today.

Through my wife's business, I met a true southern gentleman. When I first met him he was a higher-up in an investment company with which my wife did business. He is the kind of man you are just drawn to get to know. His interests are diverse and his intellect is something to behold. To top it off, this gentlemen is also a man of some means; not considerable means, but enough resources to make life comfortable for him and his family.

We had the opportunity to have this gentleman come and speak to a group of my wife's older clients. He had just published a book describing what he had learned about people who have lived more than 100 years. This book came out of extensive research he did as he traveled around the country on business. To gather the data for this book, he would locate those who were over 100 years old in the areas where he traveled, and would get permission to sit with them and hear their life story.

What a fascinating project. This man shared with me that some of the relationships he established working on this project have had a profound effect on his life. The stories he shared at this meeting from those who lived 100+ years are something I will never forget.

Since this gentleman was in the financial business, he would ask these long-lived people about money. One of his questions dealt with prosperity. He asked the centenarians this question: "At what level is someone rich?" In other words, what amount of money did they think it would take for someone to be considered truly prosperous? He was amazed to find that these 100-year-olds almost universally said that $100 million is the line at which one could be considered truly rich. Why $100 million? Our friend could never could get a clear consensus as to why, but isn't it amazing that almost every one of those interviewed had a picture of what true and lasting prosperity, in the financial sense, looked like?

Wouldn't it be great if we, too, all had a sense of what real and lasting prosperity looked like in our lives? Ask yourself how you feel about prosperity right now. Are you a prosperous person? Is prosperity a term that you would use to describe your life?

I would be willing to bet that way down deep inside, even if you have reached that magical $100 million mark set by those our business acquaintance interviewed, you would still have a twinge of doubt as to whether you are prosperous or not. There is something about human nature that just doesn't allow contentment to be a lasting and change-making part of our lives even in the best of circumstances.

CONTENTMENT AND PROSPERITY

There's the rub for those of us trying to live as victors in this world. Contentment in terms of what prosperity really means is a potentially disastrous prospect for those of us trying to live in victory. Even when we are in a place of prosperity, do we really have contentment? A feeling of doubt can creep into our lives even in the midst of tremendous prosperity. This is where we are living on the edge of victim thinking. Prosperity, and the discontent that comes with our view of prosperity, is probably the single most significant situation in which we can begin to feel victimized by the world.

When it comes to contentment in the context of prosperity, the Christian minister and author Bill Gothard has it right. He says, *"Contentment is not the fulfillment of what you want, but the realization of how much you already have."*[7]

---

[7] http://www.joniandfriends.org/radio/5-minute/detours-life/

The key to changing from victim thinking to living life as a victor starts with a change in our perspective when it comes to prosperity. Something has to change in order for us to find a place of contentment that isn't based on getting what we want.

Could it be that one of the strongest allies we have in this battle to remain a victor is our own attitude about what we have? I believe that contentment is a powerful place to start, but we can't stop there. Prosperity based on what we have is also a place full of potential victim thinking snares.

I have come to realize that even those with the most resources in their lives can have doubts when it comes to what they own. It is human nature to look for more than what we currently possess and to strive to protect all that we have amassed.

How do I know this? Just think about how you felt in 2008 when the markets crashed in this country. After more than a decade of incredible wealth generation we experienced one of the greatest downturns in the economy since the Great Depression. What were your thoughts when 30-40% of your invested assets disappeared in a matter of hours?

BILL GATES: VICTOR OR VICTIM?

According to Forbes Magazine, Bill Gates, founder and Chairman of Microsoft Corporation, is worth an estimated $72 billion today.[8] That's a number most of us just can't understand. To put that figure into perspective, consider a couple of facts about Mr. Gates' wealth as shared online by PolicyMic.com[9]:

- Bill Gates could give everyone on earth $10 and he would still be worth $2 billion.
- Assuming he lived another 33 years (to age 90), Bill would have to spend $6 million per DAY to use up all his wealth.
- If Bill earned a 6% return on his money, his wealth would be increasing at an amazing rate of $114 per SECOND.

---

[8] http://www.forbes.com/profile/bill-gates/
[9] http://www.policymic.com/articles/45397/10-ridiculous-facts-about-how-rich-bill-gates-is

- If Bill Gates were a country he would be the 37th richest country on earth. One man beats out over 200 countries in total wealth.

These facts about Bill Gates' wealth seem to confirm the thought that he is wildly prosperous. But does Bill Gates worry about prosperity like the rest of us? Does he think of himself as prosperous deep down inside? I've never been in a position to ask him and probably never will, but knowing human nature as I do, it wouldn't surprise me one little bit if he has the same thoughts as you and I who have so much less to our names than he does.

Here's why I say this. In 2008, Bill Gates' net worth was estimated to be around $60 billion. After the markets had made their significant corrections, it was estimated that his net worth was at $40 billion in 2009. One third of Mr. Gates' net worth, gone in a flash.[10] How would you feel if you discovered that you lost $200 out of your pocket one day? Multiply that times ONE MILLION and you can imagine how Bill Gates might have felt. It's a staggering thought.

Don't get me wrong, I'm not crying for Bill over his losses. $40 billion is still an astounding amount of money to have. But to wake up one day and see one third of your wealth evaporate into thin air has to do something to your thinking as it relates to prosperity.

How did you feel when you saw how much your 401(k) and other investments declined during this crazy time in American history? I bet you lost way less than Bill Gates did, but I am also willing to bet that you felt something between mild concern and outright panic. When prosperity is challenged, victim thinking isn't far behind.

Prosperity is one of those topics that can create amazing feelings about who we think we are. That's why I want to take a closer look in this chapter at how victors need to deal with this issue.

---

[10] http://wiki.answers.com/Q/How_much_money_did_Bill_Gates_lose

PROSPERITY FOR VICTORS

To begin with, we need to review one important point made earlier in this book. Victory isn't what makes a victor. Bill Gates isn't a victor because he has 72 billion reasons to prove that he has experienced victory. Bill Gates is a victor because of who he is. I'll bet that Bill didn't let victim thinking linger long (if at all) when his net worth plummeted $20 billion in 2008/2009. In fact, his victor attitude is what probably played a key role in the fact that his net worth today is some $12 billion more than he was worth before the crash in 2008.

Victor thinking goes a long way in how we deal with the challenges life tosses at us. I'm in no way saying that victor thinking guarantees financial success. There is nothing in this world that can make that kind of connection no matter how much we want it to happen. However, I believe that finding ways of getting victim thinking out of our lives puts us in a place where real prosperity can be experienced no matter what our bank statement looks like.

So what does prosperity really look like? What does it mean to be a prosperous person? The answers to these questions, and others dealing with prosperity, are what places us in the best position to live the life of a victor, even when the world makes us feel like a victim.

If we have worldly pictures of prosperity as our guide to how our life needs to look in order to feel like we are victors, then we are doomed to victim thinking. As I have said time and time again, there is no guarantee of a good life in this world. There is only one Bill Gates. If we hold out that prosperity needs to look like a Bill Gates kind of victory, then odds are we will be disappointed. Disappointment leads to discontentment, and discontentment makes us think less of ourselves. Discontentment leads us to do things to try and prove to ourselves and the rest of the world that we are capable. Striving to prove our worth ultimately leads to more disappointment and discontentment; a vicious cycle that breeds victim thinking and ultimately victimization. I believe we need an "other-worldly" view of prosperity in order to put ourselves in a position of living a life as victors as much as possible.

Money, power, significance, impact, accomplishment are characteristics of prosperity that just can't be relied upon if we are to avoid victim thinking in our lives. Victors need to look elsewhere for prosperity in order to find the strength to live as victors when money, power, significance, impact and accomplishment elude them. This is where God's perspective on prosperity is so important in the life of a victor.

In the Book of Daniel we see the conquering king, Nebuchadnezzar, opening the story of Daniel with a description of a dream that greatly troubled him. In the first four verses of Daniel, the King uses the word "prosperity" twice, according to some translations of the Bible. Check out these two verses:

*King Nebuchadnezzar, to the nations and peoples of every language, who live in all the earth: May you **prosper greatly**! Daniel 4:1 (NIV)*

*I, Nebuchadnezzar, was at home in my palace, contented and **prosperous**. Daniel 4:4 (NIV)*

There is no doubt that Nebuchadnezzar had all the attributes of prosperity. At the time he was one of the most powerful and rich people in the known world. His reach and rule was vast, to say the least. He was the Bill Gates of his day and more. But often in the Bible, God's view of an issue is different than our perspective. So it is with the word prosperity as described in this section of Daniel.

In the 4:1 verse the words "prosper greatly" come from an Aramaic word "shelam," which means welfare, prosperity, peace, and well-being. In fact, in the King James Version of the Bible this word is translated as "peace". Prosperity in this first verse has to do with peace and well-being, the welfare of one's life rather than anything having to do with assets and position. Hold on to that thought for a moment as we look at the second use of the word prosperity.

In verse 4 we see the second use of this word. In the original language the word "raanan" was used by the author of Daniel. That word was originally translated into English as "flourishing." The scholars who produced the NIV translation took that word to mean "prosperous." Two different words with similar surface meanings, but when you look more closely you see a picture that is much more in line with what a victor needs in order to fight off victim thinking when it comes to prosperity.

I believe God is giving us an eternal perspective as to what prosperity looks like. Let's bring the two words together in order to shed some more light on victor living. Basically, God is saying that prosperity is all about "flourishing in a place of well-being and peace." Nowhere do I see that this flourishing in peace has anything to do with holdings, position or how well things are working out in our lives.

If flourishing in a place of well-being was connected to how much was in our bank account then the vast majority of the human race would be doomed to victim thinking, since there are very few of us that will ever achieve what we think is needed to be prosperous. And even if we did achieve what we think is prosperity, would we be able to be content at that point?

It's my opinion that God is trying to get our attention focused onto something more profound when it comes to prosperity with these two verses from Daniel. Instead of allowing possessions and power to shape our view of prosperity God is saying peace needs to be the foundation of prosperity in a victor's life. God wants us to be driven by and find contentment in a place where we can flourish in peace.

How in the world do we get to that place? Before we go there, we need to do a little soul searching. You'll see what I mean by this in just a moment.

I believe that prosperity is about having a peace in the soul and flourishing in that place. If we can grasp this concept it is so much easier to believe we are prosperous no matter what our bank balance indicates. Having our soul in a place of peace is the single greatest defense against victim thinking a person can have in their lives. But before we can talk more about prosperity and the soul, we need to dig into what the soul is really all about.

THE THREE PARTS OF A HUMAN BEING

I believe that humans are made up of three parts: flesh, soul and spirit. From the research I have done it makes sense to me that each of these three areas are distinct in our lives, and each plays a role that we need to understand in order to live the life of a victor. Much of what I have learned about these three parts of our being comes from an excellent book called *Soul and Spirit* by Jessie Penn-Lewis.[11]

The flesh is the most obvious part of our being since this is what the world sees and interacts with. The flesh is the *world consciousness* aspect of our lives. Put your hand on a burning stove and you feel pain. Our senses (sight, smell, hearing, touch, etc.) are there to allow our flesh to deal with input from the world, and the flesh shows the world our actions in response to that input.

Next comes the soul. This is the *self-consciousness* aspect of our lives. The soul is comprised of our will, our intellect and our emotions. I believe our soul takes input from the world, through the flesh, and helps to generate what our response to the world should be.

Once you have placed your hand on a stove and felt pain, the soul is responsible for creating a connection that tells us to be careful about touching hot things in the future. The soul's main job is to bring together input from the flesh, and run it through the computer of the will, intellect and emotions to generate a response that places us in the best position of keeping bad things from happening again and again in our lives. The soul is a powerful ally AND enemy to those of us trying to rid our lives of victim thinking and live a life as a victor. We will look more deeply into the soul in a bit.

Then there is the spirit. This part of our being is quite strange and somewhat unknown to the average person. In fact, many people mistakenly think the spirit and the soul are the same. I don't believe they are. In fact there is strong biblical evidence to back up the idea that the soul and spirit are two different parts of our being.

---

[11] http://www.worldinvisible.com/library/jessiepenn-lewis/soulspirit/soulspirit.c.htm

The spirit is the *God consciousness* aspect of our lives. Most of us haven't really thought about the spirit part of our lives. Sadly, this fact is what creates so much turmoil in the world when it comes to victim thinking. Let's look at how the three parts of our being work in our lives.

In order for the world consciousness part of our being to be impacted by the God consciousness part of our being, it has to pass through the soul. Our soul, the self-consciousness aspect of a human being, is the gatekeeper for letting God out of us and letting the world into situations where God can be seen. I don't believe this was the way God intended it to be. In fact, I believe the story of Adam and Eve is the beginning of a time when victim thinking took hold and our souls have been trying to protect us from being victimized ever since.

The way I read the Bible, it is clear to me that Adam and Eve enjoyed a time when their spirits intermingled openly and freely with the Spirit of God. The Bible says that God and Adam walked together, or communed, in the cool of the day. I believe this is more than God just showing up in physical form from time to time. I believe that this communing was something that was available to humans at any moment – their spirits were intermingled with God's like smoke from two candles. I see it as though one wouldn't be able to tell the Spirit of God in Adam and Eve from the spirit of man that resided in them. That's the way Heaven will be.

To think that we were destined to have this amazing and powerful way of living on earth and lost it is something that is so crushing to me. As a result of the choices Adam and Eve made, we are now living a life that requires us to be always on guard against the possibility of victim thinking. Let's look at the circumstances that forever changed the course of human nature.

IN THE BEGINNING...

In Genesis 3 we read the story of the temptation of Adam and Eve:

> *Now the serpent was more crafty than any of the wild animals the LORD God had made. He said to the woman, 'Did God really say,*

> *'You must not eat from any tree in the garden'?' The woman said to the serpent, 'We may eat fruit from the trees in the garden, but God did say, 'You must not eat fruit from the tree that is in the middle of the garden, and you must not touch it, or you will die.' 'You will not certainly die', the serpent said to the woman. 'For God knows that when you eat from it your eyes will be opened, and you will be like God, knowing good and evil.' When the woman saw that the fruit of the tree was good for food and pleasing to the eye, and also desirable for gaining wisdom, she took some and ate it. She also gave some to her husband, who was with her, and he ate it. Then the eyes of both of them were opened, and they realized they were naked; so they sewed fig leaves together and made coverings for themselves.* Genesis 3:1-7 (NIV)

For reasons known to God, He didn't want Adam and Eve to have the knowledge of good and evil at this time. That tree was meant for consumption at some time later in their lives. Satan knew that for Adam and Eve to have the knowledge of good and evil is actually a good thing. And, in many ways, it is!

What Satan wanted Adam and Eve to believe is that God couldn't be trusted for ANY goodness in their lives because He chose to withhold one thing (the tree of the knowledge of good and evil) from them at that moment in their lives. Satan wanted to sow distrust for God and cause irreparable harm to the relationship that Adam and Eve had with God. He did this with hopes that God's plan for this world would be forever changed. When will Satan ever learn that God is so much bigger than that?

Look what happened to Eve when she pondered what Satan said about the tree of the knowledge of good and evil. She saw that it was "pleasing… and desirable."

Prosperity is always pleasing and desirable. When we can't have prosperity or when prosperity comes in a form we weren't expecting, we are put in a position where we are willing to do things that might bring long lasting harm to us and to those who will come after us. So it was with Adam and Eve. The result of Adam and Eve's decision to go against what God saw as good for them was for them to feel guilt and shame. This is something that had never been felt before, but which today is a characteristic of our lives that threatens to control us through victim thinking.

THE CONSEQUENCES OF SHAME

I believe the shame that Adam and Eve felt crushed their spirit. There are two things mankind was never supposed to experience. The first is death; we were made to live forever. The second is shame. Shame is a direct affront to our identity. Adam and Eve's identity was as pure as it could ever be in the garden. They were God's creation, His much beloved children. Shame entered the picture through disobedience, and their identity, and ultimately ours, has never been the same. This crushing blow to our identity absolutely destroyed the spirit aspect of humankind. Mankind was forever changed by the feeling of shame resulting from the wrong view of prosperity and how that impacted our understanding of God's goodness. The impact of that long-ago and forgiven action is still being felt today.

Remember, the human spirit is the God-consciousness aspect of our being. With the collapse of their spirit, there was a vacuum, a hole inside Adam and Eve that had to be filled. The soul took over where the spirit was once in charge. The soul, the self-consciousness aspect of our being, was never intended to be the controlling factor in our lives. Our spirit was supposed to be in control.

In other words, our very makeup—our will, intellect and emotions—was supposed to be controlled and shaped at the direction and oversight of our spirit as it was intertwined with God Himself. Now, the self-conscious part of our being controls how God is seen and how our lives are impacted by the things that happen in this world. This isn't how it was supposed to be, and we suffer in ways that can result in us surrendering to victim thinking.

It isn't that shame crushed Adam and Eve's spirit because their spirits were weak. It is that our spirits were never intended to have to deal with the weight of guilt and shame. Shame is about identity.

When we feel guilt for long enough we start to believe that the thing that caused us guilt in the first place is a result of the fact that we are no good.

Just ask an alcoholic who is at rock bottom. Shame has taken over in ways that make the first few months of recovery critical in whether or not permanent change will occur. Shame affects our identity, and as we have covered time and time again in this book, knowing our identity is the only thing that makes it possible for us to move from victim thinking to victor living.

Again, the spirit wasn't weak in Adam and Eve, it was just never made to carry any kind of identity other than that of a child of God's. It's like slowly lowering a 1000-pound weight onto a table that was designed to handle 10 pounds. As soon as the fullness of the weight hits the table, it will be crushed.

Adam and Eve's spirit just couldn't handle the dramatic change in weight between being God's child and an identity driven by shame. We are still feeling the pains of this reality as we fend off the moment-by-moment attacks on identity that we face every day.

This world has an amazing ability to bring about circumstances that elicit shame in our lives. Left long enough, that shame will alter our belief in who we are and greater levels of victim thinking will be the result.

COPING: THE JOB OF THE SOUL

That's where the soul comes in. Interestingly enough, the soul (the self-consciousness aspect of our being) is amazingly suited to implement coping mechanisms in an attempt to fend off the effects of the various onslaughts of identity issues we now face. I said earlier, the soul is really good at processing information given by the flesh, and "learning" from that data. The soul uses this knowledge to create ways of dealing with future input based on past lessons learned. Touch a hot stove once and the soul learns that hot things are to be handled carefully.

As the spirit collapsed in Adam and Eve, the soul rose up to take on a task that God never intended it to have. The soul is now the front line of defense, trying to protect our spirit from ever having to face the searing sting of wondering who we are.

Unfortunately, the coping mechanisms that the soul is so good at creating just aren't good enough to keep the feelings of doubt and worthlessness that continually attack our identity from affecting our actions. God never intended for us to cope, He intended for us to prosper! That prosperity is a flourishing of peace in the soul that simply won't happen by creating coping mechanisms to defend our soul's interpretation of who we are.

THE SOUL NEVER STOPS STRIVING

Here's what happens when we choose to let our souls take control. When things aren't going the way we like our will tells us, "Just try harder. Don't give up. Go after it (whatever it is) one more time and maybe, just maybe, you'll get it." Our intellect takes in all the data and tries to come up with another way to approach the problem to help us get what we want. Our emotions kick in and scream in our ear, "You have to have this, don't you dare stop until you have made it happen!"

When combined, these words in our heads get overwhelming and put us into a place of flight or fight. The chemical factory that is part of our flesh kicks in to help the soul get done what it thinks needs to happen for goodness to be seen in our lives. Left long enough, these actions take their toll on our lives. Depression, anxiety, sleep disorders, eating disorders, addictions, sickness, and who knows what else can happen to our bodies because of the fact that the soul drives our bodies to a point of exhaustion in order to achieve what it thinks we need for prosperity to prevail.

There is no doubt that the process briefly and unscientifically described above plays an important and useful role in our lives. Many times these motivating thoughts are reasonable approaches to problems that come our way, and there is nothing wrong with applying what God has given us to help us move forward in our lives. Our wills and intellect and emotions can team up to help us do big and profound things. Worldly prosperity often comes as a result of a strong-willed personality not taking "no" for an answer.

But what happens when time after time our best efforts, our most intelligent reasoning and our most passionate ways of approaching the same problem end up in failure? Those are the times when our souls get weaker and weaker. I believe our flesh follows suit.

It isn't long before that drill sergeant of a voice coming from our soul sounds more like a distant whisper. Soon, the quietness of a depleted soul is replaced with the ever-growing voice saying that you are no good. Victim thinking can be the result of a soul that has grown weary of trying to bring world-driven prosperity into the life of a human being. I'm here to state that it just doesn't have to be this way.

Victors have realized that we have to convince our soul to relinquish control to God. Victims think they have to do more or be better in order to prosper in the ways they think are best for them. Victors have decided to try and put their life in the proper order, with the soul under the control of the spirit. Victims allow the soul to do its best to dominate the world's circumstances in ever more powerful and self-controlling ways. The spirit shrinks back and the soul is off and running. But God's will can't be done if our will is in control. It just can't.

Our life was supposed to be one that is controlled by an intermingling of spirits—ours and God's. Our will, intellect and emotions (our soul) isn't supposed to be what controls us, as it does in our lives today. The real power for change in our lives and in this world comes when our will, intellect and emotions are emboldened by a prompting from the intermingling of spirits to take action. Prosperity comes when our souls are so invaded by peace that we allow the spirit of God, through us, to move us in ways we would never have considered if it were left solely up to the self-consciousness aspect of our lives.

It appears to me that King Nebuchadnezzar in the Book of Daniel understood the concept of prosperity being a peace in the soul. The words he used to describe prosperity point to the fact that no amount of power, prestige or prominence is able to satisfy that ever-present need for living in the light of true identity. How do we help our souls grasp that desire to flourish in peace? The answer to that question is the key to living a life of prosperity

CLING TO GOD

I have found that the first step in getting our souls to flourish in peace is to just get the soul to rest. Have you experienced those times when you just couldn't shut off your brain? That's the soul recognizing the potential for harm (big or little, real or perceived) in your life. When this happens, the will, intellect and emotions are kicked into high gear in order to try and fend off potential harm.

It is so hard to get the soul to just be quiet. The explosion of addictive coping mechanisms (drugs, alcohol, sex, work, food, spiritual, etc.) along with the ever-growing demand for a medical answer to depression, anxiety, sleep disorders and more are proof to me that having our soul in control of our being is an experiment that has utterly failed human nature. Something has to change. That's where God comes rushing in.

One of the most powerful means of getting the soul to find peace is growing in the ability to trust in God's goodness for your life. Adam and Eve were challenged by the potential that something God withheld from them made it possible for them to wallow in the lie that maybe there were more good things God didn't want them to enjoy. Though they had all they needed and more, the one thing that they couldn't have looked way too enticing (desirable and pleasing) to them and drove them to act in ways that changed how humans deal with the world today.

That doubt about God's goodness drove Adam and Eve's souls to move in a way that brought shame into their lives, and that shame crushed their spirit. Oh, how things would have been different if they were to have had a growing trust in God! What would we be like today if Adam and Eve had chosen to allow the spirit to speak against the attack of Satan in the area of God's goodness? Their identity would have been secure, and we wouldn't be facing the challenges of identity that rob our souls of peace today.

The same can be said for you and for me. How do we get to a place where we can trust God's goodness when it appears that He is withholding something good (our view of prosperity) from us? It's all about getting to know this God to whom we are to surrender our lives in the first place.

I wrote about the story of Jesus in the garden a couple chapters ago. There, He fought the biggest battle of His entire life the battle against the soul. It was everything Jesus could do to submit to God's plan for His life.

Jesus knew that He was about to face a brutal and torturous death (his intellect was giving input here), not to mention He would be completely forsaken by His Heavenly Father (an emotional roller coaster for Jesus, to be sure). I bet Jesus' soul was coming up with excuse after excuse to go against God's plan so that He could live (his will was fighting to take control). It is widely understood that upon one word for help, the entire army of Heavenly soldiers would have come charging in to protect and save Jesus, the Son of the King. Can you imagine how Jesus' will, intellect and emotions were working overtime to try and get him to utter that one word? Instead, Jesus chose to make this amazing and soul-calming statement: *"Father... not my will, but yours be done." (Luke 22:42 NIV)*

With those simple words, we also put our soul into the position of being able to stand aside so that the spirit can take over. When the spirit takes over, the very presence of God can pass through us to impact the world. Of course it would be great if God's presence in the world meant that our lives would be exactly what we want them to be, but that just isn't always the case.

Jesus was more prosperous to all humanity in death than He ever would have been had He lived a long life on earth. A peace came on Jesus when He calmed His soul with the resolution to follow His Father's plan no matter how bad it looked for Him. That's what flourishing in peace can do for a human's life. We get connected to a power that makes big things happen in this world.

That same peace, and power, is meant for you and for me. Our souls are standing in the way of achieving the level of prosperity that Jesus experienced that night in the garden. How could Jesus go from sweating blood, wrestling with God over the death He was about to face, to completely giving in? I believe the ultimate secret lies in the first word of what Jesus uttered in the Luke 22:42 version of the story in the garden. Jesus started His proclamation to follow God with the word, *"Father."*

Jesus knew the Father. The Father knew Him. This wasn't just a cursory knowledge; they really knew each other. God knew Jesus would choose Him in any circumstance. Jesus knew that no matter how bad the circumstance, He could trust God to provide the kind of peace in the soul that can only be described as prosperity.

That's the kind of knowledge God wants us to have in our lives. This is the knowledge that puts our souls at ease so that we can live the fullness of His plan for our lives.

Our destiny isn't determined by our ability to get our will, intellect or emotions in line with what we believe our destiny is supposed to look like. Our destiny is determined by our knowledge of God. It's also in our understanding of His love for us and in our willingness to move in the ways He leads us to move. That knowledge gets our soul in a place where it can let the spirit lead. Then, and only then, can we live a "not my will, but Yours" kind of life.

I came across a Bible verse a few years ago that has become one of my favorites. As a result of this verse I began doing something kind of weird. I now talk to my soul. Yes, I admit it. I actually talk to my soul. What do I say? Before we go there, let's take a look at the verse in question.

I cling to you; your right hand upholds me. Psalm 63:8 (NIV)

A simple verse, but filled with profound meaning to me. As I read this verse one morning I thought about my soul. It is so hard for my soul to just be quiet; to calm down so that the peace that is prosperity can flourish in my life. I found myself saying to my soul, "Cling to God, just cling to God!"

Look at what the verse from Psalms says happens when our soul clings to God. He upholds us with His right hand. For most of us, our right hand is our "power hand." That's the hand that is the strongest and most capable of doing things to make progress happen in this world. If I could just get my soul to hold onto God, then His powerful hand will be seen in my life.

Yes, talking to my soul is a bit weird, but it puts me in a place where I can choose what I think is the natural balance of things; my soul being controlled by my spirit. That's the only way I have found that makes sense to me when things are going terribly wrong.

When I stop the frenetic activities my soul gets me into and choose to move directed by my spirit connected to God, I have to believe that the results are in God's hands. This brings a tremendous peace to my life, even when things aren't looking as good as I would like them to. That peace is the difference victors have over those trapped in victim thinking. That peace only comes and stays when our soul is allowing God to bring in peace no matter what the storms of life look like.

Try it for yourself. Next time you recognize that panicked feeling that comes as a result of this world attacking your prosperity, tell your soul to cling to God. Envision the "self" part of you holding on to the Father for dear life. Then realize that's the exact place He wants us to be all the time. There, and only there, will we find prosperity—that flourishing in peace described in the first chapter of the Book of Daniel.

VICTIMS CONFUSE BLESSING WITH PROSPERITY

Victors' souls are waiting for the spirit's command so that the righteousness from God can bring blessing. That blessing is used to bless others when the God consciousness aspect of the victor's being is able to get out and touch the world consciousness parts of their lives.

Victims need blessing so their comfortable life isn't challenged. When a victim's comfortable life is impacted, they are reduced to the nothingness of victim thinking that screams that they have missed the mark or that they somehow don't measure up. Their very identity is at stake. This sends the soul into a mode of ever-increasing panic.

Victors seek after the same comfortable life, but they hold it loosely so that God's will can be done through them. Even when the comfortable life is not there, victors know that they are loved by God, and they allow themselves to be controlled by His spirit so that peace is the byproduct of their efforts.

Our spirits are unlimited. Backed by God's spirit, the sky's the limit when it comes to prosperity as described by the freedom of a "flourishing in peace" kind of life. Trying to judge what can be done in our lives by analyzing our abilities limits God's will because we see ourselves as limited by our weaknesses. This is the height of victim thinking. Victors realize they are limited, but leave room open for the limitless power of the spirit to make a God-sized dream happen through their blessed life.

And there's the rub when it comes to victim thinking: we confuse blessing with prosperity. I know Christians who search Bible verses dealing with prosperity and claim them to be their own. They are so hungry for the blessing of a good life that they are in a perfect position to miss the fact that blessing comes in the presence of God, not in the goodies He provides. His blessing is His presence, and that can be felt both in abundant worldly prosperity and in the absence of it.

If there is any truth to the Bible, then powerful things happen when God's presence is felt. Mountains move, seas part, the blind see, the lame walk. It is in the presence of God that prosperity can be best felt and most often realized. Prosperity isn't a result of how good we are or how competent we can become. I believe that victim thinking can happen when we work hard to become qualified only to find that the qualification we worked so hard to acquire doesn't guarantee the level of prosperity our worldly identities crave so completely.

We all have God-given qualifications, but victors realize that the power of qualification comes when our abilities are empowered by something greater than ourselves. Just like Jesus, victors realize they just can't lose when they set aside their will for that of our Heavenly Father's.

Jesus' qualifications meant nothing in this world. He was killed way before He could complete what those closest to him thought He came to do. As He hung on that cross, Jesus realized that He just couldn't lose because His identity was secure. His position as the Son of God made it possible for him to completely fail at worldly prosperity and still be prosperous in God's eyes.

That's the only kind of prosperity I have found that seems to work in this mixed up world we all live in. You have something that works better than that? If so I'd like to know about it. I have to tell you, though, I'm skeptical that it will work for the long run. Give your scheme a few years, I bet it will ultimately let you down. Every scheme I have tried up to this point has failed me. Even if I'm wrong about all this God stuff, the flourishing in peace I'm feeling right now is worth the shame you might want me to feel as a result of this line of thinking. Frankly, whatever shame is put before me will have no effect on me as they lay me in the ground when I die. Shame, too, is a temporary role we play from time to time, and ultimately has no impact on our identity from the eternal perspective.

Prosperity, and the drive for it, is all about identity. If we are smart enough, are inexhaustibly determined and exhibit enough passion to motivate us through hard times (all soul attributes), then we will look good and people will love us. That's the soul in control, and victim thinking will ultimately be the result no matter how prosperous we become.

I'm not presenting a pie-in-the-sky kind of life with all this discussion. Of course victors want the goodies of this world. I want as much worldly prosperity as I can get, and at times I find it easy to justify doing what it takes to get it. The difference is that victors are ultimately satisfied with whatever God provides because their souls have been prospered by His presence. Victors still go after the goodies of this world, but they have a solid place to hang onto when the goodies don't show up. That solidness is the prosperity of the soul that only comes from God.

PROSPERITY: BECOMING MORE THAN YOURSELF

Victim thinking as a result of the lack of prosperity is insanity. Trying to live a life chasing worldly prosperity can drive us crazy. But, oh how good it feels at times to live life as a victim! Those trapped in victim thinking often get the pity of others. This pity gives us what we want so badly—attention—a feeling that we matter even though the world is doing its best to show us that we don't.

But even this feeling of "success" through the pitying attention of others is temporary to those trapped in victim thinking. Eventually our victimhood gets old. The ones who would pity us, now shun us. We are too much work for those who are more concerned with how to handle their own victimhood than they are with wasting time on dealing with ours. Worse than that, we remind other victims how easy it is to be victimized, and no one wants to be around anything or anyone for long that reminds them that they, too, are disasters just waiting to happen.

Victors are nothing more than past victims who have found sanity. Humility that leads to contentment and earnestly seeking God turns the tide of insanity. It takes us from victimhood to living like a victor. This change from victim to victor is a process, one that we have to choose to start, and have to fight to continue, all our lives.

I can't say it any better than the Apostle Luke does:

> *But if you're content to be simply yourself, you will become more than yourself.* Luke 14:11 *(THE MESSAGE)*

Worldly prosperity is about trying to bolster your identity with things. We want to be more than we feel we are so we amass as much as we can in the hopes that this proves we are more. My soul is tired just thinking about how that last sentence has been lived over and over again in my life.

Trying to satisfy a world-imposed identity leads to being discontent. That discontent can put us in places where we think we are no good. Failures that happen along the way seem to prove how worthless we are. We think the more we have the better we will look. And that is true on the outside. But on the inside, those who have more often feel the emptiness of an empty life more than those who actually do have less.

It is my experience that God wants my life to be filled with prosperity. He doesn't want my definition of prosperity to make me think any less of who He has made me to be; a child of His. When worldly prosperity seems to be a challenge in my life, it doesn't mean that I have missed the mark or I have somehow disappointed Him. It just means I live in a fallen and damaged world.

This life is a training ground for all eternity. There will come a time when we will live in a place where our spirits will be constantly and visibly intertwined with that of God's. Our souls will be perfectly content with that, and we will be empowered in ways that we never thought possible.

Why not try and live that life now? It's not only possible; it's a reality that we can reach for and achieve to one degree or another. Of course we will fall short from time to time, but that doesn't seem to be a problem for God. Why should it be an issue for us?

Next time questions surrounding prosperity start to fire up your soul, remember that it is the spirit's job to be directing the soul, not the other way around. Let God's definition of prosperity be what brings you to a place of peace where you and yours can flourish. May you sense the abundance of prosperity that is God's presence as you move from victim thinking to victor living in your life.

CHAPTER SEVEN

Generosity

Just when I'm about to give up on the human race due to the crazy and evil things we can do to one another, some story of a person's senseless act of generosity makes me temporarily suspend my harsh judgment of mankind.

Take for example the "secret Santa" story I saw on a morning news show recently. This man from Kansas gives away $100,000 in $100 bills to random people around the country each and every year around Christmas. The stunned faces of the beautiful people of all shapes, sizes and colors softens my heart when I see the results of one stranger doing something good for another.

One hundred dollars isn't going the change the lives of anyone. The secret Santa from Kansas knows this fact all too well. What this person's generosity does for 1,000 people is to show that someone cares. Sometimes that's all we need to unleash big changes in the lives of those around us.

Those caught in the trap of victim thinking can sometimes be jolted out of that state by the senseless act of generosity from one human being to another. Nothing does more for how we view ourselves when we are in a bad situation than realizing that there are people out there in much worse condition than we are, and then doing something for someone else.

There are countless victors today who have found generosity to be a key to escaping the trap of victim thinking. What I have found to be so fascinating about the characteristic of generosity is that both victim thinkers and victors alike can exercise generosity in profound ways in their lives. I want to take a look at how we can use generosity either to continue in our victim thinking ways or to break the bonds that are keeping us from living the life of a victor.

Have you ever noticed that people who live a generous lifestyle have a peace about them that is hard to explain? When life hits them hard they just seem to roll with the punches. Then there are generous people who seem to lose their way when life gets hard. How is it that one set of generous people can react one way, and another set of generous people react in a totally opposite way? I believe it has to do with what we discussed in the last chapter.

Victors have found that prosperity has to be viewed in a different light in order to keep from continually falling into victim thinking. In the last chapter we presented a different way to look at prosperity. It isn't our possessions that make us prosperous. Prosperity comes when we work to put ourselves in a place where we are "flourishing in peace and wellbeing." This kind of prosperity drives itself way down deep into the soul. Peace in the soul, or lack thereof, is what I believe makes it possible for one set of generous people to live like victors and another set of generous people to use their generosity to perpetuate and/or deal with victim thinking.

GENEROSITY AS A STRATEGY

I have gotten to a point that when I see the secret Santa's of the world doing what they do best, I have to ask myself, "Why are they this way? What is it about their lives that puts them in a place where they can appear to be so generous? Is their self-sacrificial giving due to the fact that they have peace in their souls, or are they using their generosity to cover up or deal with victim thinking?"

I hate to be so jaded, but I am living proof that people sometimes use generosity to compensate for how they really feel about themselves. I'll bet you have done so in the past as well, and I guarantee you will do so in the future unless you take to heart what I'm presenting in this chapter.

Looking back on my life, I can see times in which I have used generosity to bolster what others thought of me so that I could feel a little bit better about who I thought I was. As I have described in bits and pieces in this book, there was a time in my life when I was pretty lost. I didn't know who I was, and my attempts to find myself just weren't working out. Slowly but surely, everything around me began to appear bland and lifeless. I lived for any spark of whatever it was that made me feel alive. I was searching for fulfillment, and I jealously guarded anything that I thought might make me feel okay about myself.

During that time, circumstances were such that I had a lot of free time. I volunteered here and there and stayed pretty busy doing things that one might consider to be generous. One friend of mine described me as the "busiest unemployed person he had ever met!"

At that same time, I somehow found myself in a leadership role at my church. That role enabled me to counsel people that were dealing with problems of many types. Talk about the blind leading the blind; I was the poster boy for that statement during this period of my life.

For whatever reason, those I counseled found their time with me to be productive. I started to hear statements like, "You are so wise," or "Everyone says I need to talk to you," or "You are such a godly influence in the lives of so many people…" One of the most common statements was, "You are so generous." Looking back on that time all I have to say is, "If they had only known!"

There were so many times back then that meeting with those people was all I had. Nothing else in my day came close to giving me the feeling that I was worth something or that my life had some level of meaning. I was desperate for something to help prove to me, and maybe to others, that I was worthy of the love I understood that God has for me.

Yes, there was a bunch of depression speaking into this time in my life, but which came first, the thinking that drove my actions or the depression itself? Either way, I was in a place where I was using people through my generosity to get something for myself that God never intended me to get anywhere else but from Him.

I have since found that our loving God simply won't allow us to remain in a place where we are able to get that fulfillment anywhere outside of our total reliance on Him. He simply can't stand to see us suffer the effects of grasping for counterfeit ways of finding fulfillment outside of His provision. Nothing but His fulfillment will ever come close to satisfying our needs in the way that produces the internal peace I believe we all are struggling to find in this world.

I hope that my meeting with those people back then brought some level of assistance into their lives. I hope my time with them was productive for them and that through it, they found some kind of connection to God. From my perspective looking back today, I was using them to get something for myself. Our time together had little to do with them and a lot to do with my own selfish and misplaced need for acceptance.

You see, I was so mired in victim thinking during those days that I really didn't care about the people I was "helping." The truth is that what I really cared about was feeling good about myself. I needed the time that I invested in them to both keep me busy and allow me to accomplish something by having an impact in their lives. Their gratitude and appreciation were all that I had.

That's a pretty sad way to live, and a pretty poor motivation for generosity. It borders on being downright evil for someone who calls himself a follower of Jesus Christ. Christians should know who they are, and that knowledge should be what drives them to be generous with others in their lives. But that's not how I was living back then.

Most people never saw the "dark side" of my life. I wouldn't let them. They might not have wanted to meet with me if they had known. The façade I let them see was one of a peaceful, calm, and available person who somehow gave way beyond what anyone else seemed to be able to give. But my "generosity" was actually a cleverly disguised ruse to put me in the best position to get what I thought I had to have to suit my needs. My family, on the other hand, saw something completely different at times. They were the ones that saw my sadness and misunderstood where it came from. They were the ones who had to deal with my nastiness when their needs drew me away from those things that brought any kind of fulfillment into my life.

I was a jealous defender of what I thought I needed. I demanded that everyone else take a back seat as far as what I perceived to be important was concerned. Isn't it interesting that immediate family often fails to receive the benefits of some nice façade that we share so quickly with total strangers? I was quick to be generous with people I really didn't know, but I jealously guarded all the same things I gave to others from those closest to me. I wonder what kind of victim thinking I unleashed through the victimizing acts of jealousy I allowed my family to experience during this troubling time in my life?

Are you starting to recognize the characteristics of victim thinking? Are you beginning to see what victim thinking can look and sound like? I hope so, because the truth is that we can put a halt to the madness generated by victim thinking, particularly where generosity is concerned.

To be in a place where we have the ability to impact the lives of total strangers is a wonderful place to be. But if that type of generosity has the potential to damage relationships with those closest to us because of our internal struggles, it is really not worth the good it might create. I just don't see how the ends justify the means when it comes to generosity tainted by wrong motives.

I have found that victims see things through a paradigm that is best described as, "There just isn't enough to go around." In the victim thinker's eyes there is not enough money, not enough time, not enough love, not enough of anything that is important to them. They are jealous of those things that bring them a sense of wellbeing and even in their generosity their jealousy will be seen in one way or another.

I know that this sounds weird, but the resources that the victim thinker draws upon to be generous with are actually jealously guarded at the same time. For me it was time. I was generous with my time with others, but I jealously guarded that time when members of my own family needed it. Victim thinking takes things and twists them into pretzels of logic that make perfect sense at the time to the victim thinker.

Victims have been trained by this world to grab for all they can and be sure no one takes more from them than they deserve to receive. Who is the judge of how much is enough to give out? The victim thinker. Sadly, their ability to judge is clouded by their own messed up filters. So much so that even their own generosity will become a burden to them as they find that they are getting less and less out of their generous actions. Eventually all coping mechanisms, even generosity, will fail the victim thinker when it comes to finding peace in the soul.

GRABBING FOR ALL WE CAN

I have two young friends that are amazing people. I was given the honor of marrying this couple a number of years ago. I always knew Andrew and Amy were special, but they have way exceeded my expectations of what their lives would look like in the area of generosity.

Andrew and Amy were blessed with the birth of a beautiful son. Finley brought to this couple the usual excitement, awe and panic that any firstborn introduces into a new family. Soon after Finley's birth, Andrew and Amy started feeling the draw to grow their family.

Amy got involved with a group called Reese's Rainbow. They promote adoption of special needs children from around the world. This group does amazing work at rescuing children that would otherwise have been left to fend for themselves in a state run facility with some of the most dismal conditions you can imagine.

More and more, Andrew and Amy were giving in to the feeling that they could do something more than just support a group doing good work. They were feeling the call to do some good work of their own. Adoption became a way of exercising generosity that literally changed the lives of two innocent people in this world.

Just a few years ago, after a long and drawn out ordeal, Andrew and Amy adopted two beautiful children from Russia. Amy is one of the most gifted bloggers I have ever read. If you want a blow-by-blow account of their adoption story and their journey since, check out her blog called "Tiny Green Elephants."[12] Keep a box of Kleenex nearby. The stories regarding the pre-adoption time are so moving.

The older of their two new precious gifts from God is a little girl who spent her entire 10 years living in Russian orphanages. She was used to not having enough: not enough food, not enough money, and worst of all, not enough love.

When my friends brought her home they noticed she was "stealing" food and hiding it in her room. They were told that this is a common occurrence for kids who have been raised with too little. Life had taught this little girl to take advantage of times of plenty because the famine times were always just around the corner. Even though she knew in her head that she was in a different place, a place filled with all she could ever want, her life experience made her fall back on old patterns that said, "The bad times are coming, they always came in the past, you'd better take care of yourself while you can."

That kind of thinking was essential for her survival in the Russian orphanages. It isn't a bad thing that she thought this way. Victim thinking can be a very practical tool when one is constantly being victimized. But when times change and the abuse is gone, if we stay stuck in victim thinking the results of that thinking will spread to take over more and more of our lives to a point where it is totally destructive to ourselves and to those around us.

What happened to Andrew and Amy's little girl? My friends never corrected her when they found evidence of her hoarding the first year she joined their family. They would always tell their new daughter how much they loved her and offer her more and more. When it came to food, they always said yes in the early days to whatever she asked. There were meals where she ate only ice cream. They constantly reinforced the fact that she now has a mommy and daddy who will do their very best to make sure she has all that she needs in this world.

---

[12] http://tinygreenelephants.com

In addition to food, Andrew and Amy gave their daughter a gift that is more precious than gold. They gave her time. She needed time to realize that she is really loved. She needed time to grow in the fact that this love isn't temporary. She had to learn that this love they were showing her wasn't being used as a tool to try to get her to do something or to be someone for the convenience of a cold and calculating system.

She needed time to realize she is worthy of more than just being warehoused in an orphanage. She is worthy of a mommy and daddy who love her and want the best for her. It takes time for victim thinking to be rooted out when past abuses have made that kind of thinking the key to survival itself. Andrew and Amy blessed their daughter with time and filled that time with love.

As time moved on, their daughter started to realize that food wasn't an issue in this house. Eventually, Andrew and Amy started saying no to unhealthy food requests and reinforced the fact that she can trust them in their love for her. She stopped hoarding food and began to trust their words AND actions. The new life this little girl was experiencing was so foreign to her. The welcome words and actions based in love was something she had never had experienced and they starting to become a common part of her thinking. Victim thinking was slowly giving way to victor living.

What this little girl was doing with food is exactly what I did with the time and other resources I needed to appear generous. She was hording it up in case there came a time when there wasn't enough. She was being jealous with the provision she was given because her past taught her that provision will always dry up no matter what people said. That's how I acted with those things that I needed in order to act generous. I was hoarding up the feelings of goodwill I got from being generous because life had taught me that those feelings always go away.

Victims tend to remain in a pattern where they have to rely on their own cunning to get by even in a place where they are being lavished with love. Victims hoard all the stuff they can to make sure they have a little extra when all the stuff that proves that they are acceptable seems to disappear. Victims don't fully trust the love they are receiving now. History has proven that the little love they have now doesn't come close to filling the gigantic need they have inside. When there are conditions placed on that love, it makes it even harder for the victim to ever trust a real and lasting love when and if it comes their way.

Thanks to Andrew and Amy, their daughter has a different picture of what love means. This little girl is learning that she is worthy of love. This is what changes victim thinking in a person's life. It is what changed that little girl's life and it is what is changing my life as well. Andrew and Amy's daughter isn't through with victim thinking by any stretch of the imagination. Neither am I! Challenges will come into her life that will put her right back on the victim thinking path again in one form or another. Same goes for me. Though I'm looking for ways to live like a victor, I still slip into and out of victim thinking. Writing this book is probably the biggest step forward out of victim thinking I could have ever done for myself. My hope is that these words help to unleash a bit of this type of freedom in your life as well.

FAITH AND GENEROSITY

One of the things that I have learned from Andrew and Amy's situation and from my own growth in living like a victor is that people in oppressive situations shouldn't give up on being cunning when it comes to taking care of their needs and the needs of others around them. In other words, victim thinking can create ways of dealing with situations that serve us well when we are in places where victimization is the norm.

Just read the writings of POWs from the past wars who have been put in horrific situations. There they had to use every bit of their cunning to stay alive day by agonizing day. They are responding to being victims of oppressive and evil authorities. It's when these victims return to a "normal" life and stay stuck in ways of thinking that were necessary in captivity that problems arise. This is when the unhealthy characteristics of victim thinking can rob them of the peace that is within their grasp.

Victors find healing and move into the fullness of the love, freedom and plenty that they experience in free life. They don't see those who are so willing to pour out on them the love they need as being temporary providers, not to be trusted in the long term. Victors take the jealous ways that protected them in captivity and slowly trade them for generosity in their strange, new, free life. Victors find the strength to overcome the fear of the past to live true and manipulation-free lives. They know there is no guarantee for what tomorrow holds, but they are willing to press on, even when tomorrow turns out to be less than what they want it to be. Victims, on the other hand, use past trials as proof to justify their jealous ways of hoarding and doling out whatever it takes to get what they need to find fulfillment.

Victims, like victors, have faith. Victims have been taught faith in themselves; faith to provide for themselves the essentials of their life. Victors have faith that the love of the Father is a freedom-based and inexhaustible love available for them in times of plenty as well as in times of poverty. Victims see the bad times as proof they had better hold on to all they can get now because there is no guarantee for tomorrow. Victors realize that the bad times have no bearing whatsoever on their ability to be loved. Victims are jealous of others who might get even a crumb of what they need. Victors are generous; sharing all they have and more, knowing that they are loved by a Father who is willing and able to provide more than they could think to even ask for.

God is more generous than we will ever know. His generosity isn't clouded by motives based on the need for acceptance, love, or worth like ours can be. My pastor, Aaron Jayne, once said that generosity is all about grace. Without the understanding and application of grace in our lives we will do many generous things driven by victim thinking motives. Let's take a closer look at how grace makes it possible for victim thinkers to move into victor living.

THE GRACE CONNECTION

Grace is the key to generosity. Grace, by definition, is when we receive something totally undeserved. Isn't that the underlying characteristic of generosity in the first place? We don't give because someone deserves to get what we have to offer. Nor should we give with the expectation that we will get something in return. Those descriptions don't represent what true generosity is at all. Yet, so much of the generosity we see today is driven by one or both of those motives. Generous people are generous because they have a grace about them that makes it possible to give freely.

Even victim thinkers, who are using generosity to suit their own needs, are applying an element of grace even though they themselves don't have a clue as to what grace means in their own lives. Remember, I'm speaking from experience here. This thinking is the result of the advanced degree I have received from the "School of Hard Knocks" when it comes to victim thinking.

In order for our generosity to be all that it can be as an agent of change in this world, the generous person must understand what grace is in his life. The way I read the Bible, we are in a position where we deserve to be extinguished because of the presence of imperfection in our lives. Instead, God loves us. That love is the epitome of grace. We don't deserve His love, we deserve His wrath. Victims and victors alike need to understand God's perspective when it comes to grace in order for grace to have real meaning in this world.

Victims have been so beat up by this world that they can come to believe that they don't deserve love. Yet they dedicate every part of their being to try to get that love for themselves. Even though victims think that they don't deserve love, they desperately hold on to the thought that they really aren't that bad. They work tirelessly to prove that they are okay, that they deserve something better than what they are experiencing right now. The worst thing that can happen to a victim thinker is for that façade to be challenged and ultimately disproved. Then the unworthiness that they feel deep down inside is revealed for everyone, including the victim thinker, to see.

Transparency is a terrible enemy to the victim thinker, except when transparency is used as a tool to get the sympathy that might make them feel okay about themselves.

Here's the really strange thing I have learned about my victor-based relationship with God: when it comes to worth, both the victim and the victor are exactly alike. Hold onto something solid—I'm about to share a statement that might really trouble you. From God's perspective we are totally worthless. That's right. There is nothing of worth in the victim or the victor when compared to a perfect and infallible God. But before you go jumping off a bridge or tossing this book in the trash, I want you to ponder that statement a bit in light of the next paragraph.

What do you have to offer that God is so desperate to have in His life? What part of God's life is so messed up, so incomplete, that having you or me in it brings some sense of wholeness that He was missing before we came along? What part of our "right living" is so flawless that it comes close to the perfection of an all-knowing, all-powerful and perfect God?

I said this in an earlier chapter, but it is worth repeating. God doesn't need us—He wants us! He doesn't need anything good you have to offer in order to bring some kind of completeness into His life. Freedom can only be had for victim and victor alike when we start living with the understanding that we are worthless to God. Yet in the midst of that worthlessness our God wants to love us and desires us to love Him. That's grace beyond anything that can be given by even the most generous person here on earth. We will talk more about the subject of worthlessness in a chapter to come entitled "Brokenness".

Before I move on, I have to make sure I've made myself completely clear. We have nothing to offer in a relationship with God. We are worthless to Him, but that worthlessness doesn't disqualify us from His love. I don't understand how He can be that way, but I am more free today than I have ever been because I'm holding on to the fact that even on my lowest day, Jesus would still come and die for me. That's a grace that I just can't fully comprehend and will never, ever be able to live up to.

I'm hoping this book helps me to stop trying to live up to that kind of grace. I hope it does the same for you. God doesn't want us to even try to earn the grace He so freely gives. It is a waste of time for us to try. I pray that you will find yourself in a place where you see the uselessness of trying to repay the overwhelming grace God has lavished in your life.

AGREEING WITH SATAN

I have to tell you, I am so tired of trying to prove my worth to this world and to myself. There was a time when darkness was in control of my life; a time when the feeling of worthlessness would come on me with a vengeance. I believe that those times exemplified the evil in this world heaping on more and more burdens in my life just to get me to bow down and give up.

One day the same old attack came my way. I heard that voice in my head saying over and over again, "You will never amount to anything. You are worthless as a husband, a father, a man and a follower of Jesus Christ." Normally that thought would drive me to try and do something, anything, in an effort to prove the voice wrong.

On that particular day I think I was just so tired of trying to prove that I have some worth in my life that I said words that would get me kicked out of many Christian fellowships. I said, "Okay Satan, I give up. I agree with you. I am totally no good. I am of no earthly good at all and I'm not going to do a single thing to try and prove my worth to you. I'm just too tired. I agree with you 100%. I am no good."

Then I said the words that cleared the fog from my heart and I believe poured more fuel into the fires of Hell. I said, "But even as worthless as I agree with you that I am today, as worthless as I feel right at this moment, my Savior would still come and give His life for me."

That sent Satan scurrying away from me. The moment I got the idea in my head that God loves me for what He placed in me, not for what I bring to the table, I turned down the path of healing that has brought me to this point today.

I still have a long way to go, but I have to tell you that healing is happening in my life. Throwing off the burden of believing that we have something to offer to God is the most freeing thing a victim thinker can do in the journey to becoming a victor. If we approach God with the reality that His grace is sufficient, we are well on our way to living the life of a victor He has made for us.

MUCH HAS BEEN GIVEN

How does all this relate to generosity? Let me paraphrase a verse in the Bible. To those who have been given much, much will be required.

God has given us His all. He came to us Himself and paid the price for us to be able to enter into relationship with Him. We didn't do a single thing to deserve the terrible death He endured. Each and every one of us has turned our backs on Him and gone our own way. That's what created the need for a savior in the first place.

Grace is realizing that God's kind of love is a gift of enormous proportions. Armed with this knowledge, we can go forward and let our generous ways be fueled by God's love itself, not our need for something in return.

That those who receive much give much doesn't mean a whole lot to victim thinkers. They see their lives as not being all that bad. Even though they feel worthless in their own eyes, they fight for proof that there is something good inside of them and by gosh they will do all they can to find that proof.

The victim thinker's rationale goes something like this: "I'm not as bad as some others in this world." We can always find someone with worse character, or someone who has done more bad in this world than us. Therefore, victim thinkers don't see the depth of the sacrifice Jesus Christ made for them. Victims don't believe that they need grace, not grace that would make them believe that they are of no worth at all. They aren't that bad so they don't see the fullness of the grace God gave them.

So victims can't be truly generous because they don't see that they have been given much. Generosity for the victim thinking person is a tool to use in the process of trying to get what they think they deserve.

Grace is the key for us all. Victors realize that even on their best day they deserved hell. The fact that they have been saved is so amazing that they want to give. Generosity pours out of them in God empowered ways that I believe has the potential to change the world. Victors don't give because they have to or even need to. Generosity in the person living as a victor comes from the fact that they have been given much more than they deserve and they want to show a little of that kind of love to others as a result.

Victors have come to realize that the grace God has for us is unlimited. Victors strive to live in the reality that everything we need to be generous is made possible by an all-loving and resource-rich God. We don't have to be jealous or stingy in our generosity. Even our family deserves the best we have to offer because we don't need to be generous in order to feel like a victor. We are victors because of God's grace poured out through the sacrifice of Jesus Christ. Victors realize that through God's grace they have an identity that is complete now and forever more. The foundation of identity is a powerful place from which real and life-changing generosity can be made possible.

What it all comes down to is love. Do I truly believe that there is enough love to go around? Can I be generous with the love God has given me when it comes to all the needs I see in the world today? Can God love me as fully as I need to be loved with billions of other people needing just as much, if not more love than me?

That's what my victim-living life forced me to ponder. My doubt as to there being enough to go around is what usually drove me to react badly to my family when I thought they were impinging on my ability to be generous with the time, talents or treasures I had been given. Because I didn't understand, or trust God's unlimited grace as expressed in His Love for me, my generosity was badly tainted with self-centered motives. I have since learned that God has what I like to call a "synergy" of love that is available to us all. God was real specific with me one day about what this synergy of love looks like as he gave me a quick glimpse into Heaven in the middle of performing a generous act.

THE SYNERGY OF LOVE

One day I was going down to visit a church friend who was in the hospital. This friend is an amazing woman of God. She was married for many years to a man named who suffered with a debilitating disease that ultimately claimed his life. I had an amazing relationship with both these people in some of the worst times of their lives. To be honest, the generosity they might describe as coming from me was happening at a time when I was steeped in victim thinking. I have to admit that I was part of their lives for the worst of motives. Thank God, He is bigger than my mistakes!

As I was pulling onto the freeway heading to the hospital to visit my friend, I saw a glimpse of what I think Heaven might look like. I immediately saw her husband waiting to meet my friend as she entered into Heaven. Looking back on this vision, I'm glad I didn't share this with my friend at that time. No one in the hospital should be burdened with someone coming to pray for them who has just seen them enter Heaven. I wisely chose to wait to share this vision until a more appropriate time.

In the vision, I saw my friend's husband excitedly grab her hand and run her through the streets of Heaven. As you can imagine, the streets I saw in this vision were overwhelmingly beautiful. It reminded me of a scene straight off a postcard from some quaint European village. The place was immaculate and opulent to boot. Though the streets looked nothing like my hometown, the place gave off a very powerful feeling of being at home. It is hard to explain it, but it just seemed right to me.

All of a sudden, my friend's husband heard something. He looked at my friend and said, "You have to see this." With great excitement they took off. As they came to the end of the street they rounded the corner and there was this beautiful and expansive field. It stretched as far as the eye could see.

In that field were people enjoying the amazing day. The amount of people there was mind-boggling. Somehow, I got the feeling that there were one billion people in this one place. It just felt like that was the exact number of souls enjoying this particular corner of Heaven. The weird thing was the field didn't feel crowded at all. One billion people were comfortably milling about in this one place smiling and having a wonderful time.

My friend looked at her husband for some explanation as to what he wanted to show her. Her husband just gazed off into the distance without saying a word. My friend adjusted her gaze to try and see what her husband was so intent on looking at. Then she saw it. In what appeared to be a giant wave, people were falling to the ground as though in worship. Just then, her husband released her hand and dropped to his knees, then to his face. It was at that moment that she saw what everyone else saw. There, walking among the billion people bowing down in that field was a man. My friend knew instantly it was Jesus.

She didn't really know what to do. A touch of confusion came into my friend's mind. What was proper etiquette in this situation? As she stood there, frozen, she got the distinct impression that Jesus was looking for someone as He passed by the hoards of people falling at His feet. Just then Jesus caught my friend's eye. A broad smile came across His face. He had found the one He was looking for. To my friend's great surprise and confusion she realized Jesus was making His way through Heaven, through this sea of people just to see her. She really didn't know if this was a good thing or a bad thing. All of this was so new to my friend.

So many thoughts ran through her mind as Jesus walked straight up to my friend. She suddenly realized that she was the center of Jesus' attention. This made my friend feel very uncomfortable. It just didn't seem right for her to be standing in the presence of her Savior when everyone else was on their face worshiping Him. She started to kneel down but Jesus caught her hands and pulled her back to her feet. With amazing compassion, Jesus embraced my friend. All trepidation she felt before was washed away by the amazing love she felt and understood so completely in His arms.

Suddenly the entire crowd of people, one billion strong, got up and began surrounding Jesus and my friend. It was as though the love of Jesus pouring out on my friend was drawing people to them. Can you imagine how big that circle of people must have been for one billion people to be huddled up like that? Think about it. People might have been miles deep surrounding those two standing in such a beautiful embrace of love.

Then it hit me. What about all those people on the outside of that circle? How sad they must feel to be so far from the center of Jesus and the love that He was showing my friend. At that moment, tears started flowing from my eyes so fully that I almost had to pull over. I thought to myself, that's how I feel all the time! I'm connected to the circle but oh, how I wish I was able to get the fullness of that love like my friend had at the center of that circle. Victim thinking was about to take hold. Poor me, was all I could think.

Then it dawned on me that there was no jealousy from any of the people on the outside of that circle. The love Jesus was lavishing on my friend wasn't for her alone. It was as though that love flowed through everyone equally. The person miles away from Jesus was experiencing the exact same power of His love as was my friend who was in Jesus' arms. Then the tears really started flowing. That same love is there for me as well. God's love isn't limited by the number of people it flows through nor the distance we feel we are from that love.

There was a "synergy" of love in that vision. We often allow our circumstances to negate that love here on earth. In that circle, miles deep, no one could get any more of the love Jesus was showing my friend and no one could do anything to feel any less. It didn't matter if you were in Jesus' arms or a million miles away, His love was as complete and tangible no matter where you were. I hope that is a real picture of Heaven. I can't wait to experience something like that.

The reality is that we have access to that kind of love right now in this life. We may not be able to feel it as tangibly now as we will in Heaven, but it is available to us through a relationship with God. God's love is just like His grace: it is unlimited. We don't need to feel jealous about the amount of love we think we have available in order to be generous. We don't have to ration out His love through our generous acts to others because we think that there isn't enough to go around. Jealously guarding the outpourings of God's love deposited in us isn't something we have to do. The synergy of God's love makes it possible to be generous without guarding the resources we have to give to others.

Victors somehow just know this. They live on the edge of "running out" of the Heavenly resources they have in their lives. Victors realize that those resources are endless. God's resources come with a synergy that somehow makes up for times when we are so far on the outside of the circle logic would say those resources will never be there.

Victims see themselves on the outer reaches of that huddle around Jesus and believe that they will only feel a slight touch of God's love, if any at all. They see those in front of them as being obstacles. They are jealous of them because they might be experiencing more of the love victims so desperately want in their lives. Victors are in the same position, but have found a way to believe in the unbreakable synergy of God's resources no matter what their circumstances look like.

REAL LOVE

I said earlier that both victims and victors have faith. It takes faith to believe that we have enough to be generous when it appears that our tanks are running low. Victors have found a way to take things one step at a time when the bad times come. This enables them to offer generosity even when they are at their lowest points. Best of all, that kind of faith helps make the generosity they offer something that is as free as it can be of self-centered motives like those I experienced not too long ago.

When it comes to being generous, both victims and victors can react in ways that others will see as something positive. The difference is always the motives for that generosity. I came across the following Bible verse that really speaks to why I believe we are sometimes in a position where we might use generosity as a means to calm those condemning voices that can plague us all. Check out this verse from 1 John:

My dear children, let's not just talk about love; let's practice real love. This is the only way we'll know we're living truly, living in God's reality. It's also the way to shut down debilitating self-criticism, even when there is something to it. For God is greater than our worried hearts and knows more about us than we do ourselves. And friends, once that's taken care of and we're no longer accusing or condemning ourselves, we're bold and free before God! We're able to stretch our hands out and receive what we asked for because we're doing what he said, doing what pleases him. Again, this is God's command: to believe in his personally named Son, Jesus Christ. He told us to love each other, in line with the original command. As we keep his commands, we live deeply and surely in him, and he lives in us. And this is how we experience his deep and abiding presence in us: by the Spirit he gave us. 1 John 3:18-24 (THE MESSAGE)

Debilitating self-criticism is what makes it possible for those of us caught in victim thinking to move in ways that just don't make sense. My being generous as a method of finding some kind of self-worth is a perfect example of the debilitating self-criticism that is the focus of the verse above.

The answer to this ailment is the practice of real love. In order to practice real love we have to believe in it. An athlete doesn't practice for the long hours he/she does without believing that they have a chance to compete at the highest levels possible. Same goes with practicing love through generosity.

Here's an important key for us all to grasp: we don't need to practice love to get love. We are already loved. Victors have gotten to a place where they somehow get this fact. We are already completely loved. We don't have to earn it and we can't do anything to disqualify ourselves from the love we all so desperately need.

It says in the 1 John verse that God is greater than our worried hearts. God already knows who we are. He knows we are of no value to Him on our own, but He loves us all the same. Why worry about earning that love when it is given to us freely? This is the key to being able to see the power of God through the generosity that we feel led to be a part of in this world.

Next time you are about to do something that might be considered generous, ask yourself, "Why?" Why are you doing what you are doing? Is it to feel better about yourself? If so, then you are giving in to victim thinking. Fight that off and do what you were about to do, knowing that you are completely and totally loved. This will help weed out the underlying motives for your generosity and put you in the best position to see the power of God's synergistic love flowing in, around and through your life.

CHAPTER EIGHT

When Bad Things Happen To Good People

Why do bad things happen to good people? Have you ever asked yourself this question? Maybe you are the good person bad things have happened to. That question of "Why?" Is something that can haunt us and, frankly, it is a question that can hinder us as well. So many victims are missing their opportunity to live life as victors due to that simple, three-letter question, "Why?"

Countless numbers of people a lot smarter than I am have attempted to shed some light on this universal question. If you are looking to the words of this chapter to provide a clear and definitive answer, I have to completely honest with you – you will not find definitive answers here or anywhere else, for that matter. I don't believe we will ever get a clear answer to the daunting "WHY?" questions that burden us all from time to time in this life. But I do believe that we can catch a glimpse of the big picture when it comes to bad things happening in our lives. That's why I wrote this chapter. It's time for us all to catch a glimpse of something bigger behind all the bad that happens to good folk all around us.

I don't think it was a coincidence that as I sat down to write this chapter I was notified of three different bad things happening to three different good people. My morning started out with a quick meeting with a friend of mine I've known for over 25 years. He shared with me that his family was just informed by the doctors that his wife has a significantly aggressive form of breast cancer. As I returned home from that meeting, I received an email from an elderly friend who just learned her husband has stage 4 prostate cancer that has spread to his bones and his liver (he has since died). And, just to prove the old adage about bad news coming in threes, an acquaintance I have been counseling just learned that the two jobs that were "in the bag" both called and said they were going with another candidate. He is now homeless.

Three pieces of devastating news. Three genuinely good people. I'm sure that they, like all of us, have done something here or there that might be considered bad, but bad enough to be facing homelessness or death? I don't think so. Just thinking of these situations, I, too, have to wonder: why are these good people facing such dire and devastating circumstances in their lives? Honestly, I can't come up with a rational answer to that question, and at times that really bothers me.

All I know is that for the person trying to live life as a victor, the question, "Why?" is the single most dangerous question we will ever face. It's not that we should never ask why when we are hit with bad times in our lives. We wouldn't be human if we didn't stop to ponder the meaning of bad times when they come. Though I will always believe that we will never find the definitive answer, I have found that there are things we can learn from considering why's. Oftentimes, pondering them could reveal something about ourselves that might set us on a course where victor living could be more attainable. However, when we fail to see any silver lining surrounding the cloud of "Why?" it is so easy to find discouragement and despair resonating in our lives.

It is during those times when we allow the question "Why?" to linger in ways that can dictate our outlook after bad things have happened that we find ourselves flirting with real danger. It's when we become so obsessed with finding the answer to "Why?" that our lives can spiral into the pit that is victim thinking. The victim thinker is paralyzed in life trying to make sense of the senseless.

Victim thinking doesn't come from pondering the "Why's?" of bad situations; it comes when we stop all life around us as we demand answers that, way too often, just aren't there. Those who think like victors realize that there comes a time to move on from trying to find answers to questions that just might not be answerable in the first place.

THE MOURNING PROCESS

I'm starting to believe that our dealing with the question, "Why?" is part of a mourning process that we all have to go through when we face bad times. Mourning is all about dealing with a loss. As we feel sorrow when bad times hit it is really that we are mourning the loss of the goodness that we so readily took for granted. It is totally natural to mourn by asking, "Why?" You are not a victim thinker if you are questioning some recent bad circumstance; you are a victim of the bad thing that happened and because you are human you are going to wonder "Why?" it happened.

My friend and his wife are mourning the fact that their good life of the past has been lost as a result of the battle they now face against this aggressive cancer. His wife has to mourn the fact that she might not see her new grandbaby grow up.

That elderly couple have to mourn the fact that their simple life just got a whole lot more complicated. They have to mourn the fact that their ability to live independently might be forever changed.

My friend who lost his job and is now homeless has to mourn the loss of the comforts of home. His new reality is living out of a car, and that is a loss that will hit any man very hard.

I have been taught that mourning is a step-by-step process. If you are interested in learning the steps in the mourning process, do a quick Google search on "mourning process." There are tons of great online tools to guide you through mourning a loss in your life. What you will see from almost any resource on mourning is that there is no set time for each step, nor is there a clear transition from one step to another. Mourning is a process that is up to the individual. You just can't force the mourning process.

What I have seen, however, is that people often get stuck in the process. This is when the characteristics of victim thinking covered in this book can really exhibit themselves in a person's life. When a person gets stuck in the mourning process they are often stuck trying to find an answer as to why the bad thing has happened to them. Sadness takes over. Despair often rules the life of a person determined to deal with the "Why?" that now haunts them so completely. The person stuck in the mourning process is ripe to become a victim thinker. And as we have seen before, victim thinkers can often become victimizers through the actions and attitudes they exhibit in their close and important relationships.

I've been there in my life. I've had to deal with a loss of one kind or another that has put me into the mourning process. I've had to deal with, "Why?" more than once in my life, and as long as I'm breathing I know I will have to do so again. I heard a quote just this week that went something like this: "You are either coming out of, entering into, or are in the middle of a crisis now in your life." Sorry if you see this as pessimistic thinking, but this is the absolute truth. Bad stuff is going to happen to us all. It's how we react to that bad stuff that sets victors apart from those trapped in victim thinking.

Please don't mistake this chapter for me saying that if you are dealing with the "Why?" of a tough situation in your life, that you should just snap out of it. We have to be so careful when we are tempted to tell someone to "just get over it and move on." The mourning process is just that, a process. Who am I to judge how quickly you need to move from one step to another? Telling someone that they need to move on before it is their time can be such a damaging piece of advice.

Talk about victimizing someone; telling a person that they need to "just get over it" is one of the most hurtful statements we can make if it is not yet time for that person to move from where they are to where they will eventually be. If someone is giving you this kind of advice (move on and get over it) at this time, and it doesn't feel right, you might need to consider finding a new advisor. Mourning is all about the need to deal with the "Why?" of your situation in a way that is right for you.

If, however, you are stuck on the question of "Why," then this chapter is just for you. Only you know when it is time to move on, and the reality is that you do have to move on. Victors who are dealing with bad situations in their lives aren't afraid to consider whether or not they are a little bit stuck in ways that have them teetering on victim thinking.

All I want for you as a result of this chapter is for you to be freed up enough to face your response to the badness in your life in light of victim vs. victor thinking. If it isn't time for you to move on yet, that doesn't necessarily make you a victim thinker. It just might be that you need more time in this part of the mourning process. But know that there will come a time when you need to move. It's not that victors are prepared to move on without all the answers they feel they need, it's just that they know when it is time to take a step forward even when their desire to know "Why?" just isn't being met.

I came across the following Bible verse that might help during the times we have to mourn the loss of something in our lives:

> Can <u>*anything*</u> *ever separate us from Christ's love? Does it mean he no longer loves us if we have trouble or calamity, or are persecuted, or hungry, or destitute, or in danger, or threatened with death? No, <u>despite all these things, overwhelming victory is ours</u> through Christ, who loved us. And I am convinced that nothing can ever separate us from God's love. Neither death nor life, neither angels nor demons, neither our fears for today nor our worries about tomorrow—not even the powers of hell can separate us from God's love. No power in the sky above or in the earth below—indeed, nothing in all creation will ever be able to separate us from the love of God that is revealed in Christ Jesus our Lord. Romans 8:35-39 (NLT)*

Take a look at the list of things that just beg the question, "Why?" in this verse: calamity, hunger, being destitute, facing danger, persecution, even death. What is clear from this scripture is that we ALL will face such things in our life. But the amazing promise we can hold on to is that in spite of the prospect of these bad times, nothing can separate us from the love of God. In the vernacular of a victor, "I am a child of God, that's my identity! Nothing can change that fact. Not even the horrors this world can throw at me." Victors take great solace in this fact, and use it as a foundation from which they can mourn and move on as God allows in their life.

Honestly, I don't know how I could face my spouse dying or the loss of my livelihood and home without the fact that God's love will never go away from me. I know people do so every day, but I just think I would fall completely apart without the promise of God's love in my life. I know this isn't much comfort on the first day you learn about bad things to come, but as you move through the mourning process, I have found that the fact that God loves me is what has sustained me on more than one occasion when I had to deal with a big "Why?" in my life.

A STARTLING SERMON

I once heard a visiting pastor give a message at our church. This young man was from Australia. He really looked the part. Handsome... amazing accent... tanned... great hair! As I sat there listening to what, I'm sure, was a good sermon (honestly, I can't remember most of what he was talking about), I heard this pastor go down a "bunny trail" I totally didn't expect.

During the service I attended he stopped in the middle of his talk and asked, "Why do bad things happen to good people?" Now he had my attention. I later found out that he didn't even mention this topic in any of the other three services he spoke at that weekend. I felt like God Himself wanted me to learn something, and I was all ears.

This pastor was basically asking this: why do Christians face the same kinds of trials (and sometimes worse) that non-Christians face in this world? Aren't we supposed to be on God's good side by following Christ? Why would bad things happen to people inside the Church as frequently as they do outside the Church? As far as I know, cancer, job loss, children going astray, death and other why-prompting events are just as statistically possible inside the Church as outside, right?

This pastor was hitting on a topic that was close to my heart as a result of writing this book. I really wanted to see if he gave some kind of glib, standard, Christian-ese answer or not. He started off saying that in order for us to deal with the question, "Why?" we have to agree on two points.

The first point this pastor asked us to agree upon was that bad stuff is going to happen in this world whether you are a good person or not. It's just the way it is. Bad things happen to believers and non-believers alike. Breathe long enough and you will find yourself in a crisis that will force you to deal with your own, custom made, "Why?"

This got me to thinking what the Bible says about this life. In many places the Bible calls us sojourners, travelers passing through this life to the next. In other words, this place isn't our home. We are aliens in a strange land. The problem is that most of us have decided to settle into this home in ways that we weren't meant to. We have gotten comfortable in our surroundings and have started to believe that we deserve the goodness that others have when times are good in their lives. When bad times hit, our foundation is shaken. For Christians who look to this world for their fulfillment, satisfaction and guarantee, this life will prove itself to be one cruel journey.

I know human beings can never completely eliminate the desire for comfort and the good life from their wish list. However, Christians who want to live a life of the victor to which God has called them must start living in the reality that this isn't their home. When bad stuff happens to Christians in this world we need to be in a place where we are less likely to blame God and/or try to find some fault in our relationship with him that might have caused those bad things to come into our lives in the first place.

Trying to pin the "Because..." on God or our relationship with him for the "Why's?" that come up in life is just a waste of time. If God loves us, as the Romans verse above says, then the situation we are in has some purpose greater than our desire for goodness. Fact is, we might not ever get the "Because" when the "Why's?" of life seem to be in control. The bad things that happen in this life aren't meant as punishment, nor are they there to teach us a lesson. Bad stuff is just going to happen as long as we are alive.

Victims see this world as their only hope in life. They cling to the hope that the goodness that they are experiencing right now will always be there. They go to church hoping to worship God in a good enough way as to stay under His radar. They hope that their own personal goodness is enough to convince God not to mess with the good things they have in their life. This is the basis for one messed up relationship; a relationship that is doomed to fail when the bad times we ALL will face come into our lives.

Victors have come to some kind of peace with the fact that this world is not their home. We are destined for something better. Even the best day of a victor's life doesn't compare to what God has promised for us in the future when we are reunited with Him. Since this is not our home, victors have also made a certain amount of peace with the fact that bad stuff is eventually going to happen to them and to the ones they love. This isn't pessimistic thinking, it is just reality. That's what this pastor was saying. Live long enough, and bad things will happen no matter how "good" or "bad" you are.

That was the first point the visiting pastor said we had to agree on in order to open our eyes to a different perspective as to why bad things happen to good people. The second point he said we needed to agree upon is found in the Bible. He said, "In order to properly deal with the question of why bad things happen to good people, we have to agree on what the Bible says." He then pointed us to 1 John 4:4:

> *You are from God, little children, and have overcome them; because <u>greater is He who is in you than he who is in the world</u>. (NASB)*

In other words, the Christ that is in each of us is so much stronger than the evil that has dominion over this world. That is such a freeing and powerful thought to live by. God is stronger than the evil that controls this world. God has a plan that lets evil have dominion over Earth. Why? Ultimately I think it is for us all to see the difference between darkness and light. He wants us to fully grasp the contrast between good and evil and to learn to choose good every time. This life, and the challenges we face here on earth, is nothing more than practice for all eternity in Heaven.

Do you realize that in Heaven you and I will have the ability to choose? You may be asking, "So what's the big deal about that?" You have to understand that choice is a really big deal. God is banking His entire plan for all creation on our choosing Him. Satan is working his best to try and get us to choose anything—work, health, sex, money, even church—over God. God is allowing Satan to have His way to help us refine our ability to choose so that when we are with God we will still maintain that ability and we will always choose Him.

Everything bad in this world has resulted from the power of choice. Adam and Eve decided to choose to go against God because they were tricked into thinking that God wasn't good enough. Satan twisted things in such a way as to make them think that God's withholding the Tree of the Knowledge of Good and Evil from them was a sign that God's goodness couldn't be trusted. They chose to take things into their own hands and disobey God. They wanted to be like God and chose to turn away from His love through their misunderstanding of what God's love looked like.

The problem with choice didn't originate with Adam and Eve. Satan's battle of choice is what originally made this amazing creation of God's something of a problem in the Heavenly realm. You see, Satan wanted to be like God too. He wanted to have the same power and providence of God and he chose to go against God in order to get what he wanted. A bunch of Heavenly beings (actually ⅓ of them) chose to follow Satan in this direction and they were all kicked out of Heaven. Guess where they ended up? That's right, here on earth.

As a result of Satan and others choosing to disobey God, the remaining Heavenly beings don't have the power to choose. They HAVE TO do exactly what God tells them to do. God then created man and gave him the power of choice in a place that is controlled by evil. What a crazy plan that is!

Why would God risk giving choice to humans when it turned out so badly with angels? How can I say this without sounding blasphemous? Let me put it this way; God so craves relationship with a being that He created who would choose Him that He has staked His reputation on us to use the power of choice for His good no matter what kind of bad comes our way. Absolutely reckless, wild and wonderfully filled with love is this relationship in which we have the chance to partake!

But there is a more important reason why God had "no choice" but to take such a risk with His love. You have to appreciate the fact that love without choice simply isn't love at all. If I am forced to love my wife, is that really a love that is worth having? Love based on the choice to love is something that is real and worth risking all for. This doesn't make God weak or somehow dysfunctional in His love for us. It just confirms the fact that love without choice isn't something worth living for and God simply won't accept a counterfeit love like that.

I once was asked the question whether I thought there would be evil in Heaven. Interesting question. The Bible is clear that Satan and his followers will be separated from God forever in the end times. So from that standpoint, the controller of evil on earth will not be there. But Satan isn't the creator of evil. It is clear that God isn't the creator of evil either. I believe it is the choices we make that brings evil into existence. In other words, you and I, along with the choices we make, are actually the creators of evil.

I believe that there won't be evil in Heaven, but we will have the choice to do evil by choosing to turn away from God as Satan did. It is my opinion that evil won't be removed unless choice is completely taken away. As long as we have choice we will be able to choose to go against God, and that is evil.

So will evil be in Heaven? I believe the ultimate answer is no, but the possibility to do evil will be there with every choice we get to make throughout eternity. Here's the wonderful news about choice in Heaven. I believe that due to our walk here on Earth, we will be in a position to never choose anything other than this amazing God that loves us so. Our walk with Him here on earth is putting us into a position to allow us to only choose Him for all eternity. That thought absolutely fires me up. It gets me excited about the unlimited power of choice when that choice means we will never get it wrong. That's the picture of eternity that makes this life worth living, as far as I'm concerned.

I believe this visiting pastor was making a point about choice. When bad things happen we have a choice to believe or not to believe. The reality is that bad stuff is going to happen because this place isn't our home. Because of this fact we can now choose to act in the reality that Jesus is more powerful than the bad that surrounds us, that His plan will prevail even when our prospects look bleak; or we can choose to believe that our relationship with this God is somehow broken and without meaning when bad times hit.

If we choose to believe our relationship with God is broken, not only will we suffer the effects of the bad things that have befallen us, but we will be crushed with the unbelievable weight of thinking we are alone and forgotten. In that place of perceived rejection, burdened by the bad things happening to us, we are perfectly poised to take on the identity of a victim and the downward spiral that can result is nothing short of amazing to behold.

There is a different way. That way begins with choice. This pastor made a point about bad things happening to good people that had victor written all over it. He said; "If we can agree that bad stuff is going to happen to us all AND that the Jesus that is in us is far superior to the evil behind the bad stuff that happens, then bad things don't happen to good people, GOOD PEOPLE HAPPEN TO BAD THINGS!"

When I heard this, I immediately thought, "Now, that's victor thinking if I have ever heard it!" That's the kind of shift in perspective that we all need in order to move from victim to victor when we find ourselves saddled with the bad stuff that will inevitably, come our way.

God was using this wonderful man from Australia to help me see how choice has the power to turn things on its ear. If I choose to believe bad things are happening to me for no reason at all then I'm the victim of an infraction way bigger than just the bad thing that has impacted me. I'm actually the victim of a loveless and senseless God. What parent would willingly stand by and let harm come to their child? If this is the God we serve, then Heaven isn't going to be all that great of a place to spend eternity.

But if I choose to believe that Jesus is greater than the evil that has come into my life, then there has to be a reason for that bad stuff. Maybe, just maybe, I'm happening to that bad situation more than that bad situation is happening to me. Maybe I'm part of the process of bringing light into a dark place. Maybe my involvement in that bad situation is bringing a glimmer of hope into this world that would have otherwise gone missing if that bad thing hadn't happened to me in the first place. Maybe God's plan for me is such that bad things don't victimize me in respect to my relationship with Him. Maybe I'm part of the plan to crush evil in this world. Bad stuff isn't happening to me, I'm happening to the bad of this world because of the powerful love of God that flows through me. Wow, that's a perspective change that has some power in helping me stay on the victor side of the equation even when bad things come and go in my life.

PLANTING THE SEED OF A NEW PARADIGM

Back to the triad of bad news I received about some friends and acquaintances just today. Each of these three sets of people know and love God and He loves them. So, should the lady with breast cancer or that man with prostate cancer or that poor person who is now homeless be happy about their situation? Of course not. Each of these people is facing a big battle and losses will result. Those losses have to be mourned. As we have already discussed in this chapter, the fact that they will mourn losses doesn't make them victims.

The reality is that this new revelation (good people happen to bad things) isn't something they might be able to grasp at this time in their mourning process. You see, each of these people is a victim of some horrible things. Cancer is one of the greatest victimizers in our world today. That lady with breast cancer and that elderly gentlemen with prostate cancer are victims in every way. So is that friend who is homeless. He is the victim of a strange economy and of being in the wrong place at the wrong time. They have every right and need to mourn their situation. They need to take all the time required to get in a position to move forward through the process. Right now the statement about good people happening to bad things won't mean a thing to them, but it will one day.

If you are in a bad situation as you read this chapter, I don't expect this perspective to mean a whole lot to you at this time either. All I'm hoping for is that a seed be planted. Let the fact that God isn't victimizing you with the badness you may have in your life be something that takes root and grows so that the next time bad things happen you will be in a place let the choice to love God overwhelm the forces of evil trying to get you to choose otherwise.

There will come a time for these three individuals, and for us all, to be ready to move out into victor thinking. Until that time comes, we, the friends and acquaintances of people in bad times, can come around them, love them and accept them in ways that show God hasn't left them or forgotten them.

Choice plays such a critical role in how we live, particularly when bad times strike. We can choose to live as victims or as victors. Bad things in our lives are a stark reminder of where our heart is focused, and of how easy it is to be deceived into thinking that our relationship with God isn't all that it should be.

For these three people who have come upon bad times, and for those of us who will face similar or worse situations, there might come a time when we will fall into victim thinking. We might start to believe that we are doomed to a life as a victim simply because bad things have happened to us in the past. It is specifically for those times in a person's life that I have written this chapter and, to a greater purpose, this book.

Bad stuff is going to happen. This has nothing to do with your relationship with God or your knowledge of Him. I guarantee you will learn lessons about who God is and who you are in His eyes as a result of the bad stuff you have gone through. But, hear me loud and clear:

God hasn't doomed you to a bad life because of your misunderstanding of Him or because of any bad thing you have done in your life. If that were the case, then the verses from Romans we read earlier are nothing but a cruel a lie. That option isn't an acceptable paradigm of life for me as it relates to believing in a loving God who created and saved me. I hope it isn't acceptable to you either.

THE LION

One day my family came face to face with a particularly difficult situation. My wife found she had a lump in her breast. For quite some time after that revelation the question, "Why?" was the underlying part of what seemed like every thought she and I had. As I pondered the spiritual side of this occurrence, I immediately thought, "How dare Satan toss such horrible news into the middle of our nice, neat and comfortable life!" The more I thought about Satan's involvement in this situation, the more scared I became.

Coincidentally (or not), it was during that time that I had taken on a larger role in the oversight of my church. I was told that my family and I would be a bigger and more appealing target for Satan and his evil ways because we had stepped up in leadership. Breast cancer began to be the fulfilled promise of attack, and fear began to sneak into my life. This new and big "Why?" in my family's life began to be reinforced with the question of, "What's next?"

As I fought to deal with those and other victim kinds of thoughts, I vaguely remembered a Bible verse about Satan:

> *Be alert and of sober mind. Your enemy the devil prowls around like a roaring lion looking for someone to devour. 1 Peter 5:8 (NIV)*

Could it be possible that Satan found a way to devour my wife through cancer? What else might he devour in my life as a result of taking a stand for God? Would my health be next? What about the health and safety of my kids? The more I pondered the power of

Satan, the more scared I became. Victim thinking was quickly taking hold.

As we progressed through the treatment for my wife's cancer, we found that she was one of the lucky ones. In less than 10 weeks, she was pronounced cancer free. Now, some 15+ years later, other than the scars of the battle, that time is becoming a more and more distant memory.

It wasn't until I started writing this book that God showed me something really important about that fear I felt with regards to Satan being a lion looking for someone to devour. God wanted to set straight a lie that I didn't even know had snuck into my life at that time. While gathering information for this chapter, I came across this verse:

> *Then one of the elders said to me, "Do not weep! See, the Lion of the tribe of Judah, the Root of David, has triumphed. He is able to open the scroll and its seven seals. Revelation 5:5 (NIV)*

When I read this verse it all became so clear. I grabbed my Bible and looked up that verse in 1 Peter that described Satan being a lion and one very important word jumped out at me. Problem was that I had misread and misunderstood that verse for all these years. 1 Peter 5:8 doesn't say Satan IS a lion, it says he is **LIKE** a lion. Satan is like a roaring lion. **Jesus IS THE LION**!

There is a world of difference between being like something and being the actual thing. One little word changed my entire perspective in a way that made being the victor Jesus died for me to be something more attainable. I had been giving power to Satan that he just isn't due. How about you? Are you doing the same? Satan might be like a lion but Jesus is the Lion! Yes Satan is the one that controls the evil that made cancer part of my family's life, but greater is Jesus in me than the evil that is Satan in this world. That's a foundation from which victory can be assured, even in the midst of being a victim of all the badness that happens in this world.

One of Satan's greatest ploys here on earth is to imitate God. After all, Satan was cast out of Heaven for taking steps to be like God.

Now he does his best to try and trick us into believing his power is unlimited and his plan is guaranteed. People, that's nothing more than a lie.

Satan's defeat is, without a doubt, something that is going to happen. He knows that all too well and that one fact drives him crazy. His goal is to confuse us all enough that we will choose to follow our own ways rather than God. Satan does this with the hope that he can bring us to a point where our choices will separate us from God for all eternity. Satan knows his end is assured. All he can do is try to get as many of us to go his way as possible. "Misery loves company" is certainly an expression designed with Satan in mind.

Satan planted a seed in my life during my wife's battle with cancer. He wanted me to believe that he is a giant, a lion that can go here and there and devour anyone he wants. God wanted me to see that Satan is doing a poor job of imitating a lion. Jesus is the Lion. He has all the power, He has all the perspective, and He has all the ability to save and/or carry us through the bad times that will come against us in this life. All we have to do is choose which way we want to go. Do we want the life of a victim exemplified by a toothless wanna-be lion like Satan, or do we want to live the life of a victor like the real Lion of the Tribe of Judah, Jesus?

Satan is LIKE God. God IS God! That's the beginning of a victor's approach to dealing with bad things happening in his or her life. Victims see Satan as more than he really is and feel defeated as a result. Victors see Satan in the real light of Jesus Christ and this brings hope, even in the bad times. Don't get me wrong, Satan has real powers, powers that aren't something to mess with. But his power is limited to and overshadowed by a God who is banking on us to choose His love in spite of all the mess evil will toss our way.

THE VICTOR'S PERSPECTIVE

I've said it before and I need to say it again: I'm a pretty simple guy. I'm not deep enough to find definitive answers as to why bad things happen to good people. But I can understand the possibilities I've presented in this chapter. Let me list them out in the hopes that you, too, can face your bad times as a victor and not let victimhood rule when difficult times are part of your life.

1. God loves us. Nothing can change that. There is no bad thing in all the universe that can separate us from His love. God's love is guaranteed by the fact that Christ died to make us His Children. Bad stuff isn't a sign that His love for us has changed in some way. His love for us is unchangeable, unstoppable, and undeniable.

2. This is not my home. Putting my faith in a good life is a waste of time. Eventually everything good in this life will be gone due to circumstances beyond my control. At death all things I consider good will be gone and replaced with a permanent goodness called Heaven. I will repeatedly feel like a victim and act as one if I believe I am due a good life as a result of choosing to love God. I am an alien living in a world that is not my own. My settling for goodness that comes from this world is a waste of time since it will all be gone when I'm where I belong in the first place.

3. Bad stuff is going to happen. Bad stuff happens whether I'm good or not. Bad is a result of the evil that oversees this fallen world. Since this isn't my home, bad stuff has no bearing on whether I'm a good person or not.

4. My relationship with God is secure. My relationship with God also has no bearing on whether I am acting like a good follower of His or not. He isn't putting bad things in my life to teach me lessons or to make His revelation in my life something I will desire to a greater extent. There is no doubt I will learn all kinds of lessons as a result of going through bad times, lessons about myself and about God. God sees me as perfect and blameless, not because of who I am but because of the finished work of Jesus Christ on the Cross. For that reason, my relationship with God is secure and that makes me a victor.

5. Jesus is Greater than the evil of this world. Jesus is the Lion of the Tribe of Judah. Satan is trying to imitate Jesus by being LIKE a lion. The Jesus in me is greater than the evil behind the bad things I will come against in this world. For that reason, He will either save me from the badness I am in or His presence will be with me as I pass through it.

6. Bad things aren't happening to me, I'm happening to bad things. I might just be bringing in an element of the light of God into a dark situation that would have never been there had that bad thing not happened to me in the first place. Light is the only thing that destroys darkness. Take a covered candle into a dark room and watch the darkness flee when the light of that candle is revealed. The bad in my life might just be a chance for the power of God to be seen in a way that changes the world around me forever.

This is the roadmap I now want to follow when bad things come up against me. I believe this is how I will be best able to fight my natural tendency to fall into victim thinking and move out into victor living. God didn't create me to live a life based on hopeless principles. Victim thinkers build their entire life on things like that. God made me to live as a victor even when the badness of this world makes it look like I'm not.

I sure hope this chapter has introduced a few thoughts that will help you consider your position with God when the bad of this world comes knocking on your door. Satan relishes the idea that we might choose victim thinking due to the evil he controls in the world. It confounds Satan to no end and amazes the remaining angels in Heaven when we choose to Love God even in the midst of all Hell breaking loose in our lives.

Nothing makes a person more able to cross the line from victim to victor than coming through bad times with our relationship with God intact and even more solid as a result. In spite of all the pain you may be feeling during your own bad times, I want you to hold on to the fact that you are a victor. Nothing can take that away, except your choice to think otherwise.

May the life you are experiencing right now be one that brings you to the crossroads of choosing the freedom that is the life of a victor over the prison of victim thinking. That's what God wants for you—freedom. He is staking His entire plan for everything around you on your ability to choose His victory for you over the trap of victimhood Satan wants you to live with for all eternity.

CHAPTER NINE

Brokenness

I almost didn't include this chapter in the book. Why? I felt it was geared way too directly to people inside the Church. If you are a person checking out this God thing and have made it to this point, I hope you will read this chapter. At the very least, you might catch a glimpse behind the veil of the Church and come to a better understanding of how we have been able to cause so much damage in the world over what many of us misunderstand and misappropriate when it comes to the issue of brokenness.

When I think of the word broken, I think of a horse. We all have seen movies where the grisly cowboy jumps on a stallion and rides it to exhaustion. The cowboy knows that if he can stay on that horse until it is exhausted that he will have, in essence, reached down deep into the horse's very being and changed something so profound that that horse will never be the same.

All that horse has ever known is freedom. Now a fear grips the soul of that amazing animal to the point where it will now do things that just a few moments earlier would have been unthinkable. From that day forward, the broken horse will allow a creature so much smaller and weaker than itself to control its every move. The will of that horse is now completely changed. This picture of brokenness is the perfect example of victim thinking taking over a life.

This is how many in the Christian world see our walk with God. The underlying belief is that this life is about breaking us from our wild and self-centered ways so that we can come fully under the control of this God that made us and thus serve Him all the more. There's a sadness to this kind of brokenness that touches me deeply. Is this the way God sees us? Is this what life is all about, a never ending parade of harsh happenings designed to break our will and make us submit so that we can be more useful to Him?

There are a lot of Christian leaders in the world today who think this way, but I have to question whether we really worship a God who sees the need to break His precious children so that we can be better servants. This just doesn't sound like something that would come from the hands of a loving Father like the one I know God to be. I may be totally wrong about this, but I believe there is a different view of brokenness with which we need to come to grips. That's what I'd like to explain in this chapter.

THE MEANING OF "BROKEN"

Isn't it amazing that the simplest words often times are the hardest to succinctly define? That's the case with the word broken. There are so many different meanings of this word. I had to stop and look it up in the dictionary[13]. Here's what I found. Broken means:

    1: violently separated into parts: SHATTERED
    2: damaged or altered by breaking: as
        a: having undergone or been subjected to fracture <a *broken* leg>
        b: *of land surfaces* : being irregular, interrupted, or full of obstacles
        c: violated by transgression <a *broken* promise>
        d: DISCONTINUOUS, INTERRUPTED
        e: disrupted by change

---

[13] http://www.merriam-webster.com/dictionary/broken

    f: *of a tulip flower* : having an irregular, streaked, or blotched pattern especially from virus infection
3 **a:** made weak or infirm
    b: subdued completely : CRUSHED, SORROWFUL <a *broken* heart> <a *broken* spirit>
    c: BANKRUPT
    d: reduced in rank
4 **a:** cut off : DISCONNECTED
    b: imperfectly spoken or written <*broken* English>
5: not complete or full <a *broken* bale of hay>
6: disunited by divorce, separation, or desertion of one parent <children from *broken* homes> <a *broken* family>

Broken is a really strong word with specific meanings that are hard for me to reconcile when it comes to my interaction with God. Want to really bring into clarity how weird these definitions are in light of a loving relationship? Go back and reread each definition and insert it into the following sentence:

"I will (insert the definition of broken here) the one I love so that they will be better at loving me."

Let me take one definition and insert it into the sentence above and show how weird the concept of brokenness is with God in mind. Can you possibly see God saying, "I will make weak or infirm the one I love so that they will be better at loving me?" That is not something I could ever envision the God I know doing. Sure, the Old Testament is filled with acts that might be considered "breaking," but in light of the finished work of Jesus Christ, brokenness is something that I believe is quite different than what Christians have thought and acted upon in the past.

The definition in #3b above is the one that I believe most closely defines what a horse experiences when it is broken. I believe this is also the definition that we Christians have a tendency to put on each other when we see bad things happening to people. It is so easy to say, "God is breaking that person of their evil ways" when we see someone going through a hard time who isn't quite living up to our notion of what it looks like to be a mature follower of Jesus Christ. How often have I thought that of another human being? How often have I put on God the misguided thought that He is there turning the screws in a person's life to somehow make them better at loving Him? Forgive me, God, for such thinking about you and about the ones you love.

Let me pose a few questions based on the definitions of the word broken to help frame the discussion I want to have in this chapter. Is God the kind of being who is in the business of completely subduing His children? Is it God's plan to have us completely shattered in ways that make us see Him better? Is being cut off from him the best thing for us in God's eyes? For those of you who aren't followers of Christ, how does the kind of relationship that requires God to break His children sound to you? Not too appealing is it?

When Christians speak of being broken they typically point to a set of circumstances a person is going through that the Christian thinks will make that person come closer to God. In other words, God is using the bad circumstances in life to teach that person to submit more fully to the God who loves him. Does anybody else find that kind of thinking perverse?

We just finished a chapter that I hope debunked the notion that bad things happen to good people because we aren't all that good in the first place and need to be put into our place. The fact is that we are blameless and without fault. Why? Because of what Jesus has done for us.

Our blamelessness and being without fault doesn't happen because of our coming to our senses and submitting more fully to God after a particularly hard time in our lives. We are blameless because of Jesus' actions, not ours. Of course God wants us to give our lives fully to Him, but not out of brokenness from exhaustion like a battered horse that has had its will forever altered. God wants us to come to Him because we choose to do so. Yes, this world might drive us to him at times, but God isn't the one doing the driving.

Take a look at what the Apostle Paul said about the subject:

> *You let the distress bring you to God, not drive you from him. The result was all gain, no loss. Distress that drives us to God does that. It turns us around. It gets us back in the way of salvation. We never regret that kind of pain. But those who let distress drive them away from God are full of regrets, end up on a deathbed of regrets. 2 Corinthians 7:9-10 (THE MESSAGE)*

We have a choice in this world. We can let the distress that will happen in our lives drive us to God or drive us away from Him. It is just hard for me to think that God is sitting in Heaven planning wave after wave of distress to break me of my will so that I will finally decide to choose Him. I hope that kind of God is just as unappealing to you as it is to me.

THREE CATEGORIES OF CHRISTIANS

I came across this quote from Larry Crabb from his book, *"Shattered Dreams."* It really helps set the stage for what I see as the reasons and consequences of our misinterpretation of the term brokenness in the Christian community:

> *The western church has become a community of either the victorious or the acceptably broken. With each other we're more proper than real, more appropriate than alive.*[14]

Here's what I have seen happen inside and out of the Church. We all have had trials of one kind or another. How we portray our lives to others in the Church typically falls into one of three categories. The first category is made up of those of us who have come through the trials and have found success afterwards. These are the victorious Crabb is talking about in the quote above.

I have been part of the victorious class at times in my life. For me, and maybe for us all who have been victorious, the underlying

---

[14] Taken from *Shattered Dreams* by Larry Crabb. Used with permission of Penguin Random House. All Rights Reserved.

thinking might be: "I weathered the storm of hard times with God at my side and I'm now living the blessed life as a result of getting my life on the right track." Wow, is that statement packed full of future victim thinking opportunities. A person who thinks they are successful because they have gotten right the obedience side of walking with God is a victim waiting to happen. Unfortunately, the vast majority of the victorious class can't see the wall they are rushing headlong towards because they are blinded by self-righteousness.

Those who think they are living the victorious life because of something they have done are targets for Satan to come in and rob them of their peace. Jesus came across a young man who felt he was living the victorious life. This early member of the victorious class is called the "rich young ruler" in the Bible. Take a look at his story in the verses below:

> *As he went out into the street, a man came running up, greeted him with great reverence, and asked, "Good Teacher, what must I do to get eternal life?" Jesus said, "Why are you calling me good? No one is good, only God. You know the commandments: Don't murder, don't commit adultery, don't steal, don't lie, don't cheat, honor your father and mother." He said, "Teacher, I have—from my youth—kept them all!" Jesus looked him hard in the eye—and loved him! He said, "There's one thing left: Go sell whatever you own and give it to the poor. All your wealth will then be heavenly wealth. And come follow me." The man's face clouded over. This was the last thing he expected to hear, and he walked off with a heavy heart. He was holding on tight to a lot of things, and not about to let go. Looking at his disciples, Jesus said, "Do you have any idea how difficult it is for people who 'have it all' to enter God's kingdom?" The disciples couldn't believe what they were hearing... Mark 10:17-24 (THE MESSAGE)*

Jesus isn't against prosperity and good living, as some are so quick to say as a result of this story. It is the grip that riches can have on a man's soul that Jesus hates to see in our lives. Jesus wasn't telling this influential young man that he needed to be broken down to owning nothing before he could see God clearly. He was pointing out that this man's "victorious" living was getting in the way of him living like a victor.

Why do I believe this young man thought that his victorious life was part of who he was? Look at his words. The young man said, "I have… kept them all (God's commandments)."

It is my opinion that the victorious in the Church today feel they are victorious because of the word "I." Remember that being victorious isn't the hallmark of a victor. We are victors because of Jesus's death and resurrection, not because of any goodness in our lives. Thinking that we have done what we need to do in the spiritual realm to reap the rewards of a God blessing us in the physical realm puts us in a place to relate to our God in "proper and appropriate" ways rather than "real and alive" ways.

This is why it was so hard for the rich young ruler to consider Jesus' words. Sell everything? I can hear the cries in this young man's heart at the prospect of selling everything: "Do you know where I came from, Jesus? Do you know how hard it was to get to this place of prominence and prosperity? If you only knew the hardships I faced along the way to get to where I was willing to do all you commanded. If you really knew the trials I faced you would never ask me to give up this one thing that gives me peace."

Jesus knew that if you take away all the goodies in the rich young ruler's life that his relationship with God would be something that this young man couldn't possibly want or understand. The "victorious" camp believes that their good and victorious life is a result of their efforts in obeying God. This camp leans heavily on the belief that their obedience has been shaped by the bad things that have brought some level of brokenness into their lives and that their current blessing is a result of God's pleasure when it comes to their efforts to follow Him.

The victorious class is the first "type" of Christian that I believe exists in the Church today. The second camp I believe Christians can fall into is what Crabb calls the "acceptably broken."

The acceptably broken are people who are either in hard times or who have recently come through hard times but who haven't reclaimed the success that the members of the victorious class have in their lives. The acceptably broken are too weary to cause too much trouble inside the Church. They are willing to change their ways to fit into the norms that the local body of believers has instituted as tradition when it comes to their way of worship. The acceptably broken won't sing too loud, get too crazy in the spirit or create any kind of ruckus in our nice and neat worship service because they are too shell-shocked from the hard times they have just come through to risk rocking the boat with God anymore.

The acceptably broken look at the victorious with envy and hope that their day will soon come when they, too, can praise God for turning their lives around in such dramatic fashion. The acceptably broken are more than willing to get involved in Bible studies, prayer groups and discipleship training programs because they see the victorious doing so. They want to do whatever the victorious class are doing in an effort to ensure they will never have to go back to the hard times they faced just a short while ago.

Although the Bible studies and prayer times and discipleship training will be something that feels real to the acceptably broken Christian, there will come a time when victorious living takes over and the realness as well as the feeling of life in these activities will fade. Why will it fade? Because the motivation for being involved in these activities was misplaced. The Bible studies, prayer groups and discipleship training weren't being done to build relationship with God, they were being done to try and appease this God who, they believe, might take them back into places of greater and greater brokenness. The lot in life of the acceptably broken is to spring up quickly in growth and "maturity" only to wither because the roots of that growth were placed in the wrong soil.

The victorious and the acceptably broken fill the seats of our Christian services every weekend. The sad thing is that I'm one of them most of the time myself. That's what makes it possible for me to think like a victim for long periods of time in my life. Chasing victorious living isn't what a relationship with God is all about. Until we get that kind of thinking out of our worship times with God, we are doomed to see victimization rule in our congregations. But there is one more class of people we need to consider.

The third class of people that come and go from our churches is what I call the unacceptably broken. These are the people who haven't come around in a sufficient way as to fit into the mold of what we think Christian life is supposed to look like. They are the outcasts. Take, for example, that homeless guy that keeps coming to your service, who smells bad and can cause a bit of a disturbance from time to time? Or what about that gay couple that sits in the back of the room, not sure of what they are doing there in the first place? Just the presence of any number of examples of the unacceptably broken can make the other two classes of Christian squirm as their comfortable worship services are challenged by the diversity that can come from this third class of church attendees.

How often have I looked at such people with the thought that they haven't had enough BAD happen in their lives to make them "hit bottom" and see God clearly? Obviously, they haven't come to that point since their lives are still filled with "sinful" ways and "out of the norm" kinds of living. When we have a view of people that is shaped by a misunderstood meaning of the word broken, the Church can become such a closed, unwelcome and victim-promoting entity.

With the wrong view of brokenness in our churches, we don't have to worry about the unacceptably broken people for too long. They won't hang around for any length of time if we believe that they (and we) are like horses in need of being broken in order to get their life into alignment with what we think a relationship with God should look like. They will get the message that they just don't belong there until they get their lives straightened up. We don't have to say it that directly. They understand where we are coming from. The unacceptably broken quickly find the back door of the church and leave.

This is so far from the reality of the "come as you are" kind of love Jesus wants us all to have that it blows me away. I believe part of the reason we shun the unacceptably broken is that we just don't know what brokenness looks like in the first place.

BROKENNESS

Look, I'm not saying that we don't need to change. That homeless person and that gay couple need to change just as much as you and I do right now in our lives. What do they need to change? That's really between them and God, not between them and you or me.

Nor am I saying that challenging circumstances are not useful in helping us see God in a better light. What I am saying is that there is a spirit in me, and in you, that makes us wild stallions. Where do you think that spirit came from? God's the one who put that spirit in us in the first place. Why in the world would He take steps to destroy that spirit so that the wildness that was put there by Him is forever forfeited? That view of brokenness just doesn't make sense to me. For that reason, I'm trying desperately to stop putting that kind of a view of brokenness on others as well.

As I was writing this chapter, I took a break to spend some time with my wife and we watched a movie on a rare rainy California afternoon. After the movie was over, I took a quick look at my Facebook newsfeed and saw a picture I'd like to describe to you. At the bottom of the picture was the caption, "Sometimes the chains that prevent us from being free are more than mental and physical." In the picture was a big, and I mean BIG, horse quietly standing with his reigns tied to a small plastic chair.

Can you see that picture in your mind? A 1200 pound beast being held in place by a 2 pound plastic chair? If that doesn't sum up how warped a view we have when it comes to brokenness, I don't know what does. Is this how God wants us to be? So broken that all our natural power is forfeited in ways that defy logic? I just can't get my mind around the possibility of a loving God thinking this is the best for His children.

Maybe it's time that we get introduced to different perspective on what brokenness is and how Christians are to live as "broken" people. I just don't see any way for Christians to move from victims to victors if we look as hopeless as that poor horse does in the picture I described above. What I believe God is really saying about brokenness can change our perspective in such a way that victor living will allow us to break free from the weak ties holding us all down in one way or another.

TWO SIDE OF BROKENNESS

So, how is a person who is following God or who is considering becoming a follower of God to view brokenness? I believe brokenness needs to be considered in two realms, the physical and the spiritual.

In light of all I have said in this chapter to this point, I have to admit something that still kind of bothers me. Physical brokenness that looks like the horse picture described above isn't necessarily a bad thing. The fact is that that horse, broken as it is, is now a more valuable commodity to those who own it. The reality is that life is such that we all have to be broken in one way or another in order to bring us to a place where we will become more valuable to society and those who are close to us. Though I hate making that statement, it is a reality we need to face head-on.

Children have to be "broken" to learn to sit in a seat so that they can be taught math, science, humanities, etc. Newlyweds need to "broken" to learn to selflessly serve each other for the betterment of their union. New recruits in the military go through a carefully planned, very elaborate and extremely physical means of being "broken" in order to take them from individual thinking into group thinking that will give them the best opportunity to survive in some terrible situations.

How a person is brought to that place of brokenness can be a controversial and misapplied process. If it is done wrong, victimization will result that can lead to the kinds of victim thinking I'm speaking against in this book. The results of some level of physical brokenness are generally something that we all can agree is useful and has some element of universal appeal from the point of view of group advancement. If we approach spiritual brokenness in the same way as we do physical brokenness, I believe we open the door to a level of victimization that threatens how we view our lives and can actually turn us away from a vibrant relationship with God.

We discussed the difference between the three aspects of our being in an earlier chapter. We are all made up of flesh, soul and spirit. Physical brokenness that is good for society, done right, is a process that enables us to let our flesh and soul change in a way that makes us more useful for the greater good. Done wrong, brokenness is something that can cause incredible damage to our flesh and soul, as well as to our spirit.

Spiritual brokenness can never look like that picture of the horse above. I just don't believe God's intention is for us to be broken so that we can be made more useful to Him. I come to this conclusion because I view God as my Father, not my boss or master. I am His son, not His slave. God's intention for me isn't to be broken so that I can better meet His needs. His intention is for me to come into a relationship with Him that is more real and alive than ever before. Brokenness, in the spiritual sense, is more about how I view myself than how God views me.

I have come to believe that brokenness in the spirit realm is the convergence of two vastly different thoughts. Brokenness to me has become an effort to live life as a person who, at the same time, is totally NOTHING to God and totally EVERYTHING to Him. Confused? I hope so. Spiritual brokenness is something with which I think we need to wrestle deeply. Let me explain the two sides of what I think brokenness is supposed to be all about.

THINKING TOO LITTLE OF OURSELVES

On one hand we are totally nothing to God. Remember, we are nothing but dust, formed in an image and given the breath of life straight from the mouth of God. How could dust be important to God? How could a handful of dirt mean anything to the creator of all the universe? I asked in an earlier chapter, "What is it that you and I have that somehow makes this perfect, all powerful and all-knowing God more complete? What is it that God is missing that we bring to the table?" One side of brokenness, in the spiritual sense, is the realization that we mean absolutely nothing to this God who made us.

How does that statement make you feel? Kind of depressed? Do you feel a sense of hopelessness creeping into your soul? I hate to be so direct, but, good. Brokenness requires that we feel the despair that comes with being completely without hope and purpose. We need to feel like the dirt that God formed us from in order for us to come to a place where brokenness can have the power in our soul it needs to have. But hear me loud and clear: this place of hopelessness, despair and confusion isn't where God wants us to stay.

Unfortunately, too many of us choose to remain on the "I am nothing" side of brokenness. Spiritual brokenness isn't meant for us to walk around with our head hung low. Those of us who allow this side of spiritual brokenness to rule in our lives tend to react to the pain of being utterly worthless before God in one of two ways. We either completely give up or we double down in our efforts to try and get through this life in ways that prove our worth. Unfortunately, I've reacted to these feelings of worthlessness in both ways. And when I have, the results in my life have been less than stellar, to say the least.

The Church is filled with people who are reacting to the gnawing feeling of worthlessness in their lives in these ways. Those who have just given up have decided to live a Christian life that, on their best day, is just barely mundane. They are satisfied with a good message now and then and have given up on the thought that God can or will interact with them on a personal level. They feel like their life has no purpose and have resigned themselves to live with as much peace as they can while eking out a day-by-day spiritual existence. They see their melancholy ways as somewhat of a badge of honor; even though they can't feel or see God, they continue to follow Him. There has to be some reward for choosing God in spite of the fact that their lives can't prove His existence. Hear the haunting strings of victim thinking in such a response?

I hate to make such a callous observation, but those Christians who respond to and are stuck on the idea that they are of no use to God are amazingly valuable to the Church. They have resigned themselves to the fact that they are worthless and are the quiet, stalwart attendees. Though their demeanor is one of heaviness and lacking in joy, they can be depended on to support the Church and will do so with minimal disruption. They may not get overly involved in many aspects of Church growth, but they will be there, not causing any trouble. They are easy to overlook but won't react badly when they are not seen.

Then there are those who, though deep down inside feel they are nothing before God, just can't stand to believe that God would view their existence as worthless. They get busy working to prove to themselves, their loved ones, to their Church and to God Himself that His choice of their life was a wise one. They are the type A personalities. They are here and there, doing this and that.

Those who react to the feelings of worthlessness by trying all the harder to prove otherwise are a pastor's dream. They are the ones who will dive into any and all aspects of Church activities. They are more than willing to work hard for God and for the Church as they try to earn enough "atta-boys" to cover the growing evidence that God just doesn't need them. From time to time their accomplishments quiet that ever persistent voice inside saying that they are no good. But the silence is short-lived. Sooner or later, accomplishment has no effect on their lives. Sadly, many of these people either burn out before they come to the end of such useless thinking or stay in this kind of production mode beyond the point where results have any impact on whether they feel worthy or not.

Even when these type A personality people burn out from "doing," they typically become like those who remain on the "I am nothing before God" side of the scale. Either way they hardly ever leave the Church—that would be one more proof of their failure to make a difference. Whether they stay overly involved or move to the background to deal with the feeling that they don't matter to God, these people make great church-folk. You might know many in your congregation today who are coping with the "I don't mean anything to God" category by applying one or both of the actions described above.

Floundering in the knowledge that we mean absolutely nothing to God is a victim thinker's paradise. Living to prove we are valuable in

God's economy creates a wake of victims as we work hard to prove our worth. Choosing to remain on the side of the brokenness spectrum that says we are nothing before God kills our ability to live as the victor we were created to be.

So, one side of the spiritual brokenness spectrum says that we mean nothing to God. The other side we have to consider is that we mean everything to Him. It amazes me how much God loves us. Though we have and will continue to abandon Him, He still stands for and wants the best for us. How do I know this? God Himself came to save us through Jesus Christ.

A STORY OF THE TWO SIDES OF BROKENNESS

Remember the story of Abraham taking his son, Isaac, up on the mountain to sacrifice him at the request of God? You can't help but see an amazing mix of meaning nothing and, at the same time, meaning everything to God in that story.

As you may remember, God speaks to Abraham one day and tells him to take his son, Isaac, up on a mountain that God Himself will point out and to sacrifice Isaac in the name of God. Talk about not meaning much to God; Isaac didn't seem to rise to much worth in the eyes of God if you look at God's request on the surface only.

You have to realize what God was asking Abraham to do. He was telling Abraham to kill the very person that seemed to be the fulfillment of the promises that God had made to Abraham about the future of his legacy. God had promised that He would make a great nation out of Abraham and his descendants. Abraham waited over 100 years to see his son born. It was a miracle Isaac came into the world in the first place. Did God think so little of Abraham, not to mention Isaac, that He would allow Abraham to commit such a heinous act, thereby destroying any chance for God's promise of a great nation to come about?

As they get ready to go up on the mountain that God has selected, Isaac (probably a young man of 13 or so) starts to get a little suspicious. He says to his father, *"Look, (we have) the fire and the wood, but where is the lamb for a burnt offering?" Genesis 22:7 (NKJV)*. Abraham says something that is amazingly profound. He says, *"My son, God will provide for Himself the lamb for a burnt offering." Genesis 22:8 (NJKV)*

Sounds like a perfectly fine statement of faith Abraham made in verse 8. Many have viewed Abraham's response to Isaac's questioning about the sacrifice to be a belief that Abraham had unwavering faith that God would provide. Some even postulate that Abraham so believed in God that he expected God to raise Isaac from the dead after he sacrificed him to God. Can you imagine what was going through the head of both father and son as Abraham stood over Isaac with the knife raised to kill him? What an impossible situation for a father and a son to be placed into.

At the last second God intervenes and shows Abraham a ram that "just so happens" to be caught in a thicket next to where he was about to do his son in. The fact that we don't mean much to God is steeped in this story. The proof that we mean everything to Him isn't that the ram showed up at the last second; the proof of our worth to Him comes in what seemed like a faith-filled response of a father to his son.

If we take a close look at Abraham's response to Isaac in Genesis 22:8 we see something interesting. The original language has a word missing that the English translators decided needed to be placed there for continuity. The word "for" is missing before the word "Himself a lamb" in the original language. Let's reread the verse without that extra word. The verse actually says, "God will provide Himself a lamb for sacrifice."

Why is this proof to me of the fact that we mean everything to God? God was saying, "I will provide <u>myself</u> as a sacrifice in your place." Jesus, being part of the triune nature of God, was called the Lamb of God. In other words, God offered Himself, through Jesus, to us as a sacrifice to save us all. That ram caught in the thicket was a sign of the lamb (Jesus) who would come on the scene thousands of years later. Jesus' death on the Cross wasn't an accident. It was being foretold on a remote mountaintop through a drama being played out by a father and a son.

Want to have your mind blown even further? I once heard it taught that it is speculated that the mountaintop on which God instructed Abraham to sacrifice Isaac, was actually the exact same hill on which three crosses were erected outside of a town that didn't even exist at the time of the telling of this story—a hill called Golgotha outside of a town called Jerusalem. This is the place where Jesus met His long foretold and gruesome death. It is thought, by some, that the place God took His Son to be sacrificed is the exact "mountain" where another father (Abraham) was willing to sacrifice his son (Isaac).

Coincidence? I think not. God goes to big and extreme measures to prove how valuable we are in His eyes. He is even willing to go to the length of allowing His own Son to die in our place to prove the faith He has in us! That kind of love is radical and sometimes hard to believe. That's how much we mean to God. God Himself was willing to do whatever it took to make it possible for us to have a deep, meaningful and lasting relationship with Him.

THINKING TOO HIGHLY OF OURSELVES

The other side of the spectrum of brokenness is that we are EVERYTHING to this God who made us. When the truth that we mean everything to God gets into our lives it can be like a cup of water to a parched and thirsty soul. That first sip is like nothing we have ever experienced before. Sadly, just like choosing to remain on the side of meaning nothing to God, those who elect to live a life of meaning everything to Him are just as liable to be caught in victim thinking as those entrenched on the other side of the spectrum of spiritual brokenness.

People who choose to live lives rooted in the fact that they are everything to God are dangerous to be around. These are the people who allow arrogance to come into their lives and control how they relate to others around them. I have always thought that the atrocities done during the Crusades have their roots in a superiority that comes from thinking that our relationship with God trumps everything, even the life of someone else.

Other religions have adopted this kind of thinking and the result has been killing, abuse and victimization in some of the most horrific forms, all in the name of God. How sad that we can get to a point where our standing with God would drive us to do things that make victims out of others in this world.

Remember what we covered earlier in this book. Victims caught in victim thinking can become some of the biggest victimizers themselves. Those who have gone from thinking they are nothing before God (a life filled with victimizing events) to a place of realizing they are everything before that same God can often get the purpose of this shift in thinking all wrong. When they do this, it can lead to victimization of others in ways that might not rise to the level of mass murder, but can be just as painful for those caught in the sights of individuals or groups who live solely on the side of being everything to God.

People who choose to live on the side of thinking they are everything to God tend to be extreme in their thoughts and beliefs. They are the religious zealots of the world. They latch onto causes and factions in ways that can cause others pain. They are the legalistic ones who have to maintain a level of purity (real or perceived) in an attempt to prove to others that they are everything to God. There is an arrogance in them that repulses some people and draws others in. Those who remain on the "I am everything" side of the spiritual brokenness spectrum can be a handful, to say the least.

CONVERGENCE, NOT BALANCE

As I was pondering all of this some time ago it seemed logical to me that the answer to the dilemma of how to live with the two opposite sides of brokenness must be found somewhere in middle. After all, the state of our political system in the U.S. seems to be saying that right and left are too extreme so we all have to find some way to come together in the middle, right? I don't know about you, but I haven't seen too much good coming from our middle-focused political system. I highly doubt being middle-focused when it comes to spiritual brokenness will work either.

No the answer isn't trying to walk a narrow line between thinking too lowly and too highly of ourselves. How can one possibly do that on a consistent basis? As I pondered these two sides of spiritual brokenness it came to me that it isn't balance we need, its convergence.

What I need is to be in a place where I can be spiritually broken in a way as to allow the fact that I'm NOTHING before God to converge with the fact that I am EVERYTHING to Him. The two have to be a single, overarching fact that leads my life. Can I do this perfectly? Of course not. But I believe that life is more powerfully and peacefully lived as I allow these two simple facts to overwhelm my existence.

I am nothing to God. He doesn't need me to do a single thing. That fact is devastating to me. That fact is also trumped by the fact that I am everything to Him. The convergence of these two points is something that I believe puts us in a place where we can overcome victim thinking and establish more victor living in our lives.

I believe the Church needs to grasp this convergence. Too many church congregations are stuck on one side or the other of the spiritual brokenness spectrum. What worries me the most is that churches will one day wake up to the two sides of spiritual brokenness and will try to do their best to help people remain in the middle. Talk about a recipe for victimization. Please join me in praying that that never happens.

Spiritual brokenness isn't about getting the pendulum to move from one side of the curve to the other. Nor is it about trying to keep it right in the middle as world events work to swing it from side to side. Spiritual brokenness is about living in the completeness that comes when we know we are nothing AND everything to God at the same time.

There is a continuity in having the fact that we are nothing before God converge with the reality that we are everything to Him. It seems to keep us in balance. When life experiences are bad we can find a peaceful rest in the fact that this isn't happening because God doesn't care. More importantly, when life is going well, this convergence of spiritual brokenness might actually keep us from thinking too highly of ourselves and creating the connection that goodness is happening because we are somehow doing all the right things in our walk with God.

BROKENNESS, HOPE AND JOY

I have mentioned Larry Crabb several times in this book. One of the books he authored is called *The Safest Place On Earth*. I came across this quote from his book many years ago and it really sums up the issue of brokenness to me. Crabb says:

> *Brokenness is realizing He is all we have. Hope is realizing He is all we need. Joy is realizing He is all we want.*[15]

Spiritual brokenness isn't about being beaten into something that is useful to this God that created us and loves us. Brokenness is about realizing who we are in the eyes of this God and who He is to us. He is all we have, all we need and all we should ever want. Anything that gets in the way of these three simple statements is setting us up for disappointment and, therefore, victim thinking.

The victors in this world have found ways to live with the converging thoughts that they are nothing to God at the same time as being everything to Him. They have found that whether enjoying times of plenty or dealing with scarcity in their lives, all they have, need or want is secure in Him. Though they might not recognize it at the time, this kind of eternal thinking is what sets the victor apart from the victim thinker.

I want to close this chapter by highlighting the glaringly obvious fact that I have not provided the "How To's" when it comes to living in the convergence of a spiritually broken life. I have purposely left

---

[15] Taken from *The Safest Place on Earth* by Larry Crabb. Copyright © 2001 by Larry Crabb. Used with permission of Zondervan. www.zondervan.com. All Rights Reserved.

out any steps I might believe could allow the two opposite ways that God views us to converge into one. Why? Because I simply don't think there is a set process for doing so. I believe that this convergence is a moment-by-moment thing. If I were to come up with a process for convergence then convergence wouldn't be the focus, the process would be. Humans are such a process-focused species.

I believe God wants us to be like Abraham and simply trust Him. Know that He will provide Himself. Then take a step and start the climb up that mountain ahead of you. As you climb higher and higher in that trust in God you will get a better perspective of what your life as a victor is supposed to look like.

Look, you're not a victim—you are a victor. You are a victor not because your capabilities and accomplishments mean something to God. You are a victor because God decided to make you out of nothing to be something so precious that He would give His own life for you. Let your brokenness be something that brings you to Him with an authority that is due the precious gift that you are. The results will be the life of a victor in the midst of a world trying to make you a victim.

CHAPTER TEN

Get To vs. Have To

I came across this paragraph in a daily devotional I read from time to time. Oswald Chambers is one of those deep thinkers who lived much too short of a life. Fortunately his writings live on and so does the wisdom of God that flowed through this man.

In the February 16th reading of *"My Utmost for His Highest,"* I read the following:

> *God does not give us overcoming life; <u>He gives us life as we overcome</u>. When the inspiration of God comes, and He says – "Arise from the dead," we have to get up; God does not lift us up. Our Lord said to the man with the withered hand, "Stretch forth thy hand," and as soon as the man did so, his hand was healed, but he had to take the initiative. If we will do the overcoming, we shall find we are inspired of God because He gives life immediately.*[16]

So what does this have to do with the process of moving from victim thinking to victor living? More and more, I'm starting to think that the keys to victor living are held within the understanding of what Chambers was communicating through this devotion.

---

[16] Taken from *My Utmost for His Highest*® by Oswald Chambers, edited by James Reimann, © 1992 by Oswald Chambers Publications Assn., Ltd., and used with permission of Discovery House Publishers, Grand Rapids MI 49501. All rights reserved.

What this quote is saying to me is that as we move, God moves. The more we sit around waiting on God to move the more obvious it seems to us that God just isn't present. When we are paralyzed waiting for God to make the way clear for us in all areas of our life, it is easy to start believing that God isn't for us; maybe we really are the victims the world seems to want to label us as, in light of all the badness that seems to come our way.

Way too many of us are waiting for the miracle to happen before we choose to get moving. I believe we do this because we have allowed victim thinking to linger way too long in our lives. So it is with the case of victors dealing with the obligations of this world that put us into a place of "having to" do something. To help victors see our responsibility in receiving the miracles God does in our lives, He placed an amazing story in the Bible that highlights an important point about the "Have To's" we face. Let's dig a little deeper into the story of a man named Lazarus and see if there aren't some lessons we can learn about moving from victim thinking to victor living.

THE LESSONS OF LAZARUS

Lazarus is a Biblical character who, like Oswald Chambers, died way before his time. Not only did he die too young, he died in spite of the fact that Jesus, Lazarus' good friend and proven healer, knew he was sick several days before the end came.

The Bible says in several places that Jesus healed EVERYONE who came to Him. Yet, He did not heal His close friend, even though Jesus knew He was sick. In fact, Jesus waited to travel and see His friend in spite of the fact that He knew His friend was coming to the end of his life. This fact is plainly stated in the verses below out of John chapter 11:

> *Now Jesus loved Martha and her sister and Lazarus. So, when He heard that he was sick,* <u>*He stayed two more day*</u>*s in the place where He was. John 11:5-6 (NKJV)*

When Jesus heard His beloved friend was sick, Jesus didn't go running to His friend. Instead, He waited two days before He started on the journey to see the one He loved so much. By the time Jesus was able to walk to the town where Mary, Martha and Lazarus lived, poor Lazarus had been in the tomb for a total of four days. What a strange way to treat a friend. Any time I run into a story in the Bible where it seems odd the way God relates to His creation, my attention is piqued. It's in these kinds of situations, I believe, God is trying to get me to learn something important about this life of a victor.

The fact that Jesus lingered before coming to see Lazarus wasn't missed by those around Jesus either. When He finally arrived where His friend had died, Jesus asked to go see Lazarus in the tomb. Those around him reminded Jesus that Lazarus had been dead so long that the stench of death was an issue Jesus would have to contend with. You have to believe that those doing the reminding must have been thinking how weird this Jesus was; with the power to heal the sick, He waited and let His friend die, and now is wanting to see his rotting corpse! I bet there was plenty of gossip and under-the-breath comments being aimed at Jesus as a result of how He handled this situation.

So, what's the big deal of Jesus waiting to come see Lazarus? The big deal is that with one spoken word, Jesus could have healed Lazarus from afar. Lazarus didn't need to die. The Bible records many stories where Jesus healed people without having to see or even touch them. The fact that Jesus waited so long to go see Lazarus that his body had begun to rot in the grave has to have significance. There has to be a reason for the delay. I believe the reason Jesus waited plays right into the main focus of this chapter.

It is my opinion that one of the reasons for Jesus' delay was to help us to grasp the difference between "having to do" something and "getting to do" that same thing. You see, in Martha's (Lazarus' sister's) eyes, Jesus HAD TO come. His showing up was imperative to her. Isn't it amazing how we so quickly put our agenda ahead of everyone else's, including the God of this universe? Martha was, in essence, saying, "God you have no choice. You HAVE TO listen to me and come heal my brother!" Can't you just hear the demanding cries of a victim in those statements that were working to control the thoughts of this grieving sister?

As far as Jesus was concerned, He didn't "have to" do anything. In fact, on more than one occasion, Jesus made it clear that the only thing He did at all was to simply do what the Father was doing in, around and through Him. I'm more than sure that Jesus felt the familiar tug we all feel when are faced with the urgent in our lives. I can only imagine the pain Jesus must have had to contend with knowing that His choosing to wait to see His friend would cost His friend his life. I'm also sure that Jesus knew He would feel the intense ridicule that would come from the pain of all those who loved Lazarus. Jesus was more than aware of the glares of disbelief and doubt He would have to endure as a result of His decision to wait. I believe one of the reasons Jesus decided to face the pain of losing His friend and the potential ridicule He would receive was to let us know the importance of dealing with the "have to" and "get to" situations in our lives. For the victors we all are in Jesus, learning this important lesson is so critical for us to keep moving from victim to victor.

Jesus was living out a fact of life that all victors need to grasp. Urgent tasks always present themselves with the words "have to." Think about it. When the last emergency popped up in your life, don't you remember saying, "I have to" do something? It isn't that victors ignore the urgent. I believe that victor living comes when we understand how to handle the "have to" situations that we all will face.

I want to challenge you to do something today. Listen to your words as you go about your day. How many times do you say, "I have to?" I *have to* go pick up my kids. I *have to* go to dinner with my wife. I *have to* go to church. Yes, there are things that we will always "have to" do, but I'm seeing that these little words (have to) can have a massive impact on our thinking when it comes to trying to live this life as a victor.

"HAVE TO" LEADS TO VICTIM THINKING

You see, "have to" comes with the stigma of obligation. When faced with obligation, the human species has a unique tendency to rebel. Tell a three-year-old to not touch something and what's the first thing they do? They touch it! It is almost like we are hardwired to fight being under the domination of anyone or anything and want to live free, even when our idea of freedom can cause damage to us or others around us.

Want to know something really amazing? We are hardwired this way. God made us to live free. His best for us is to NEVER be under the domination of anyone or anything at any time. Urgency in our lives brings us face-to-face with "have to" statements. Those statements are fertile ground for victimization and the possibility of victim thinking.

When it comes to freedom, the Bible says it this way:

> *You, my brothers and sisters, were called to be free. Galatians 5:13 (NIV)*

Now this doesn't mean that we will not ever be in a position of coming under the authority of someone or something. That's just a natural part of life. In fact, that is part of an eternal life as well. We will all come under the authority of God, but that authority is so different than the warped and, sometimes, evil authority we experience here on earth.

It's no wonder we are hardwired by God to rebel against obligations. In the really bad times that come against us from time to time, those "have to" tasks in our life can be something that make us doubt our identity as God's children.

Take, for example, my friend's wife I introduced to you a couple chapters ago. She's the one that found out she has a serious case of breast cancer. Don't you know the words, "have to" are part of her vocabulary? She *has to* go to chemo. She *has to* face the fact she is losing her hair and *has to* go buy a wig. She *has to* deal with the pains that come with the possibility of not being there to see her lovely granddaughter grow up. All the "have to's" take a toll on those of us struggling to live a victor's life in this crazy world.

I'm in no way saying that she is in the wrong for feeling the weight of the obligations that come with the diagnosis of cancer. Any and all bad news comes with a list of "have to's" for us to confront. I'm saying that we need to be aware of how the "have to's" can crush our ability to live like a victor in the middle of the bad circumstances that victimize us all. Worse than that, living in the "have to" mode can spill into our everyday life even when life is going well. That's when we can really take on the identity of a victim and allow victim thinking to control our lives. When "have to" thinking permeates all parts of our lives, freedom becomes something that we can only dream of.

Victors face the "have to's" in a different way. Just like Jesus, victors realize that they don't have to do anything. Victors "get to" do things. Think about it. My friend's wife doesn't "have to" do chemo. Neither did Jesus "have to" give His life on the cross for our sins. We are just like Jesus in that we "get to" do all the things in our life. This is also the case with the bad things that we are faced with from time to time. I know that these statements need some unpacking. Let's take a closer look at how "have to" and "get to" relate to moving from victim to victor.

"HAVE TO" AND THE SOUL

Remember our discussion in earlier chapters regarding the soul and spirit? Our soul has taken on the job of being the controller of our being. Our will, intellect and emotions are what controls our lives most of the time. But God intended this to be different. Our spirit is what God wants us to lean on, allowing the soul to come under the authority of that direct connection with God that lies dormant in us so much of the time. Simply stated, the words "have to" fire up our soul. That's bad for those of us who want to live like the victor God has called us to be.

It goes back to that hardwiring. We are hardwired to rebel against the obligation authority tries to put on us. God has made each of us to fight against anything that puts us in a place where the freedom we were designed for comes into question. Why did He do this? It all comes down to the word love.

Think of the most beloved thing in your life now. It might be your spouse, your child, your pet or someone or something else. Do you "have to" love that person or thing or do you "get to" love them? If you are obligated to love them then you are in a position where you will eventually feel resentment and might rebel in a way that could damage or even destroy that relationship.

That's something God just can't stand for in our lives when it comes to relating to Him. God wants us to choose to love Him, not be obligated to do so. We "get to" love God, we don't "have to" love Him. Can the person who is the object of love really trust that love if it is mandatory? In other words, can you trust the love of a person you force to love you? I don't think so. Why would God think that way?

It is because God wants us to choose to love Him that He hardwired us to rebel against the obligations that are sometimes associated with loving relationships. That's why I believe our soul gets fired up when we are faced with the "have to's" in our lives. You see, "have to" goes against that eternal part of us that was made to live free forever.

Words have power. When we use the words "have to," we are giving permission to our soul to allow our will, intellect and emotions to come to our rescue and save us from something that might be jeopardizing our freedom. For those tasks that are important for us to do, the words "have to" can ultimately make us feel like victims of life because "have to" makes our soul fight for freedom even when that freedom isn't being threatened. This can make us think in ways that may hinder our ability to relate to each other and to God in a truly loving way. When a relationship is in peril we can feel like a victim and victims can be created all around us as a result. "Have to" gets our soul riled up such that we can act in relationship-damaging ways.

Let me give you an example from my past life. I remember saying one day in front of my wife and kids, "I can't wait for the day when you kids are on your own. Maybe then I can get a life of my own."

Can you imagine the victimization my children felt over this soul-driven statement? From that moment on, I'll bet their souls were energized to find ways to earn the love of their father that these words seemed to be saying just wasn't there.

On the particular day that those hurtful words came out of my mouth, I was firmly in the grips of victim thinking. Freedom was the furthest thing from my view of reality. As I have explained earlier, my wife was, and is, the income provider for our family. I had accepted the role of taking care of more of the things at home, particularly when the kids were younger. At that time in my life I was completely locked in obligation mode. I "had to" stay home. That was my job. My wife "had to" go to work. That was her responsibility. There was a part of her that longed to be at home where I allowed myself to be seen as the victim of a messed up world. There was a part of me that longed to be in the stress-filled place my wife "had to" be. See how the "have to's" in life can grab you in ways you least expect it?

The more years that passed in which I lived solely out of commitment and obligation, the more defeated and worthless I felt. On the day that I told my kids I couldn't wait until they were gone, I was feeling like a trapped animal. My soul was in total rebellion mode. I saw my family as something that was standing in the way of my freedom, and that put my soul on high alert. The "Have To's" in my life were coming against the foundation of some important relationships. Victim thinking was in control and victimization was happening in areas I never would have allowed were I able to view my "have to's" in a different light.

"Have to" implies that we don't have a choice. When we use the words "have to," even for common everyday tasks, we are teaching our soul that we don't have a choice in life. Our souls begin to believe the lie that we are stuck where we are, and all hope for freedom begins to evaporate. God forbid a really bad thing happens when we are in that bad place of feeling stuck in obligation. It is then when we start to think that choice will never be an option that victim thinking takes hold in ways that can make us victimizers like I was with my kids on that very sad day.

THE POWER OF CHOICE

If you want my honest and brutal opinion, there is nothing we "have to" do. I can hear you now saying, "Oh yeah? I have to breathe, right?" Well, do you? Where does it say that you are required to continue living? With this powerful thing called choice that God gave us we even have the choice of ending our own life. Let me quickly say, that suicide is definitely not an option God wants us to take, but the truth is that we do have power over our own life. Please understand, I'm not trying to make some political statement regarding the sanctity of life, or lack thereof. I purposely selected a very "in your face," type of "choice" that we all have in our lives to make the point that we really don't "have to" do a single thing.

You see, we have access to an amazing power with this thing called choice. We don't have to breathe, eat, love, work, worship, sit, stand, walk, watch TV, or do anything. Of course there are consequences to any decision we make. Take work, for example. You don't have to work. That's an absolute fact. I know what you're thinking though: "If I don't work I'll lose my house. I have to go to work." You are probably one hundred percent correct about losing your house if you don't go to work. But losing your house is a consequence, not a requirement. You don't "have to" go to work. Rest assured, you will face consequences, some of them not that great, if you choose not to go to work. Choice is a powerful thing. It is powerfully useful for victors, if we more fully understand how to use the power of choice we have been given.

That's where we have to be careful of our words. You really don't "have to" go to work. You choose to go so that you don't lose your house. You may hate your job. It might be the most miserable job in the world. But continuing to believe that you "have to" work puts you in a position where you will ultimately be doomed to victim thinking. A victor is able to boil down the choices they make so that the reasons they choose to do what they do become the power behind why they continue to do whatever it is even when what they do isn't all that pleasant. Choosing to do something for a significant purpose or reason can be the difference between feeling trapped and experiencing the freedom our soul so longs to have.

No one can stand being trapped. The more you believe you are trapped, the worse your life will look to you. I'm here to state emphatically that you aren't trapped. Everything you choose to do isn't a "have to," it is a "get to." Choosing to do something puts you into a place of control, whereas having to do something makes our soul come alive in ways that can bring victim thinking into our lives.

One Sunday, after having the opportunity to speak at my church on "Have To vs. Get To," I had a conversation with a young mother. This woman shared with me a situation that made her consider the reality of "have to" in her life. She is in the midst of a terrible divorce proceeding. Her husband is acting in ways that can only be described as evil. Her children are responding to the turmoil they sense in their lives in ways that are making the mom crazy. She said to me, "I have no choice. I *have to* be the mother of my kids. That fact is just killing me!"

I was just about to challenge her about the "have to" statement; I wanted to say to her, "Do you really *have to* be your children's mother?" Just before I got the words out, her eyes opened wide with the realization that she wasn't trapped.

She looked at me with an excitement that only a free person can feel. She said, "I don't *have to* be the kid's mother. I could drop them off at my abusive husband's house and leave them there and run off on my own. I'm not trapped. I have a choice!" I then said to her, "What do you want to do?" With a confidence that wasn't there before she said, "I want to be the mother of my children."

This woman came face-to-face with the fact that we don't "have to" do anything—we "get to" do things. This realization hasn't changed a single thing in her situation. Her ex-husband is still acting like a jerk. Her kids are still driving her crazy. The only difference is now she is acting out of choice. That simple difference can be all we need to make victor living something within our grasps even when the world is victimizing us so.

This fact is just as true with the bad things of life. When it comes to my kids and the damage I caused with my senseless comment, I don't "HAVE TO" do all I can to repair that damage. I don't "have to" grovel and hope they will forgive me. I don't "have to" take every opportunity to show them how much I love them. I don't "have to" spend wakeless nights praying against the potential impact of my hurtful words in their lives. I GET TO enter into the process of what God is doing to bring my children into a living and loving relationship with Him. Yes, that process might have me groveling, showing them love and spending time in prolonged prayer, but I don't "have to" do these things; I "get to" do them as I feel God is leading me. See the difference in living a "have to" vs. "get to" kind of life? That difference is freedom, and our soul loves to live the life of freedom that "get to" brings to forefront.

If I lived a life of "having to" when it comes to fixing the damage I caused on that day (and the other hundreds of days when my soul was going haywire) I would be empowering my soul in ways I have seen that only lead to failure. Of course I want to right those wrongs, but I don't "have to" any longer, I "get to!"

That simple shift in attitude makes all the difference in giving my soul the opportunity to come under the power of my spirit. It is my belief that in that place of submission to the spirit, the power of my will, intellect and emotions can be what it needs to be to bring about maximum healing to those I have victimized in the past.

What's so amazing about the difference between "have to" and "get to" living is that we often miss the miracles of life by mistaking God's leading in our lives as "have to" obligations. The following story is a great example of how we can be on the brink of missing God's amazing work in our lives by rebelling against what we perceive as "have to's" from Him.

THE STORY OF NAAMAN

In 2 Kings 5 there is a story about a particular general named Naaman. Naaman was a great warrior. He was highly regarded by his King. Unfortunately Naaman had been stricken with the terrible disease called leprosy. As powerful and highly regarded as Naaman was, he was seen as an outcast as a result of this disease.

One of Naaman's servant girls was a captured Israeli. She told Naaman about a man of healing in her home country who seemed to have the ear of God. Naaman got permission from his king to make the trek to Israel to seek out this prophet of God named Elijah. He took with him a letter of introduction from his King and a horde of riches that he was hoping to give to anyone who could help him get out from under the burdens of the illness that was progressively eating away at his body.

Naaman was done with "having to" deal with the issues associated with leprosy. He heard of the power of this God in a far off land and he felt drawn to seek out and come under the authority of the power that had healed so many in the past. Naaman didn't "have to" go on this journey. He was in the amazing position of "getting to" go to this far off land with the hopes of finding healing.

On this long journey, Naaman must have played out in his head how this healing would come about. Would this healer lay hands on him? Would there be some religious ritual Naaman would submit to? Even if it were wacky and wild, Naaman was sick and tired of being sick and tired. He was ready for the unexpected, or so he thought.

When Naaman came to the end of his long journey, he received word from Elijah as to what he was to do to be healed. No laying on of hands. No weird religious ritual. Elijah told Naaman to go wash himself in the River Jordan seven times and the leprosy would go away.

Naaman went ballistic. "Take a bath! Are you kidding? That's the answer to this terrible disease I came so far to find? I could have bathed anywhere. Why did I "have to" go on such a long journey only to be told that I would be healed by bathing in some dirty river?" Then the soul of Naaman really took hold.

I'm sure some of the following thoughts might have ran through Naaman's mind: "Don't you know who I am? I am someone important. I have gifts to give you if you heal me. What do you think,

GET TO VS. HAVE TO

I stink? Do I smell so bad that I need to bathe? Is that what you are thinking?"

I bet with every passing thought, the will, intellect and emotions of Naaman's soul really kicked into high gear. Naaman got so disgusted with the prospect of "have to" that he packed up and got ready to head back home. He almost missed God's miracle because "have to" thinking took hold on this important trip that Naaman "got to" undertake.

Fortunately for the general, Elijah's servant was able to convince the general to just do what the healer said. Take a look at what happened from 2 Kings:

> *Naaman's servants went to him and said, "My father (kind way of referring to Naaman), if the prophet had told you to do some great thing, would you not have done it? How much more, then, when he tells you, 'Wash and be cleansed'!" So he went down and dipped himself in the Jordan seven times, as the man of God had told him, and his flesh was restored and became clean like that of a young boy. 2 Kings 5:13-14 (NIV)*

When Naaman saw that beautiful new skin appear where just a few days before he had seen nothing but rot, don't you think his perspective changed? His attitude of "have to" must have been turned around in a profound way on that day.

Naaman almost missed the miracle of complete healing by allowing his soul to fight the perceived obligation that came from what he saw as a "have to" directive from the healer. I'll bet you the next time someone tells Naaman to do something to receive a miracle, that general will say, "I get to…"

That's the difference between a victim thinker and one who is living the life of a victor. Victors work to see the tasks and circumstances, as well as the directives in their life, as "get to's." Even the "have to's" a victor faces turn to "get to's" as they live out their God given identity as His Child. Crazy thing is that the bad circumstances can even take on a "get to" attitude for the victor when they dwell in that place of love that comes with being God's Child.

CHANGE YOUR THINKING, CHANGE YOUR LIFE

It is a sad fact that real and meaningful change often can't happen until we completely surrender. Victors are faced with the need to surrender their words, actions, attitudes, and ultimately control by turning "have to" to "get to." That surrender usually comes at the end of a long journey: a journey that can take the victor through a painful string of "have to" obligations. The pain of that journey often takes us to the limit of being able to stand up under the burdens these "have to's" can bring into our lives.

"Get to" living isn't an automatic way of life. It is a learned thing. This happens as we change our words. The belief that changing our words can have impact in our lives is something that is preached by motivational speakers both secular and non-secular alike. Pick up any self-help book and you will see reams of data and stories that attest to the power of positive thinking and positive living. Words play an important role in being positive. Changing from a "have to" kind of person to one that believes they have a choice through the words "get to" is something that works.

But here's a caveat: don't change your thinking to try and make your life better. Saying "get to" isn't an insurance policy against bad things happening to you. I hope you have the same perspective I have on bad things. I believe bad stuff is going to happen to us all. Changing one word from "have" to "get" isn't going to do a darn thing to change that. All "get to" does is put us in a position where we are more capable of dealing with the fallout when the bad does hit. It is my belief that "get to" thinking puts us in a place of thankfulness. Think about it. If I say I "get to" doesn't it sound like I have an appreciation for what is ahead of me? "Get to" speaks of opportunity, whereas "have to" speaks of obligation.

Let's say you have always wanted to go to Hawaii and all of a sudden someone gives you a ticket and money to go enjoy that beautiful place. When the day comes for you to get on the airplane and head off to this paradise you have dreamed of all your life, do you say you "have to" go (as though you are obligated) or do you say you "get to" go (from a place of true thankfulness)?

See the difference in how these two simple phrases work in the very core of our being? Our soul fights against the perceived loss of freedom when the words "have to" are used. On the other hand, when we "get to" do something our soul is at the ready to help in any way to make that experience the best it can be. The soul loves opportunity and hates obligation.

One of the many differences between victim thinking and victor living is thankfulness. When we are thankful, things change. Our attitude changes. Even our very physiology can change by the way thankfulness can make us more positive. Ask any cancer survivor how a positive attitude helped win their battle. Thankfulness somehow brings a sense of hope, and hope is essential in order for us to live free, particularly when life's circumstances seem to be robbing us of worldly freedom at every turn.

There is a power we tap into when we are thankful, even for the badness that hits us from time to time. I'm not saying my friend's wife is to be thankful for the cancer she has received. That's kind of crazy. But she can change her words to make it possible for the power of thankfulness to come into her life in ways that somehow ushers in the power of God.

Instead of saying, "I have to go to chemo," she can say, "I get to go to chemo." This simple change in words opens the door for our souls to be put on high alert in a good way. If my friend's wife is going to chemo for some reason ("get to" implies that there must be some benefit to the task), then her will, intellect and emotions become energized to look for that reason.

When my wife went through breast cancer, there were many times she came home from her treatments saying, "You won't believe what happened at the doctor's office today." There were God given opportunities for her to be at the right time and place for someone who was having a bad day. Purpose was felt. Maybe, just maybe, there was a reason for this horrible disease to be in my wife's life. I'll bet it is the same with my friend's wife who is dealing with cancer. "Have to" can close the door for us to see God's Hand in our lives. "Get to" opens that door as we exercise our power of choice and thankfulness, particularly in bad situations.

That's the power of "get to" living. We get hope. The Bible says this about hope:

> *Hope deferred makes the heart sick, but a dream fulfilled is a tree of life. Proverbs 15:13 (NLT)*

I wish it were enough that Christ died for us to give us the hope we need to face the ups and downs of this life. But sometimes that gift isn't enough. God knows that's how we think at times. He doesn't seem to be overly concerned with that reality. Why should we be concerned with the fact that we need more hope at times?

It is my belief that God gives us opportunity after opportunity to see hope in the everyday tasks of our life. We kill that hope by turning opportunity into obligation when we live a "have to" kind of existence.

Just like the words I spoke to my kids that terribly bad day have the power to squash a soul, words have the power to set the soul free. I believe it is time for us to do a word check in our life. It's time to change our "have to's" into "get to's." You may not say "get to" every time you are in a position to say "have to," but thinking about it will make the difference when it comes to moving from being a victim to being a victor.

THE HUMANNESS OF JESUS

The more we come to the reality that we have a choice in everything we do, the more comfortable our souls will feel about coming under the authority of God through our spirit. The soul loves the possibility of choice. It fights against the prospect of lack of choice. In fact, I have found that the soul continues to fight until it perceives that there is NO choice in life. Then the soul collapses; so do we. That's when full blown victim thinking takes hold. That's when the damage we so often do in relationships can really happen. That's also when we have the greatest opportunity to see lasting change take place in our lives—if we choose to allow change to happen.

Once again, identity comes into play in the process of moving from victim to victor. If I believe that I am nothing more and nothing less than the eternal child of God's, then I'm in a better position to believe that the bad stuff that happens to me is there for a reason. If I believe there is a reason, even when I can't see that reason, then I might be in a place where I can join the ranks of Jesus Himself and find myself "getting to" do something horrifically painful that might just be part of bringing change to the entire world.

Victors aren't superhuman. Want to hear something many will take offense with? Neither was Jesus when He walked this Earth. I once read an article in *Christianity Today* that said something to the effect that the people closest to Jesus when He walked the earth had no problem believing that He was 100% human. He "had to" eat, sleep, walk to His next destination, go to the bathroom, etc. All very human activities that made it totally easy for those around him to believe that He was basically just like them.

For us it is hard to hold on to the fact that Jesus was completely human. It is much easier for us to believe in His divinity. The people who were around Jesus when He walked this earth were challenged by His divinity. We are challenged by His humanness. Jesus had choices just like you and me. What made him better at making all the right choices in God's eyes was the fact that Jesus was totally and completely sure in His identity. He knew His security lay in the fact that He was and is God's Son. Nothing in this world could take that away. Even when the bad times hit, Jesus was secure in this knowledge. That's the same thing God wants for us.

When Jesus faced that horrible death and rejection by the Father, "have to" had a chance to come in and take control. Thank God for our salvation that Jesus lived a life of "get to." He didn't let the terrible circumstance of His life shake His position as a victor in this world, even though there were those who hated Him and wanted to make Him a victim. His stand as a victor led him to the point of "getting to" go to the cross. That made it possible for us to shake off victim thinking and live the victor's life just like Jesus did.

Next time you hear yourself say "have to," think about this chapter. Think about what those two words are saying to your soul. Is that what you really believe? Do you really believe you are obligated to do whatever it is that you are saying you "have to" do? Do you really believe you have no choice? If so, you are ripe for the evil of this world to allow you to move into victim thinking.

One of the simplest ways we can move from victim to victor is to change one simple little word. By replacing "have" with "get" we move from obligation to opportunity. That one word makes it possible for our soul to be either fired up to fight against the possibility of losing freedom or fired up to step more fully into it. Replace "have to" with "get to" in your life. This won't guarantee victory, but it will make you more and more able to live the life of a victor, even when you are being victimized by the bad that this world so often serves up in our lives.

CHAPTER ELEVEN

Destiny

Destiny—there's a topic mankind has struggled with since the beginning of time. What is my purpose here on earth? Why am I here? However you phrase it, the question of your personal destiny has either been something that you have struggled with at one time or another, or it is an issue that will cause consternation in the future.

This is particularly the case for those who have survived some serious incident in their lives. I have met more than one person who has lived when, in hindsight, everything they experienced should have resulted in their death. Whether they are spiritual or not, the question of "Why am I here?" comes up in their lives over and over again. But you don't have to be the sole survivor of a death-defying situation in your life to want to come to some kind of grip with the deeply profound questions that surround destiny.

As it relates to the process of moving from victim thinking to victor living, the issue of destiny or purpose is a critically important thing to understand from the correct perspective. Why? Because often we see destiny as intrinsic to identity. And as we have discussed time and time again in this book, when we allow our identities to be defined by anything that is of this world, we set ourselves up for the kind of persistent failure that opens the door to victim thinking.

THE DOORWAY TO DESTINY

I have had the opportunity to meet a man by the name of Ken Hubbard several times now. Ken is a "man's man" kind of guy. He is in amazing shape; in fact, you might call Ken "ripped." It is obvious that he has worked hard at keeping his body in shape. In fact, many of Ken's close friends are MMA fighters. For those of you who know what MMA (mixed martial arts) is, you know these guys are the toughest of the tough.

Ken grew up in what can only be called a very difficult environment. His father was a member of an outlaw biker club. As a result, Ken's youth was quite a wild ride, to say the least. After a rocky marriage his parents divorced. This left Ken's mother in a place where she struggled to cope with life as she tried to make a living for herself and her family. Like so many others you and I know, life was not easy for Ken growing up. I would have loved to have had a conversation with Ken about his view of destiny as he dealt with some incredibly challenging circumstances in those early years after his father left.

Through some very interesting and what can only be described as "God-sized" coincidences, Ken became a follower of Jesus Christ. Later on, Ken felt that he was supposed to be a pastor. I'd be willing to bet Ken's view of destiny and purpose changed when these events happened in his life.

After much hard work and the blessing of God's provision, Ken built a very large church organization. At the peak of his ministry, Ken had a total of 13 buildings on a state of the art campus, with throngs of people attending his church programs. By the world's standards, Ken had more than made it. Destiny shouldn't have been an issue with Ken at all, right? Let's look at a little more of Ken's story.

At the "ripe old age" of 45, Ken felt a familiar stirring in his heart. As he did his best to listen to God, he felt God was calling him to leave the established and successful ministry that he had built and move his growing family to Detroit. As Ken has shared, God wasn't calling him to some cushy suburb of Detroit. No, God was giving Ken the "opportunity" to trade the success of a big church for the chance to minister to one of the most depressed areas of inner city Detroit.

Before you knew it, Ken was catapulted from the prestige of building and running one of the most successful church organizations in his state to trying to make it while pastoring a congregation of 45 people sitting in plastic chairs in a cafe. Ken went from being looked at as a superstar in the church world to someone who is just like the rest of the "rank and file" pastors struggling to provide for their families as they serve their small congregations.

Ken has shared more than once that he has had to deal with a "crises of identity" over making this big change in his life. I am sure Ken has asked more than once, "What in the world have I done to myself and my family?" I can only imagine Ken has also called out to God, "Are you sure this is what you called me to do with my life?"

As we have touched on in a previous chapter, these kinds of questions can often lead us to a point where we start to think of ourselves as victims. I'm sure victim thinking has slipped into Ken's life more than once, but knowing Ken as I do, I have to believe that victor living always wins out. It does so not because Ken is a driven individual who seems to end up on top out of sheer will power at times, though this happens to be the truth about Ken. No, it is the fact that Ken has such a strong belief that God is for him. It is Christ's death that makes it possible for Ken to think that he is a victor even when his circumstances have victim written all over them.

Is it Ken's destiny to build another big and successful church organization? I think if you asked him, Ken would think that that is part of God's plan. But I know for a fact that whether that plan comes about in Detroit or not, Ken is confident of one thing; God is for him. No matter what happens in this life, he is a victor in his Heavenly Father's eyes.

As I started writing this book early in 2014, Ken came to speak to our church in Carlsbad, CA. On that particular day he made a statement that guaranteed Ken's story would be a part of this work on moving from victim thinking to victor living. What he said was this:

"Identity is the doorway to destiny." Don't you know these six words got my attention in a big way?

I know I sound like a broken record, but identity is the cornerstone to victor living. When we put our hopes for who we are in anything we do here on earth we are likely to feel the sting of defeat. When we feel defeated over and over again we can easily move in a direction where we may believe we will always live like a victim. So it is for the Ken Hubbards of the world who have come face to face with the victory of success only to be put in a place where success seems to be so slow in coming.

When we have our destiny tied to what we do here on earth, our identity is able to get so convoluted that victim thinking can really take over. This is particularly the case for those who have felt God leading them in a particular direction only to have that direction fall short of their expectations in one way or another.

I have to ask myself, how many people in this world are living a life filled with sadness and despair because their idea of destiny hasn't panned out the way they thought it would? How many pastors are in the pulpit today thinking they are anything less than a victorious Child of the King that our God sees them to be? I have to believe that there are thousands upon thousands of good people teaching about this Father who loves us while struggling with whether they are fully loved by Him or not simply because of their perspective on destiny. What a sad waste of powerful resources in this world.

If identity is the doorway to destiny, as Ken Hubbard preached that Sunday morning, then what's the link between the two that gives us the best possible chance of understanding our own destiny?

We have already dealt with the subject of identity in a previous chapter of this book. Our identity has to be that of a Child of God's ONLY in order for us to live this life with any hope of believing that we are the victor God created us to be. We have to fight the very natural tendency to let our tasks shape who we are. Tasks are temporary and can change like the shifting wind. If we allow tasks to shape our identity then we will spend most of our time trying to figure out who we are. That's such a waste of valuable time.

Ken isn't a victor because he built a big church, just like he isn't a victim because he moved to a small one. I have found it to be so important to remember that being God's child is the only thing that guarantees the fact that we are victors (more than conquerors, as it says we are in Romans 8). If we try to judge whether we are victors or not based on the success we achieve in our lives, we will be in the position where victim thinking could easily take over and ruin our lives should that success wane.

If identity is the doorway to our destiny, then destiny has to be viewed through the lens of eternity in order for it to make any sense at all. If the Bible is true, as I believe it to be, then everything that we are experiencing here in this world will pass away at some time in the future. Whatever His plan may be, all the success and failure in this world will have absolutely nothing to do with who God sees us to be in eternity. We are His children whether our destinies are panning out in this life or not.

WE HAVE ALL ETERNITY

I was sitting across from a friend the other day at a local bakery. This friend and I have journeyed together through many difficult times in each other's lives. Somehow our paths went in separate directions, as paths often do. The opportunities to meet seemed to become fewer and fewer. On that particular morning we bemoaned the fact that we hadn't gotten together for way too long of a time.

I had heard that this friend had come on some hard times in his professional life. In fact, I had just learned earlier that week that my friend now worked for that particular bakery on a part time basis. Not that working for a bakery is a bad thing, but for this man in his fifties, who has had a great deal of success in his past, I can only imagine the identity crisis he must have gone through to accept his current situation in life.

As we sat and got caught up on family, church and personal issues, I noticed a quiet confidence in this man. I have to admit I was a bit nervous about meeting with my friend because of his current situation. I didn't want our meeting to be some kind of embarrassment for this wonderful man of God. But the confidence I saw in my friend's eyes that day proved to me what a victor this man really is.

I'm not saying my friend was "overjoyed" with his current position and his prospects for the future. Just like you and me, he was frustrated, a bit scared and worried for what tomorrow might hold. But on that morning, he told me, "You don't know how hard it was for me to slip on that apron and hat (standard uniform for this bakery) on the first day I showed up for work." This is a man who was part of building a very large and successful business in his earlier years. To be working in an environment where his peers are now some 30+ years his junior must have been a real blow to how he viewed himself. But that quiet confidence I saw in my friend's eyes spoke to the true identity he knew his God gave him through Jesus' death for us all.

At one point in our conversation, I said something to him that sounds very egotistical as I read the words on this page. I said to my friend, "You and I were made for BIG things."

Because of our past experiences together, I know this guy very well. He is such a compassionate man, yet forceful in ways that make people gravitate to his leadership skills. I love his intellect. He is way smarter than I am, yet I always feel like I can keep up in any conversation we have together. He has a gift to make people feel at ease and can get the best out of everyone he meets. This is part of why the team he was on was able to build such a successful business in his earlier years. My friend was made for BIG things. I believe that BIG is part of his destiny. And for whatever reason, I just can't shake the feeling that BIG is part of mine as well.

Then comes the cold slap of reality. My friend is working at a local bakery. Though my financial prospects aren't the same as his, my opportunities for a BIG destiny feel just as compromised as my friend's.

Both of us believe we have felt God leading us in ways that point to the possibility that our destinies were to be filled with bigness. Did we hear God incorrectly, or is there some big flaw (also known as sin) in our lives that is keeping us from reaching our full potential? Simply judging the circumstances of our lives, one could come to the conclusion that there is something seriously wrong with us or with the God we serve. But when it comes to both these statements, nothing could be further from the truth.

My friend's quiet confidence and the very act of writing this book are examples of the fact that we both have an eternal perspective in our lives. We believe that we are victors whether we come to see the fullness of our destinies in our lives or not.

Again, it isn't what we do that makes us victors, it's what Christ did for us. This eternal perspective is the kind of crazy thinking that allows two underemployed friends destined for BIG things wonder if the dreams that they once had will ever come into play.

A few years ago, as I struggled with depression in my life, I had to deal with the little voice in my head that was saying, "The fact that the dreams you had as a young man will never materialize proves that you will never reach your destiny." Although this statement is a lie, you have to know that for any lie to be convincing there has to be some element of truth hidden in it. Let's look a bit more closely at that statement to uncover the foundations of truth that made this lie so convincing in my life.

As a young man, I truly believed that God put it on my heart that I would be in a position to have a significant impact on the lives of millions of people. I believed that this would happen as a result of my being a part of building something BIG. Maybe a business. Maybe a church. Who knows? Who cares! The simple fact that I believed that I was destined to do something BIG in my life was an exciting and identity-filled prospect.

As I proceeded through my twenties and thirties, I was blessed to be surrounded by people who had achieved significant success. This afforded me the opportunity to learn a lot about business and as a result I started several ventures on my own or with friends who shared similar expectations of BIG destinies. As I shared with you earlier, those ventures didn't pan out so well. With each failure, I felt more and more of a burden to succeed. That took a toll on my health until there came a time when I had to stop.

As I took the time I needed to get stronger, I found that my confidence in my ability to do BIG things diminished dramatically. Soon I found myself in my forties. It is amazing what happens to a person physically when they turn 40. It is my absolute belief that when I went to sleep on September 1st, 1999, I could read the newspaper without any problem. The morning of September 2nd of that same year, when I turned 40, I was as blind as a bat. I'm not kidding you, it seemed as though my sight literally went away that fast. Now that I'm in my mid-fifties, I'm living in the reality that my stamina and other really important abilities required to do BIG things seem to be fading just as fast as my vision has.

If there was one thing that I learned about trying to build something BIG it was that it takes almost superhuman energy. Both of my kids are in the process of starting their own businesses. Along with much encouragement and lavishing of the pride I have for them, I also give them healthy doses of reality by telling them this is the hardest thing they will ever do. My forties had me waking up to the possibility that I might no longer have what it takes to build something BIG.

What a slap that was to my identity. I had always thought that by doing my best to fulfill what I thought was my destiny people would view me in a way that my misplaced identity longed to be viewed. It was as though I wanted to look good more than I wanted to fulfill what I believe God had put on my heart as being my destiny in life. The truth is that, as I got older, I really did want my view of identity more than HIS view of my destiny.

As my forties rolled on into my fifties, depression seemed to grip me even more. I went from having a bad day every now and then to having them every other day. I began to believe that my dreams were nothing more than a figment of my imagination. My aging body and my belief as to what it takes physically and mentally to make big things happen seemed to be the world's proof that I had either heard things wrong or screwed things up so badly that not even God could clean up my mess. Destiny was quickly beginning to become something I simply ignored.

DESTINY

A FATHER'S DAY SURPRISE

It was the Saturday before Father's Day in 2010. I was having an okay day. That meant that I had just come out of some serious depression and knew the next bout was just around the corner. The pattern was becoming very familiar.

My wife, Barb, came to me asked, "What would you like to do on Father's Day?" I think if I would have asked to spend a million dollars she would have found a way to make it happen, that's how concerned she was for my emotional state. The miracle of my wife standing by me during this horrible time in my life is proof enough to me that there is a God who loves me.

Though I could think of a bunch of things I really wanted to do (like something, anything, BIG) none of them could be accomplished on that one day. So I said, "I think I'm going to skip church and just take it easy." This was a nice way for me to share that I felt too hopeless to even think of something fun for us all to do on a day my family was carving out to honor me.

That evening my daughter, Jesslan, came bounding into the family room where I was "resting" and jumped into my lap. As she hugged my neck she said, "I want to go to church with you tomorrow Popsidaisy (one of the many cute names my daughter has blessed me with)." I guess she hadn't gotten the memo that I wanted to skip church on Father's Day.

As I sat there with this incredible joy of a daughter in my lap, I faced what I now see as a life changing choice. Amazing how these kinds of big decisions come in such small packages. I could give in to the feeling of hopelessness and turn down a teenager's request to go to church (how often does a 17-year-old ask to go to church?), or I could give in and go for her sake. Fortunately, I told Jess that I'd love to go to church with her.

To be honest, one of the reasons I didn't want to go to church was the fact that our Senior Pastor was out of the country that weekend. We had a young guy (35 years old) coming to fill in for our services that Sunday. I knew of this guy. He had a very successful ministry up at the Dream Center in Los Angeles, CA. The last thing I wanted was to go listen to some young guy tell me how I have screwed up my life and need to get back on the Jesus train so that everything would work out in the long run, "All Glory To God"!

As we sat at church on that Father's Day, the young pastor gave a message that I later found out was one of his "canned" teachings. He had given this message maybe 100 times or more over the years. He later told me that he had prepared a totally different message for that morning, but our Senior Pastor had gone out of his way to request that he give this particular message that Sunday. God has such a great sense of humor.

So this young pastor proceeded to use a message he could give in his sleep to tell me that my dreams were not dead. He used the words he has passionately preached over and over again that went something like this, "As long as you have breath in your lungs, God's dreams for you are not dead!" To this day just saying or writing those words brings tears to my eyes.

What a lifeline God was throwing me that day. Could it really be that what I had heard over two-and-a-half decades ago was still a possibility? As I contemplated these words, I began to think that maybe I had totally misunderstood how destiny was supposed to come about in my life.

What if the impact I was to have wasn't through BIG things? What if God were using the small things in my life to create BIG impact? Heck, if He's the creator of the universe I think He could do that kind of miracle in my life.

Although this thought didn't completely sit right with me, it opened the door to the possibility that something BIG was happening even if I couldn't see it at this time in my life. Thinking that my dreams were alive was a big step for me. I wish I could say that that day cured me of my depression, but I can't. It took another several months until I could embark on the medical treatment that has brought so much physical healing to my life.

It was at church, on that Father's Day, that I started to get a sense of hope that had been missing for such a long time. That hope slowly turned into joy. Victim thinking started to give way to victor living. This book is the result of that process. But, that's not the end of the story when it comes to the issue of destiny.

THE IMPORTANCE OF PERSPECTIVE

I said two paragraphs earlier that the possibility that I had misinterpreted my dreams from God just didn't sit well with me. As I pondered many of the points that I have written in this book, that thought kept coming back to haunt me over and over again. What was it about that thought that was troubling me?

Then it hit me. It was my perspective. Just like identity, destiny has to be viewed according to how God sees it. If we view destiny or identity from the wrong perspective then we are in danger of killing off the possibility of living as a victor as we go through the hard times this world can offer up. Just as I believe identity must be viewed from an eternal perspective, it is my opinion that destiny and, more importantly, the fulfillment of that destiny, must be viewed from that same eternal perspective.

Here's what I mean by that. My mistake wasn't in thinking that God is going to use me for something BIG. It was in limiting God to these 80 or so years I have here on earth to make that BIG happen. Do you know how long 80 years is in the span of eternity? It isn't even the size of a grain of sand on the seashore. Yet we bank all our hopes and dreams on that small speck of sand instead of realizing that we have all eternity to see our destiny come to fulfillment. If you let that statement sink in you will find the same incredible sense of freedom that I found as God chose to reveal this to me.

As I sat across from my friend at that bakery, sharing how he and I were made for something BIG, I added one more statement. I said; "What if, just what if, the BIG things that we were made for (our destinies) were to be completed in Heaven rather than here on Earth? What if we have all eternity to get done those dreams God has put on our heart?" You should have seen his eyes light up. That perspective brought a new level of confidence to that man's life as he faced the hard reality of being underemployed at that bakery.

You see, my victor living has been bolstered by the thinking that I have all eternity to see my dreams happen. I don't have to hurry up and get busy with the 25 or so years I have left. I have billions of years to work with God to see the dreams He gave me come to fruition. I can't tell you how much stress this takes out of my life. I believe it will do the same in your life as well.

Instead of a sense of urgency that says, "I have to get busy making something happen," I can now live with a posture of trust that is summed up by the statement, "It's up to God to make this happen."

This new way of thinking doesn't mean that I now want to just sit back and wait for things to happen. In a weird sort of way, my looking at destiny from an eternal perspective has actually lit a fire under me to get up and keep moving.

I still don't have the energy that I think it will take to make something BIG happen in this lifetime, but who cares? Why not just put my hand to those things I have learned that bring joy to my life and that I'm good at and leave the results up to God? I'm now involved in more different opportunities and doing things in ways I would have never thought possible before this perspective change. This book is just one example of that truth.

Every one of us is looking to discover our purpose. Every one of us will one day come face to face with the fact that we might not see that destiny come to reality in our lifetime. The difference between victim thinking and victor living, for me, has to do with perspective. I simply cannot guarantee that anything I do will prove who I am, so I need an eternal perspective on my identity in order to face the failures that are an inevitable part of any human's life. It's the same with destiny. Thinking that we have the ability to guarantee destiny in this short life is a recipe for victim thinking.

Will this book or any of the many, many other things I'm involved in today fulfill my destiny here on earth? I doubt it. But, again, who knows? Better yet, who cares? I am a Child of God's, and that makes me a victor. None of the failure experienced in this world can change that. I have all eternity to see my destiny unfold.

If it were Jesus' destiny to die on this earth so that He could see the fullness of the Father's plan in Heaven, why do I think I deserve to see my destiny any sooner? If I do, praise God. If I don't, I praise Him all the more because my dreams aren't dead!

In the meantime, there is plenty to do in this life. Those people I have met who have been given a new lease on life by surviving something that should have killed them are here for just as much a reason as you and I are. Our destiny hinges on our getting to know this God that loves us so. That takes an eternal perspective that I believe trumps all the crazy things that we will come across in this lifetime.

SIMPLY BE

When are we ever going to get comfortable with the fact that God doesn't need us to *do* anything? Some of us are so hung up on doing to try and please God. The rest of us are doing to try and prove who we are. Why can't we get the fact that we are humanBEings not humanDOings? The door to destiny is slammed and locked tight when we have the wrong perspective on identity and destiny.

Don't get me wrong, I have plenty to do in the remaining years of my life here on earth. There are some important tasks that I currently have before me and many more are to come. But how, if or when I complete those tasks just doesn't have any reflection on who I am or on the dreams God has put in my heart. My identity is secure in Christ: I am a victor. My destiny is absolute: I am His child, and His promises to me will never change.

The same goes for you. Please understand that the perspective I've presented in this chapter isn't a guarantee that all will go well with you. Also understand that applying an eternal perspective doesn't guarantee that bad days will not come your way.

I still worry whether I'm doing enough of the right things that may make my destiny a reality. The difference now is that I'm emotionally healthy enough to be able to return to a firm, safe place of perspective: a place that knows my eternal identity and destiny have been established before time was ever created. I know who I am and believe that whether I do enough or not in my life has no impact on that identity and can't change my destiny.

What's your destiny? What dreams do you have in your life? Are you striving to make sure those dreams happen, so much so that you are in a place where worry is driving you into victim thinking? You are a victor. You are a Child of God's. If those dreams and your destiny are there at God's placement, like I think they are in my life, then look at your identity and destiny the way God sees them, from Heaven down not from earth up.

Identity is the door to destiny. Perspective is the key to that door. Don't let a temporal identity derail you from realizing that you have all eternity to see your destiny come into the fullness that God wants it to be. Hang on to the fact that you have been made a victor by the finished work of Jesus. When the good times come it doesn't mean that you are more of a victor and when the bad times come it doesn't mean that you are failing to see your destiny materialize. Let the eternal perspective on identity and destiny be what make it possible for you to finish your race strong.

CHAPTER TWELVE

Offense

I started this book off with a discussion on the epidemic of victimization in our society. It seems that everyone is a victim. Worse than that, it is beginning to feel like more and more people believe it is their "right" to have their victimhood acknowledged, accommodated and repaid in some way or another. All this demand as a result of victimization just leads to more and more victimization. It can't be said enough, those stuck in victim thinking will become victimizers themselves if left in that horrific spot for too long.

I used one word above that we need to unpack a little. The word "right" is such a powerfully important word for a nation like ours. Our country has been founded on the idea that with freedom comes rights. Read it for yourself. In the second paragraph of the Declaration of Independence, the guiding document of the United States, Jefferson wrote:

> We hold these truths to be self-evident, that all men are created equal, that they are endowed by their Creator with certain unalienable Rights, that among these are Life, Liberty and the pursuit of Happiness.

Those words penned over two centuries ago have been the cornerstone of our nation's independence and are the authority for the freedom we all enjoy today. "Unalienable" means absolute. Why are they absolute? Jefferson says, in this important document, that they are absolute because they come from our creator. God gave them to us, so no one should be able to arbitrarily take them away, particularly any government. Though his wording indicates that there are more rights to consider, Jefferson points to three absolute, God-given rights: life, liberty (or freedom) and the pursuit of happiness. Powerful stuff to say the least.

But, let me show you the hidden danger of putting our faith in something temporal, even something as important as the historical work of art that founded this great nation. Let's look at how victim thinking lurks even in the Declaration of Independence.

When I think of God-given I think of holy, unquestionable and undeniable. Don't you? When I use my judgment as to how my God-given rights of Life, Liberty and the pursuit of Happiness ought to materialize in my life, and then use my judgment to determine whether those rights are being met and/or accepted, I step into a place where I can become offended at my fellow man and, sometimes at God Himself.

Rights combined with human judgment are a powerful precursor to offense, and offense can lead us directly to victim thinking. At its core, offense is all about identity. Think about it. The last time you were offended, wasn't it about something that felt like a personal attack? When we feel personally assaulted it is almost always about our identity.

OFFENSE OPENS US UP TO VICTIM THINKING

As we have been discussing throughout this book, choosing to allow our identities to be altered by victimization will ultimately lead to victim thinking. When I am offended, I am either being victimized or feel like I am in a place where victimization is just around the corner. Offense is a powerful part of the human experience that has to be carefully considered in the life of a victor.

I once again need to interject a disclaimer here. I am in no way saying victimization, offense, rights or judgment are a bad thing. All humans will experience victimization and offense many times in their life. I agree with Jefferson; God has given us the ability to know our rights and to use the judgment He has given us to help determine when our rights are being trampled upon.

What I'm trying to highlight is the state of hypocrisy to which our culture has evolved when it comes to judgment, rights, being offended and victimization. We have gotten to a point where without even knowing it, we have taken Jefferson's words to heart in ways that bring an air of entitlement that is so crushing to the person trying to live life as a victor. If I am entitled to something and that thing is somehow not fully provided there is nothing I can feel but offense, and I inevitably see myself as a victim. The more I take on the identity of a victimized person the greater the power that victim thinking will have in my life.

I believe that the vast epidemic of victim thinking in our nation has come from the fact that we have twisted Jefferson's words to fit our own personal lives. Furthermore, we attempt to use our interpreted meaning of those words to fuel our motivation to go after our own personal desires. God help the person who gets in the way of a self-justified victim thinker who has judged that their rights have been somehow compromised. Let me use a personal example to show you what I mean.

AN EXAMPLE: GM VS. FORD

Jefferson says that the pursuit of happiness is a God-given right that no man or government should ever take away from the individual. I'm a Ford man; have been for as long as I can remember. I currently own six Ford manufactured automobiles. What do Jefferson and the Constitution have to do with me being a Ford fan? Let me explain.

As much as I love Fords, I hate Chevrolet. I'm exaggerating for effect, kind of… Nothing would make me happier than to see only Ford products built. Why? Because Ford parts would be more available and wouldn't cost me as much to "Fix or Repair Daily" (get it? F.O.R.D.?), as my GM counterparts would say about my brand of car.

So, when the U.S. government used my tax money to bail out GM a few years ago, I wasn't too happy. My dream had been about to come true—life without Chevy's. It is my judgment that the U.S. government squashed my unalienable right to the pursuit of happiness (remember, happiness to me is a world with no GM products). I was offended; no, I was actually victimized by the unbridled and illegal use of the power of taxation in a way that killed my ability to pursue my God-given rights as I saw them.

Jefferson himself must be turning over in his grave at this flagrant violation of the basic tenets of our nation as spelled out in the Declaration of Independence. I know Thomas Jefferson would see me as a victim of the U.S. Government. He would have to, right?

Now, before you think I've totally gone off the deep end, let me say I picked as inoffensive a topic as I could think of and dramatized it in a way so as to illustrate how hypersensitive we have become when it comes to judgment, rights, offense and victimization. I have no doubt that Jefferson could have cared less if it made me happy to see GM go out of business. I just want you to see how our basic freedoms can take on a power of their own when our judgment as to what our rights are lead us to where we find offense. This all leads to victimization both of the valid type and of the dangerous type that keeps us from living life as the victors that God has made us to be.

Had I chosen gay rights, abortion, gun ownership, separation of church and state, race relations, government-backed healthcare, socialism vs. capitalism, or a hundred other issues that quickly polarize the political landscape, offense would surely have happened. Those who might have been offended by any example, other than the ridiculous one I chose, would not have been open to anything of substance that might come from the rest of this chapter because of their offense. Offense has that amazing ability. Once offended, a person is closed to hearing anything about that offense until such time as they judge that those who have offended them have been punished enough.

Sadly, the ability for people to have meaningful conversations and come to meaningful compromises has become one of the many casualties of the victim-thinking-driven environment we have fostered where the issues of rights, judgment, offense and victimization are concerned. I simply point to the mess in Washington D.C. as proof that victim thinking has taken hold of our nation. By all appearances we are doing nothing to help stop the effects that this epidemic of victim thinking is having and will continue to have on the people of this nation. Somebody needs to stop this madness.

As stupid as my Ford vs. Chevy example of offense is, I'm afraid that it is an accurate portrayal of the level to which our nation has stooped as we live under the rule of victim thinking. I could easily point out people on both sides of any issue who have taken my Ford example to extremes that put my silly presentation to shame.

Yet the ears of the offended have been closed, and so are their hearts. When victim thinking takes hold like I believe it has in our nation, we are closed off from making changes that ultimately allow freedom to reign.

Please don't let offense creep in right now. I'm not blaming one political party for this mess. Neither do I blame any particular worldview. Anyone who is allowing their judgment on rights to bring them to a place of offense and victimization is to blame, which means I'm to blame; and so are you! That's why this book has been such an amazing journey for me. Victim to victor is not just a bunch of words on the page. It is an actual way of living that has changed my thinking so that the Ford example I laid out earlier is nothing more than a total work of fiction as far as I'm concerned.

Victors don't think in the way that I described in my Ford example. Even on those bad days when they do think that way, they don't stay thinking that way for long. They don't see themselves as victims of a government that chooses to do something that they don't agree with. They get on with their lives. They vote the way they think will maintain as much freedom as possible. They get active in causes that promote the same kinds of freedoms that they enjoy. Even if their efforts don't change things the way they would like, they go on living as the victors they know they were created to be.

Those who are stuck in victim thinking and react like I described in my silly example aren't threats to victors. They are simply people who haven't woken up to the reality that rights, judgment, offense and victimization aren't always all they are cracked up to be. There is so much more to the life of a victor than staying focused on one's own way of thinking.

We have spent most of this book presenting how victimization can lead to victim thinking. I hope you have gotten an appreciation of this important concept. For the remaining pages of this chapter, I'd like to discuss how the issues of rights, judgment and offense are the stepping-stones to becoming a victim in our own minds. Victors need to know the truth about rights, judgment and offense in order to live life as victors when the world is changing around them in ways that allows victimization to happen. Let's take a look at each of these issues one at a time.

RIGHTS

I don't think Thomas Jefferson got it wrong. I do believe we have God-given rights. I'm just not sure that we are always in the correct place from a psychological standpoint to accurately determine whether those rights are being met or being trampled on as we go through this life. This is particularly the case when we consider the fine line that separates the selfish person from the self-centered one.

I've quoted the author and psychologist Larry Crabb several times in this book. Crabb has put together an amazing curriculum called *Soul Care*.[17] This compilation of books, teachings and other resources are aimed at people interested in helping others who are searching to move from what I call victim thinking to living like victors. These resources have been unquestionable in their ability to help me move in this direction in my life. Crabb's curriculum has fueled in me a passion to see others find the kind of freedom I'm living in today.

---

[17] http://www.newwayministries.org/soulcare-exp-curriculum.php

As I read one of Larry Crabb's books, I came across something that totally changed my way of thinking about myself. In his book *"Men and Women; Enjoying the Difference,"* Crabb highlights the difference between being selfish and being self-centered. After reading his explanation of these two very different character traits I came to a place where I am comfortable with the fact that God made me to be a selfish person. Did that statement offend you? If so, please push your offense aside so you can hear what I'm trying to say.

You see, selfishness isn't such a bad trait. Larry Crabb helped me see that the real damage occurs when self-centeredness replaces our naturally selfish ways. That's when victim thinking can creep in. When self-centeredness is fueled by victimization, we are in danger of becoming victimizers in our own life. Before we can dig in on the issues of our rights, we need to take a closer look at the difference between being selfish and being self-centered.

Selfishness is a human quality. Watch any baby and you will see that they come out of the womb selfish. When a baby is hungry they cry, and I mean cry until their needs are met. They don't care if you are busy or not. They don't care if you are in the middle of a much-needed stretch of sleep. When they are hungry they will let you know of that fact and won't stop letting you know until you do something to satisfy their need. This is a totally selfish attitude that is instinctual and completely appropriate. The baby doesn't know he is being selfish. He is just trying to survive. Selfishness is put in our lives to help us make it from one day to the next. We can, of course, abuse selfishness, but being selfish in and of itself isn't necessarily a bad character trait.

God has made it so that from the get-go, human beings learn to be dependent on relationship with a higher power for survival. I think He made us unique in this way in all creation because He wants us to see our need for dependence on a relationship with Him for eternal life. Sometimes our efforts at survival make it so that we have to be selfish in order to exercise a growing dependence on God. It isn't bad that we are selfish; it's just how selfish we are at demanding our rights that makes all the difference in our ability to live like victors.

Crabb makes it clear that being selfish isn't always a bad thing. It is when the pain in our soul is so great, and we become so caught up in our selfishness that we become demanding that we cross the line into an area where victim thinkers thrive. More victims are created by selfish people demanding their needs be met than just about anything else I can think of. It is at this point that Crabb says we cross from being normal selfish human beings to dangerous victimizers living a self-centered existence. An existence we believe is completely justified. This is particularly the case when our selfish right for identity comes into play. In *Men and Women: Enjoying the Difference*, Crabb puts it like this:

> *Self-centeredness convincingly and continually whispers to me that nothing in this universe is more important than my need to be accepted and respectfully treated.*[18]

The only thing I disagree with about Crabb's quote above in light of my own life is that that whisper was in fact a loud, screaming voice in my head as I struggled with all the issues that I believed were compromising my rights.

Self-centeredness has had its talons firmly sunk into the depths of my soul in the past. It has caused me to victimize my loved ones in ways that I have shared through some of the personal stories presented in this book. I believe self-centeredness is the cause of much of the victimization that is happening by those trapped in victim thinking in our nation today.

Jefferson is completely correct. We have the God-given right to life, freedom and the pursuit of happiness. Where many of us misapply our rights and cross the line from victors to self-centered victims is when we use our expectations to determine what our rights should look like. As we have seen with destiny and identity, perspective plays the key role in understanding our rights when it comes to being a victor.

---

[18] Taken from *Men and Women: Enjoying the Difference* by Larry Crabb. Copyright © 1991 by Larry Crabb. Used with permission of Zondervan. www.zondervan.com. All Rights Reserved.

OFFENSE

I used to believe that my right to life, liberty and happiness had to look a certain way. I've even used the Bible at times to defend my perspective on what these rights need to look like. When circumstances made those expectations seem unattainable, I became so offended that I couldn't see or hear any voice of reason, including God's.

How could that be? Why would I tune out the very one who gave me those rights in the first place? Crabb has an answer that I believe is right on the mark. From the same book quoted earlier, Crabb says:

> *The greatest obstacle to building truly good relationships is justified self-centeredness, a selfishness that, deep in our souls, feels entirely reasonable and therefore acceptable in light of how we've been treated.*[19]

When I get to the point where I feel justified at being mad at my wife for not giving me what I think I deserve, offense can take hold so deeply that I can't hear, see or experience the love she has for me in this relationship that has developed for over 30 years now. Same goes with God.

When I am so offended at not receiving the life I feel I deserve or was promised, I feel justified in my rants against God and become demanding in ways that are simply inappropriate. That offense closes the door to my being able to hear from the one who knows me, and has exactly what I need. As a person attempting to live life as a victor, I'm beginning to see that what God knows I need is so much more important than my expectations surrounding what I want.

What rights do I have as victor? Honestly, the only answer that puts me in a place where expectation doesn't lead to offense is, "I HAVE NO RIGHTS!" Maybe it's just me, but thinking I have God-given rights puts me in a place of thinking I'm entitled. Entitlement, when not met according to the way I stipulate, leads to offense. Stay offended long enough and victim thinking will be in firm control. This

---

[19] Taken from *Men and Women: Enjoying the Difference* by Larry Crabb. Copyright © 1991 by Larry Crabb. Used with permission of Zondervan. www.zondervan.com. All Rights Reserved.

connection between rights, entitlement, and offense is what I believe has made our society so entrenched in its victim thinking ways.

If life, or any other thing, is a God-given right, I had better be using God's perspective on what that life looks like or offense is going to rule the day. My perspective is going to get in the way every time, and when that happens, I'm easily offended. Same goes for freedom. I had better be basing my expectations of freedom on God's perspective, not my own. If I think freedom is lots of money and time on my hands, I'm going to be disappointed as the circumstances of this life work to rob me of both time and money. Being victimized by this world brings offense. Offense makes us deaf to those with whom we want or need to be in relationship.

Want to be living the life of a victor? When it comes to rights, be sure you manage your expectations. Life, Liberty and the pursuit of Happiness might be God-given, but are you one hundred percent confident that you know God's definition of those terms as they relate to your life? If you said yes to that question, I need to tell you that you are on a crash course for victim thinking and offense.

Victors need to be okay with the fact that rights based on their own expectations, knowledge and experience are going to fail them from time to time. That's just how it is. God has given us rights in relationship with Him. Those rights are something He reveals to us individually. They aren't temporal. In other words, the rights He is revealing aren't temporary and they weren't meant solely for this world. The rights of a victor are eternal. They will never change, just like our identity and our destiny.

Next time you feel offended at someone or something, think about this. Why are you offended? Have your expectations of what you think your rights should look like put you in a place of demanding something be changed? If so, maybe you have crossed the line that separates the victor from the self-centered ways of a victim thinker. If that's where you find yourself, that's easy to change. Re-evaluate your rights and what your expectations are for those rights. Remember, how God-given rights look in your life is an issue that is defined by God and God alone. Rights, along with so many other things in this life, when viewed from His perspective, give those wanting to live the victor's life the best opportunity to thrive.

JUDGEMENT

I'm beginning to think that our real problem isn't with rights, it is with our ability to judge what our rights are supposed to look like. It's not the Declaration of Independence that gets me into trouble. It is my judgment as to what those God-given rights are and how they are supposed to look that rocks me every time. But, that's not the only place victors can get themselves in places of offense and victim thinking when it comes to judgment. We can be lousy judges of others and their actions, too, as they relate to our needs, wants and desires. Take a look at what the Bible says about our judgment in the following couple of verses:

> *Do not judge others and you will not be judged. Mat 7:1 (KJV)*

> *Stop judging by mere appearances, and make a right judgment. John 7:24 (NIV)*

Judgment isn't a good thing for us to be doing under our own power because our judgment is flawed. It comes from a perspective that we belong here and that the bad things of this world shouldn't happen to us. When we judge our rights based on the circumstances of this world, of course we are going to be disappointed and even offended at times.

More victim thinking has resulted from judgment than almost any single thing I can think of. Yes, I know that everything I have written in this book is essentially nothing more than my judgment; that's why I firmly believe you have to let the light of God's spirit carefully and specifically illuminate all the writings of man. This also includes the Bible.

I have no control over how you interpret what I have written here. I have to trust that God is doing what He wants in leading me to write this book and that He will reveal to you what you need out of this work as you read these words. I have no ability on my own to correctly judge how this book will be received, nor can I judge how what I have presented will impact the world around me. All I can do is what I feel I'm supposed to do, and leave the results up to God.

We have to be so careful in how, when and what we judge. Judgment is tied to offense. When I am offended I have judged that someone or something has come against me in ways that are insulting or somehow damaging to my persona. Most of the offense we feel happens when this world puts us in places where we believe that we have been judged by someone else. When that person cuts you off on the freeway, could it be that your anger can be summed up with the following statement? "They could have killed me!" What that statement is really saying is that you have judged that person who just cut you off as one who doesn't care about your life. You have come to the instant conclusion that they thought their life, time and property was more important than yours. Getting cut off on the road by some "jerk" is offensive, I know; I've been there many times on the freeway, and been just as offended as you have been.

But what if that person that cut you off just didn't see you in the lane? Maybe they had just learned about a tragic event in their lives and they were less focused on driving than they should have been. I know I wouldn't be offended for long if I knew that the reason I was cut off had something to do with the two excuses I just mentioned. Isn't it so much easier to get offense out of our lives when we know the truth?

Judgment is nothing more than us trying to figure out the "why" when something happens to us that leads to offense. That's why judgment can lead to serious victim thinking. You have no way of knowing the "why" in most circumstances. Thinking you know the "why" puts you in a place of judgment that allows offense to take control.

We all have a choice when it comes to judgment. Victors work to suspend their judgment until such time as God sheds some light onto the question of "why" in that situation. That's what the John 7:24 verse quoted above is saying. Only God knows what is right, and victors are willing to suspend their judgment in ways that keep offense from taking over until God brings to light the "right" or truth of that situation.

Victors and victims alike make instant judgments. The difference between victim thinkers and those living the life of a victor is that victors are willing to suspend acting on their judgment about a situation until such time they have the God given information that makes their ability to judge as free of the influences of offense as possible. Victims believe their read on the "why" of a circumstance is correct and are quick to react on their judgment. They just can't see that they are required to make so many assumptions in order to reach their judgment that their judgement is of no real use at all. I apologize for the crassness of this old adage, but you know what happens when we assume: we make an ass out of you and me (ass-u-me).

As with everything else, judgment always comes back to identity. God didn't make you an ass. He made you His child. Could it be that we get so easily offended when we have to judge from assumptions simply because we know deep down inside that this makes an ass out of us? Could our spirit be so taken aback at the affront to the true, powerful and eternal identity of God's child that even the subconscious possibility that we are an ass is what drives us to lash out in victimizing ways at times?

Think judging others is a bad idea? One of the worst things we can do is to try and judge ourselves. If we are constantly put in situations where bad things are happening to us, it is often easier to just blame ourselves rather than face the fact that this is a hard world in which we live. Of course we need to evaluate our situation and learn from our mistakes. But anything that brings our true identity into question needs to be pushed as far away from us as possible. Victors evaluate every situation and learn from what they find. They work to keep doubt from entering their way of thinking in ways that might bring into question their true identity as God's child.

This fact was clearly illustrated by Pastor Layne Scharnz from Church of the Highlands in Birmingham Alabama. Pastor Layne was visiting our church in Carlsbad one Sunday and gave this illustration.

He pulled from his pocket a crumpled, well-used $100 bill. He asked the question, "How much is this bill worth?" Everyone responded $100. Now at this point my son, Jay, who had just finished his freshman year at Point Loma Nazaren University, leaned over to my wife and said, "Has he taken into account the future earning potential of the present value of that bill?" You've gotta love the youthful exuberance of new knowledge!

Pastor Layne went on to point out that it doesn't matter that this bill might have been used in a drug deal at one time or another. It is still worth $100. It doesn't matter if this bill came from the gutter. It's still worth $100. It doesn't matter if it is ripped and torn. It is still worth $100. It doesn't matter if it came from the hands of the richest person in the world or the poorest. It is still worth $100.

Such is our value to God. It is set and secure. It doesn't matter where we came from, what we look like, how battered we are, or what shape we are in. Our value has been set by the price paid by the death of His Son. We are priceless!

It doesn't matter how others judge us or even how we judge ourselves. We are victors and our value is beyond comprehension. Why do we allow ourselves to be put in situations where we devalue ourselves as we try to judge the "why's" as they relate to the bad things that happen in, around and through us? We do that exact thing to ourselves and to others when we make assumptions as we try to figure out the meaning that surrounds the bad stuff that comes into our lives.

Judgment without knowing the truth is what ties judgment to offense. Only God knows the ultimate truth behind what we face in this life. The only way I know to live as the victor God sees me to be is to judge only as He leads. In all other cases, I leave the judgment up to Him. Since He is the only one who knows the "why" of all situations in this life, I need to surrender my "right" to make judgment as to the "why" behind the offending things that come up against me.

OFFENSE

Getting offended seems to be an easier and easier thing to do these days. One group of people is offended at the sight of a generic religious symbol on a hill. Certain groups of people are offended at the name of a professional football team. Certain religions have actually resorted to causing death and mayhem by being offended at the sight of mere cartoons.

All this offense comes from years and years of victimization that has led to what I see as an inferiority complex due to misplaced and misunderstood identities. The roots of this inferiority come straight out of victim thinking. The results of this inferiority often shows itself in ways that cause others significant pain and loss. Victims creating victims. That's the power of victim thinking that is often behind the feelings of the offended.

Each of the generic groups above have had serious and, in some cases, long term periods of discrimination as part of their past. Some of these groups have faced tremendous periods of persecution that have created generation after generation of victims. When we lose our identity through long-term victimization, victim thinking quickly makes itself available to fill the void and provide an identity.

When we are offended, it hurts. This is a reality that we all have to face. I'm not trying to minimize the pain the offended feels by anything presented in this book. But as we hold onto any pain caused to us, as we wallow in the offense, something happens to the offended. Bitterness starts to take hold.

Bitterness is described as a root in the Bible. Have you ever seen a root grow? It starts out as a tiny hair and grows thicker at the base and pointy at the end. The root pushes its way through everything around it: rocks, house foundations and other seemingly impenetrable objects. Roots end up twisting and turning in ways that anchor the plant into the ground. Left for a long time, that root can grow bigger than the actual plant that it was designed to support.

So it is with offense. The longer offense is allowed to linger in the life of the offended, the bigger the problem of bitterness can become.

Just like the plant root, bitterness seems to find its way deep into every action of the offended. It grows larger than the offense that it was designed to support. It gets into areas it just wasn't intended to go. The result of bitterness from long-term offense is a destructive force in every part of a person's life.

You've met people who are really, really bitter over something, right? Maybe that bitter person is reacting to the offense created through a horrible divorce. Left unchecked long enough, that bitterness begins to turn towards the kids of the divorce. The offended sees their kids going to the ex's house more than to theirs, and they are further offended.

Then that bitterness can turn towards other family members. They start to see that family, who were once there at the drop of a hat, are not as willing to make the long drive to help them with yet another emergency in their lives. Family members are now offenders. The same thing can happen at work. Co-workers and bosses get fed up with the negative attitudes that spill out of the bitter person. Steps, even kind ones, to help them see that they need to change are met with offense. "Aren't I good enough for you anymore?" is the cry from the one whose heart is entangled with the root of bitterness.

Before too long, that bitter person is someone no one wants to be around. The isolation that the bitter person sees happening in their lives is yet another reason to be offended, and bitterness continues to spread. It's a terribly destructive, self-feeding cycle that repeats itself in the lives of way too many people in the world today.

Offense is the killer of relationship. The more we know about someone or about a group of people the less chance we have at being offended. The less we know, the greater the possibility of misunderstanding. It is when we don't know all we need to know about a person, group or situation that the possibility for offense is at its highest.

When we are offended the tendency is to just close the offender off from our lives. That isn't a terrible thing in and of itself, but it doesn't end there. When we are offended, we begin to create rules in our lives. We institute generalized regulations about people who remind us of the one who offended us in the first place. Entire groups of people can become off limits to the offended because of the offense of a single person. The root of much of the prejudice that offends so many today lies in the rules of engagement that someone has had to create due to the offense in their own lives or offense that happened generations ago.

It is unfortunate, but the vast majority of offenses that people carry with them today are the result of misunderstanding. What is even sadder is that the person who is perceived to be the offender most likely doesn't have a clue that they have done anything wrong. This has to be one of the most ridiculous methods of victim thinking we can ever let into our lives. Yet I'll bet you are doing exactly that thing right now. I know I do it all the time.

The good news is that there is an antidote to offense. Notice I didn't say cure? Cure implies that if you take your medicine you will no longer suffer the effects of the original ailment. Unfortunately, with offense, the cure only comes with long-term exposure to the antidote. One dose rarely does the trick when it comes to offense.

What's the antidote to offense? The antidote can be found in one totally misunderstood and completely hated word in today's society. That word is forgiveness.

FORGIVENESS

Nobody likes to forgive an offender. I understand. We seem to think that by withholding ourselves through unforgiveness we are somehow causing the offender personal harm. I've heard it described this way: "Unforgiveness is the poison we take hoping to kill those we need to forgive." I have also heard another description of unforgiveness. It goes like this: "Unforgiveness is the process of lighting yourself on fire, hoping that the one who offended you dies from smoke inhalation."

These descriptions of the unwillingness to forgive would be kind of comical if it weren't so sadly true. I've also heard one other saying about forgiveness that we need to consider: "Forgiveness frees the captive of offense; that captive is you." Forgiveness is really about freedom; not freedom for the offender, but your own personal ability to live freely.

Reality is that when we hold onto the bitterness of offense all we are doing is causing ourselves damage. Forgiveness frees us from having to carry the weight of the offense for the rest of our lives. That's why forgiveness is a process, not an event. Depending on the offense, forgiveness might need to be done time and time again until we feel the gates of that prison open and we can start to enjoy the freedom we are offering to ourselves.

I have a neighbor who is very interesting, to say the least. A few years ago we had a boundary dispute that caused me much angst. I'm not a person who is hard to get along with, but when you deal with me in a bullying way, something goes off in me that makes me just want to fight for the sake of fighting. I know now this was and is an identity issue. I'm working on it, okay?

After many months of arguing, a costly property survey, some attorney fees and a couple calls to the police we finally got to a point where there was some peace and quiet at my house.

I have to tell you, I was offended by my neighbor's actions. He had no right to accuse me of the things he accused me of, or to demand the things he demanded of me during that time. His very attitude was such that my buttons were pushed every time I saw his face. I was carrying this offense with me on a moment-by-moment basis.

After about a year I realized that this was killing me. I noticed that as I drove up my street to turn into my driveway, I dreaded the possibility of seeing my neighbor on my property. I was actually not looking forward to coming home each time I left my house. With every noise that came from the direction of his house my heart stopped and I would think, "Oh no, here we go again."

Finally, one day I realized what I had to do. I needed to forgive my neighbor. I had to let myself out of the prison I had created because of the offense I had experienced at the hands of this random guy. I needed to stop taking the poison that I was hoping would kill my neighbor.

As I prayed about what I needed to do, I told God I just wasn't ready to go see this guy face-to-face. I just couldn't go knock on his door and tell him I forgive him. What good would that have done anyway? To him, I was the offender. Telling him I forgave him would have done nothing but escalate the situation as far as I could judge (remember how faulty our judgment is).

I felt God saying that I just needed to forgive, and so I did. I forgave my neighbor for many things that I feel caused me offense. I felt better, lighter in my daily walk. Then those old feelings would come back again. I'd have to forgive him again, then again. Time and time again, over these past couple of years, I have forgiven my neighbor. Not once have I seen him face-to-face since that unsettling time, but I continue to forgive him.

Then God did something ridiculous. He told me I need to bless my neighbor. Bless him? You have got to be kidding! But that feeling wouldn't go away. Again, I told God I just don't think I can face him yet. God let me know that that wasn't necessary at this time. That very day I started praying for my neighbor's blessing every time I drove down my driveway.

I mostly work out of the house, so I'm constantly driving here or there to this meeting or that. There are times I pray for my neighbor's blessing five to ten times a day! I have to admit I pray that God's blessing would be that this neighbor get some big promotion with a big house in some faraway distant land! There are also times I have been brought to tears at the pain I know this man has in his heart as I pray God would reach out and bless yet another victimized human stuck in victim thinking.

I'd like to say all is well with my neighbor. It isn't. But all is well with me. I am free to live day-by-day. I don't wake thinking about the possibility of what this guy will do next. Nor do I carry the weight of offense that sends me into victim thinking. Forgiveness has set me free, as free as I can be at this time in my life. What's tomorrow going to look like? I have no idea, and neither do you. All I can do is have faith that whatever offense hits me tomorrow can be diffused as powerfully as the offense I felt by this neighbor through the antidote of forgiveness.

Forgiveness is hard. Not because of what forgiveness is. I think we find forgiveness so challenging because of what forgiveness is NOT.

Forgiveness is NOT an admission that the offender is right and that you are wrong. The things my neighbor did and said are one hundred percent wrong. I didn't deserve those things he offended me with. Now there is plenty of wrong in my reaction to him that I need to ask him to forgive me for and maybe that will be a possibility someday down the road. So when you are faced with offense and need to forgive, remember forgiveness isn't an admission that what you felt was incorrect.

Forgiveness also is NOT a requirement for you to have a relationship with the offender. This is particularly the case when the offender is someone dangerous or has the potential to bring more harm into your life. You may not have to see or talk to the offender to usher the power of forgiveness into your life. Victors simply need to forgive and let God direct when, and if the time will come for a relationship with the offender to happen.

As for my situation with my neighbor, I simply can't stand the sight of him right now. I have run across people that mildly resemble him and that anger starts to flare up inside me all over again. And again, I forgive. Who knows what God will do when it comes to relationship with my neighbor in the future. For now, all I can do is forgive and let God take me where He wants me to go in the future.

I know that my on-going attitude towards my neighbor is a problem that needs to be, and will be dealt with by God in my life. My job as a victor is to listen to God and respond to his direction. Led by God's Love, forgiveness has the power to do mighty things, including the restoration of a relationship. It all starts with forgiveness followed by an openness to God's direction. This makes it possible for the victor to leave offense behind and see God's work be done in and through his life.

Finally, forgiveness is NOT a mandate to forget what has been done to you. Forgive and forget is only done by one person, and that is God Himself.

For the offenses of many, it would be foolish for the forgiver to forget what the offender did to them. Offense can be such a vile thing that it must be rooted out of the life of the offender. That job is not the responsibility of the forgiver. Forgiveness doesn't mean you have to toss out common sense. Freeing ourselves up through forgiveness doesn't mean we need to put ourselves in harm's way to make forgiveness happen.

I know it's hard to forgive others of the offense you feel. But know this. You aren't letting the person who offended you off the hook by forgiving them. Forgiveness has nothing to do with judging the actions of the offender. Judgment is the Lord's and the Lord's alone. Unless the offense is something illegal, then the consequences of the offender's actions aren't up to the victor. By forgiving, the victor isn't required to take on the heavy weight of judging the offender. With forgiveness, you are freeing yourself up to be able to throw off the shackles of victim thinking, and live more like the victor you were created to be.

Victim thinking that results from offense has done nothing for me but cause me pain. It has weighed me down for way too long. Forgiveness has to be part of the life of a victor, particularly a victor who finds their victory in Jesus.

YOU DON'T HAVE TO BE ALONE

Offense is the killer of relationship. Left long enough, offense makes lonely people out of us all. And for the person who has decided to walk with God through a relationship with Jesus Christ, offense is the killer of faith. Relationships require a lot of belief in the unknown. If you have been the victim of serious abuse, violence, rejection or any number of other life circumstances in your past, you, too, know what I mean about it taking faith to have relationship. The unknown in people is a scary thing, to say the least.

But God didn't make us to go through this life alone. Not only can we trust He is with us, He wants us to value and benefit from close relationship with fellow travelers on this path of life. That requires we have faith and take calculated risks on people. That cannot be done if we have ruled out particular kinds of people because they remind us of someone who has offended us in the past.

Until we come to a place where we have been dosed with enough forgiveness to get us free from the offender that has caused us such pain, we will never have the faith to appreciate the potential good in others. Worse yet, we will never be able to see the good in God when we come face to face with all the bad that can happen to us in this world.

For so many of us, the first person we need to forgive is God. I know this sounds crazy, but we can actually get to the point of thinking we need to forgive God. So many of us have been carrying around an offense for so many years now it has totally changed our ability to see the spiritual movement in our lives. That offense has to be put at the foot of the cross.

Maybe it was the death of a child. Maybe it was the prayer for a healing that never materialized. Maybe it was the time you begged God to get you out of a particular bad situation that just didn't turn out the way you wanted it to. Whatever the case, all practical appearances point to the fact that we have been let down by God. It looks and feels like He has offended us by not meeting our needs in such a desperate time when you reached out so fervently to Him.

We have to remember that the notion that we need to forgive God is based on our faulty judgment. God hasn't done anything that warrants forgiveness. If offense is there we need to remove it and that can only happen through forgiveness. Even if we <u>feel</u> offended by God's apparent inaction on our behalf, only a healthy dose of the medicine of forgiveness will begin to break us free from the bondage of offense.

Are you carrying around offense? Offense gives bitterness permission to linger in your life. It has the unique ability to make you blind to the love that is all around you. It makes it impossible to believe that good will ever happen in your life. It drives you to do all you can to make sure you are never wounded like you were before. Walls are built all around you that keep out the very people who need you to let them in. Your spouse… your children… your God!

Isn't it time you forgave those who you think have offended you? If you believe God has perpetrated some offense in your life, isn't it time to forgive? Do you think you have kept God in some prison for all these years by not forgiving Him? You are the one locked in a cell. You have the key to get out. Forgive.

The reality is that He hasn't done anything to you that requires forgiveness. The world is what has caused you such pain. It is because you and I don't know Him like we could that we have misjudged Him. The fullness of the life of a victor always comes down to relationship when God is involved.

If it takes the action of you forgiving God for you to move from victim thinking to victor living, then forgive Him. Then let a relationship with Him happen. The more your relationship develops to where you realize that God hasn't done anything to require us to forgive Him, the more you will be able to surrender to the love He has for you in this life. You will be amazed at the difference in your ability to live as a victor as you take the antidote for offense when it comes to God and others around you.

GETTING OFF "THE HOOK"

There's a book that was published a few years ago called *The Bait of Satan* by John Bevere. I haven't read the book but love the title. The picture those words paint is one that I totally understand. Bait is a tricky thing. You have to have just the right smell, texture, look, etc. in order to get the big fish to bite.

Satan knows exactly how to push our buttons. He knows my neighbor acting like a bully was exactly what it took to make me (a peaceful man) turn into a raging defender of what is "right." Satan knew that I would bite at that particular bait and offense would be the result. He also knew I would carry that offense with me. He knew I would wallow around in that offense, allowing it to corrupt all that I am. What Satan didn't anticipate was that I would actually let God in in ways that would lead me to forgive and pray daily for my neighbor's blessing.

I took the bait of offense, so have you. Getting off the hook is something you have control of through the power of forgiveness. There is no way in the world you can live the life of a victor without first experiencing forgiveness (through Jesus Christ) and giving forgiveness to those who have offended you.

There are no doubts that I have rights in this world. There is no problem with me using my judgment, flawed as it is, to determine whether my rights are being violated or not. The key for the victor is to let go of offense as quickly as possible and do what needs to be done to move out of any place where bitterness can thrive. It is only then that the victor can grow as the free person they have been made to be.

We can easily diffuse offense when we remember that our identity has been secured by Jesus. We are God's Children and that is all we will ever need to be no matter who does or says what to us from now on. If you are offended, I'll bet you have let your victor identity be replaced in some form by something less permanent than what Christ died to make you to be.

When we know who we are, offense takes on a different role in our lives. We have choice. With choice comes freedom and power. That's the destiny of a victor. Not to be saddled down with offense, but to be freed by forgiveness in ways that make the possibility of victim thinking less and less likely in our lives.

Who is it you need to forgive? What offenses have you bound up by the roots of bitterness? Isn't it time to move into a place of power and freedom? God knows your rights. He is the judge. You are His Child. Let Him carry the burden of offense. Let him hand out the penalties of judgment for those offenses. Your identity is secure in Him. This world will always be filled with offense. You are just passing through. Don't let offense open the doors to the weightiness of victim thinking. Choose life. Choose freedom. Choose forgiveness and watch what God does in your life.

CHAPTER THIRTEEN

Bringing It All Together

If you are anything like me, you are chomping at the bit for a formula on how to live like a victor in this world that seems to victimize us at every turn. I've presented a lot of data on how victim thinking can creep into our lives, but I have presented very little on how to live like a victor.

Sorry to say it this plainly, but the lack of formulas is no mistake. I've done my best to make this book as devoid of formulas as possible. Why? Because, formulas often fuel our ability to let victim thinking rule in our lives.

Look, I've got nothing wrong with formulas. My engineering training is based on formulas. The physical and scientific parts of our flesh depend on formulas. Were it not for the formulas surrounding gravity our very existence would not be understandable and quantifiable. No, formulas in and of themselves aren't bad, it's what we do with formulas that get us into trouble where victor living is concerned.

In the opening of this book I shared with you the victim thinking pattern that took control of my life as a result of my misapplication of the formula, "Hard Work equals Success." For many of us this, along with a myriad of other formulas, has played a critical role in our lives. This particular formula is based on a truth that is unmistakable. Those who apply themselves will almost always do better than those who choose not to apply themselves.

The problem with formulas is our definition of what the outcome should look like. My victim thinking that resulted from the "Hard Work equals Success" formula came about because of my definition of success. When I found myself not achieving what I thought success should look like as a result of my hard work, I was challenged in ways that made me doubt my abilities, my life choices and, at times, my very existence.

No, formulas aren't the problem. It's our own thinking as to what will happen if we properly apply those formulas that messes us up.

At this point in the book, I hope you are sold—I hope you want to live the life of a victor. I can't provide you a formula to get there, but I can sum up this book by describing certain characteristics that all victors share. Here they are:

VICTOR CHARACTERISTIC #1: ETERNAL PERSPECTIVE

Victors view things differently. They don't let current circumstances define who they are. Victors believe that there is an eternal part of them that simply cannot be taken away no matter the extent of the constraints and challenges they face in this world. Even if they don't believe in the Christian God, victors have a sense that there is something more than these couple handfuls of decades that we are all destined to live.

Victors with an eternal perspective aren't defined by the stumbles and falls they experience in this lifetime. Yes we get upset at failure, but failure doesn't define us. Victors have a sense that there is some destiny out there greater than what this life might be capable of fully revealing. Even when this life beats us black and blue, victors hold onto the "fact" that they were created for more.

Eternal thinking gives victors the ability to change their attitude. There is something positive about people who believe that they have all eternity to discover and apply their destinies. It is when we think that time is limited that we start to let victim thinking overtake our attitudes. Having an eternal perspective doesn't guarantee a good attitude but it does give victors the ability to get to a place where they can choose what their attitude will be.

This eternal perspective leads to a peace in the soul that enables the person trying to live the life of a victor to find rest. That rest is something that is noticeable to those who don't have it. There is something powerful in a person who has peace and a good attitude. They make the best leaders. People are attracted to them. Just think how powerful it would be in your world if you exuded an air of peace and dealt with the crazy things of your life with an attitude that others just don't seem to be able to muster up.

VICTOR CHARACTERISTIC #2: IDENTITY

Victors know who they are. They have spent a lot of time working to disconnect their roles and the relative success or failures found in those roles from the reality of who they are. Victors know that roles are temporary. The fact that they are a success today does not guarantee success tomorrow. Victors have learned that they can't trust what they do to define who they are.

Those victors who hold the particular belief that Jesus is their Savior know that their identity as God's child is secure. They work hard to not let their job, titles, ministries and/or anything else on this earth take away from the power that comes with being the child of an all-powerful being like our God. "Child of God" is their identity now and forevermore.

Those living the victor's life who don't have a belief in Jesus have found a definition of identity that they, too, believe will outlast their lives here on earth. They also do all they can to make sure things of this earth don't rob them of the foundation of their true identity.

Identity is crucial due to the fact that we will all face times of great success and times of miserable failure. If our identity is tied to things that can be judged by our success or our failure then we are ripe for victim thinking to take over. Victors can't stand the thought of being on the roller coaster ride of identity that will happen when that identity is tied to roles that they play. They have done that way too many times and want something different for their lives.

VICTOR CHARACTERISTIC #3: RELATIONSHIP

Victors are relational people. They value life in ways that victims often miss. Victors have found ways to be proactive in relationships. They work hard at ending the use of relationships to get what they want. They have found that others can neither completely nor consistently provide what they need to feel good about themselves.

This lesson has come at a high cost. Many relationships haven't survived in the victor's life. Some very important personal connections have paid the price that enabled the victor to learn that the actions of others will almost never be enough to bring the kind of fulfillment that they have been looking for in this world.

Victors now see the importance of being in relationship. This is particularly the case when it comes to a relationship with their God. Victors have stopped trying to use God to get what they think they need and/or deserve in this life. Now they just want to relate—to others and to God. Victors want relationship, for no reason other than that this life is better when there are connections.

Victors realize that they will always need to be connected to people and to their God. They know that connection is a blessing, not a tool for getting what they want. If there is any regret in the victor's life it is that they didn't learn the lesson of the importance of relationship before so many of their past connections were damaged beyond repair. But victors know that even these losses are not meant to be defining parts of their existence. The lessons learned work to make the relationships they have now be exactly what they are meant to be in the victor's life.

VICTOR CHARACTERISTIC #4: NOT DRIVEN BY "HAVE TO"

Victors have learned that "have to" makes freedom something that is so hard to obtain. They have found that the soul is such a powerful force in moving them towards freedom or towards bondage. Victims don't "have to" do things; they "get to" do things. "Get to" is the key to which direction the victor moves in their life.

It isn't that victors are so independently wealthy that they don't need to work or do things that aren't their first choice when it comes to their daily responsibilities. It is just that they realize that they have a choice when it comes to everything that crosses their path. They don't have to do a single thing.

Victors have realized that the consequences of their choices might not be all they would like them to be, but they know that they have a choice. This choice gives them a feeling of freedom that makes the hard choices that much easier to make. Victors aren't always happy with the fact that the things they choose to do don't measure up to exactly what they want for their lives. They have just settled on the reality that choice brings a power to self that is not found by those living a "have to" kind of life.

VICTOR CHARACTERISTIC #5: NOT EASILY OFFENDED

Offense is the killer of faith. Not only does offense make it hard to believe in something bigger than oneself, it kills the faith we might have in our own ability to move from victim thinking to victor living.

The victor has found that offense is a waste of time. Offense to the victor is something that they are quickly and systematically weeding out of their lives.

It isn't that victors don't get offended. It is that they quickly move from offense to forgiveness. This movement is what gives them the power to see what is really going on: offense is an attack on the victor's identity. Since victors have a firm handle on identity they work to remove anything that might make the victor doubt and/or tout their identity.

Victors also realize that those who are habitual offenders are nothing more than victims who haven't found their place where victor living might be a possibility. Victors know what it feels like to live in a place of temporary identity. Because they know how lost one is when they don't know who they are, it makes it easier for the victor to have compassion for the offender and move to a place where forgiveness sets the victor free.

NOW THE TROUBLE BEGINS

There you go. Five characteristics of victor living that, if applied in the right way, will make it possible for you, too, to live life as a victor.

Sad part is that now that this book has been boiled down to something like a process, you are on the road to being stuck in victim thinking all over again. Why? Because human nature is crippled with the desire to live a good and productive life. Formulas often make it easier to plan on how to move toward that good and productive life. Formulas also make it possible for us to think we can accurately measure our success at going after the goal of a good and productive life. It's not necessarily a bad thing that we try to apply formulas to make our life what we want it to be. It is just that formulas can introduce the flaws inherent in our limited ability to judge that can make it possible for even the best process to be corrupted by personal motivations. The best motives of the person trying to live a victor kind of life can end up opening the door to victim thinking when we allow the process we try to apply through formulas take over.

If you take any concept and make it a formula it goes something like this: If I do "A" then "B" will result. Larry Crabb has a new book out called *"The Pressure's Off."* In this book, he describes how we use formulas, particularly in the Christian Church, to try and make it possible for us to get what we think we need to maintain the good life we sometimes think we deserve. He calls this, "If I do A, I will get B" formula way of looking at life "linear thinking."

Linear thinking is a killer to the process of moving from being a victim to a victor. Why? Because A does not always lead to B. Go back to my formula "Hard Work equals Success." I wanted B: Success. I thought that the way to get B was to do A: Work Hard. When I didn't get B, when B didn't come about the way I thought it should, I felt victimized by all those people who made this formula part of my way of doing things.

BRINGING IT ALL TOGETHER

Do you know how much pressure I put on myself to make A give me B? So much pressure that my health, both physical and mental, was pushed to the limit. Crabb has it right. Linear thinking can't be supported in a person's life in the long run. Why? The pressure's too great. According to Crabb, there is a better way. I believe that way is what makes us able to live life like a victor and not be so victimized when our A doesn't lead to B.

Here's what is going to happen if you make the five characteristics of a victor your A to get you to the B of living the life of a victor. You are going to have a mindset of what a victor looks like. Victory is going to be a part of that definition. It is just our natural way to do whatever it takes to make victory (a good life) part of what victor living should look like.

With your B defined, you will set goals and change habits to make the five characteristics more and more a part of your life. Don't get me wrong, great things will happen if you incorporate these characteristics of victor living into your life. But what I'm saying is that eventually your definition of what victorious living is supposed to look like will miss the mark. A hiccup will occur that will make you either doubt the characteristics or, worse than that, doubt yourself. That's when the pressure is really turned up to an unbearable level.

Formulas that show any sign of not doing what we intended for them to do either make us double down on our efforts or make us give up altogether. That's why I have been so careful to not make this book about the steps you need to apply in order to live the life of a victor. I just don't want you to make the mistake of taking some valuable information and turning it into an "if I do A I will get B" kind of existence. You were made for so much more than that.

I realize that life would be so much better if A always brought about B. I'm so happy for those people whose A's are making their B's come to fruition. I just know that it will not always be the case for these people. And when B doesn't happen, the door is opened up for victim thinking to take control.

My encouragement to you is this: don't make this book about formulas. Of course do an evaluation and see if you are doing things to make these characteristics part of your everyday life. But don't give into the temptation to let your definition of victorious living be what defines how you are living your life as a victor. If you do, you, too, will be in a place of profound disappointment at some time in your life. That disappointment will eventually make it harder and harder to live like the victor I have described in this book.

WHOSE DREAM ARE YOU CHASING?

I came across this fictional story in a *Reader's Digest* years ago. I so relate to this man's plight that I want to share it with you. As the story goes, there was a man who found himself on his death bed way before his time. What was killing him? It wasn't cancer or some other horrible ailment. It was a disease of the heart that is so hard to cure when it has set itself in so fully.

You see, this man had dreams that defined what he thought a good life looked like. As a young man, he dreamed of marrying the blond captain of the cheerleading squad and having three good looking, strong, enterprising sons that would take over the long-lasting and profitable business this man dreamed he would develop.

The legacy this man saw in his life was something that hinged on a level of success that would require dedication, ability and a bit of luck. This man thought these things would come his way if he did all the things he was trained to do and did his best to do them right. The man was banking on A always leading to B when it came to his dreams.

As the years passed, the man didn't end up marrying the blond cheerleading captain. Instead, he married a wonderful woman who loved him so. Though she wasn't the bombshell he thought he would marry, the man realized that the beauty of this woman was more than just skin deep and he was okay with that.

Then children came: one daughter, then a second and finally a third. To top it off, the third daughter had a disability that required the entire family to sacrifice in ways that made it harder and harder for the man to be able to build that legacy of a business he thought he would always have.

It wasn't all of these apparent contradictions to his original dream that made the man feel like his life was so messed up. It was just that he was beginning to wonder what he had done wrong along the way to make his life so different than what he had always dreamt it would be.

As the decades came and went, a malaise permeated the man's soul. Though the love of his wife and daughters was unmistakable, the man couldn't shake the feeling that that love just wasn't enough. Resentment began to take hold of the man's heart. If only my life had been different. If I had taken more aggressive steps to marry that cheerleader, he thought to himself, maybe my life wouldn't be the way it is today.

It wasn't that the man's life was a failure. It just wasn't what he always thought it would be. His unrealized expectations were literally killing him.

As time went on, various physical symptoms started to plague the man. Aches and pains began to be there all the time. A tiredness crept into the man's life that he just couldn't shake. Though he tried remedy after remedy, nothing seemed to be able to rid the man of the feeling that his life was a waste; that his dreams were a complete charade. His physical ailments were but another sign his life had taken a bad turn at some point or another.

That tiredness started to impact the man's health in ways that brought great concern to him and his family. Finally, the man found himself in a hospital bed literally dying of a broken heart. Not broken because of a failed relationship, but broken because of the dreams that were never going to come about in the man's life. Victim thinking was literally killing this man.

As he lay there in bed, he cried out to God the question we all have when our expectations of what our good life is supposed to be aren't fully met. The man cried out, "Why? Why haven't you given me the dreams of my heart? Why haven't you been the power behind the dreams when you put the dreams there in the first place?"

In a moment of silence in that hospital bed, the man actually heard God respond. God opened the eyes of the man to the enormity of the plan that was at work in his life. God let the man see how the love of his wife had carried him and his family through thick and thin. God revealed the marvelous talents of the daughters He had given him. God opened his eyes to the fullness of their admiration for a father who had sacrificed so much for their well-being. God let the man see how his handicapped daughter had brought into his life a fullness that was so easily overlooked. God went on to show the man the impact his mildly successful business had had on the lives of people the man would probably never know. God let the man see what a victor he was in spite of the self-defined victimizing events that had such a grip on his heart

Though the man was deeply moved in a way that brought a great deal of healing to his physical body, the pain of the lost dreams still overwhelmed him and he cried to God, "Yes but what about my dreams?"

God responded with a simple and yet profound statement. God said, "I understand you had dreams for your life, but I, too, had dreams for you. My love for you is so great that I wanted the best for you and that's what I gave you. I gave you my dreams instead of yours because my dreams are so much better than yours."

As the story goes, something happened to the man's heart at that moment. When he realized that his life wasn't an example of failure but proof that a loving God provided the best for him a confidence overtook him in a way that literally turned him from the brink of death. The man begin to appreciate the dreams of God over his own expectations of what those dreams should look like. That shift in thinking took him from the bondage of victim thinking to the freedom of victor living. The same thing can happen to you and to me.

Victor living isn't about us GETTING what we think would be best for us to live the good life we chase so relentlessly. The victor's life is about LIVING the dream. Not our dream, but God's dream.

If this God is all-knowing and all-powerful and was willing to do anything to bring us into relationship with Him, doesn't it make sense that this same God would have dreams that are so much better for us than our dreams could ever be?

I'm not saying that God doesn't want us to have a good life. I'm simply saying that our definition of good might not always line up with what this life will bring our way. I believe victors have found a way to live their life in a manner that keeps their hands loosely fastened to the dream of what their life is "supposed to" look like. This way of living brings about a peace that is literally a healing balm to a hurting and discouraged heart.

I still have dreams in my life. Dreams of great impact and significance. But as I age, I am realizing that those dreams are less and less likely to materialize the way I thought they would. In the past this has devastated me. It made me feel like a failure, worthless, and a victim. So much so that I was easily able to victimize the people who are the central part of the dream God has dreamt for my life.

Victor living isn't about compromise. It isn't about trading one dream for a lessor dream. That's what victim thinking is all about. Victor living is about living life to the fullest. It's going after all that we have the drive and determination to go for. Not because we HAVE TO go for it in order to prove that we are victors. No, that kind of living is what leads to victim thinking. Victors go for all they can because there is a joy that comes with their actions. A joy that springs from the fact that victors are free and that freedom brings a peace that is truly beyond understanding.

THE MOTION PICTURE KIND OF LIFE

Remember that friend whose wife is battling breast cancer? He and I were able to grab breakfast and catch up recently. At that meeting we happened to discuss whether we see things in a "glass half empty" or "glass half full" kind of way. As I was beating myself up for being a "glass half empty" kind of guy, he made a statement that is simply profound. He said, "Maybe we need to look at it another way. Maybe we need to be looking at life as a motion picture and not a snapshot." He went on to explain what he meant but that.

As we all know, motion pictures are just what the name implies, many, many single images spliced together and ran at a speed that makes the still images look like they have motion. He said that if we just look at one image in a reel of a motion picture we are very likely to get the wrong impression of what is actually going on in the film.

Could it be that my feeling that I'm a glass half empty kind of person is just a snapshot of where I am at this very moment? What if God is in the process of filling my glass and all I'm seeing at this moment is the point where it is just halfway full? That's victor thinking if I have ever heard it.

My life isn't over yet. There are big things still to come. If I get stuck looking at an image that defines my life at this particular moment, I'm well on my way to staying in that place where I might fail to let the motion picture continue. Victim thinking does that for us. It stops the reel from moving and we get stuck in a single frame that we mistakenly think defines our life. That was what the man in that *Reader's Digest* story was doing. That kind of thinking almost took him to his death. Unfortunately, it has been the death of so many of those who have gone before us as well.

So, what's a person to do who wants to live life as a victor? I hate to make it this simple, but here it is: take your next breath. That's it! Take another step. Breathe another deep, lungful of air and let your body do what it does best—live!

Yes, your circumstances might be horrible at this moment. But this isn't where you are going to stay. Life is not a snapshot. It is a motion picture. Sometimes change in circumstance happens by just taking enough breaths to get us through where we are today and move us to where we are going in the future. Our job is to try and keep our expectation of where we want to be from being the driving force behind what makes us victors in the first place.

What are you going to choose today? Are you going to let the breaths you take today be what drives you towards a future that has been meticulously designed BY you to suit your every need? Or are you going to move in a direction where you keep open to the possibility that a far greater dream might be part of your destiny? A dream that you would never have dreamt possible? A dream that you might not have ever seen coming? A dream that, frankly, you might not have chosen in the first place? Those who want to live life as a victor, as described in this book, will choose the latter.

I don't know how many answers you have found in this book. I don't believe answers are the reason this book was written. It has been my hope that the journey I have shared in these chapters is one that you can relate to in your own life. The road you take and the road I'm on will never be completely the same. But as our paths cross, I'm hoping we will be in a position to share how our lives have been more and more defined by victor living.

I also hope that we see the places where our living like victors has rubbed off on others in ways that have set some people free. Now that's a dream we all can share and relish in. Take another breath and live! You were made to be a victor, and that is what you are!

ABOUT THE AUTHOR

John Hovis was born into a very middle class family from a small town called High Shoals, North Carolina. He spent his elementary school years in Merritt Island Florida, a town near the Kennedy Space Center. John and his family were privileged to see all but one of the Apollo moon rockets lift off from Cape Canaveral. John's Jr. and Sr. High School years were spent in North Babylon, NY. He attended College at Drexel University in Philadelphia, PA. There he received his BS degree in Mechanical Engineering.

In 1982 John moved to Southern California. After a short stint in the LA area, he moved to Carlsbad, CA, near San Diego. John is married to Barbara Williams. They met in college and were married in 1986. Together, along with another partner, Gloria Foote, they have built a successful Financial Planning and Investment Advisory firm called Financial Focus. John and Barbara have two amazing children, Jesslan Urquhart and Jay Hovis.

John has had the honor to serve at his local church, Coastline Church, in many capacities. Over the years his desire to counsel people has been augmented by studying and applying the techniques learned through various on-line and print resources. He has discovered that the kind of counseling he was attracted to wasn't about fixing anyone's problems, rather it was about discovering God in the middle of the challenges that people faced. John has said many times that he can't even fix his own problems, why would he ever think he could fix someone else's?

This is John's first attempt at writing a book of any kind. The thoughts presented within are a result of many, many conversations with others, a lot of personal soul searching and deep study into God's Holy Word. Please don't think John believes that he has life all figured out or that he is an authority on any subject presented in this book. If you disagree with any of his findings or theories, John will be the first to say you might just be right in your thinking. The thoughts presented in this book are a result of a journey that has opened his eyes to some interesting possibilities about his relationship with God and with others that has stood the test of time in his life.

John is an avid auto enthusiast. His daily driver is a restomodded 1966 Ford Galaxie. He also has a 1965 F100 pickup truck and is currently working on modifying and restoring a 1972 DeTomaso Pantera. He also enjoys working on any creation that has to do with wood, metal and/or stone and uses his "free time" to create industrial styled pieces of furniture that a friend sells in the San Diego area.

It can't be said enough: John isn't a victor because he has some nice cars, is part of a nice business or has a nice family. He is a victor because God paid a big price to make his identity as God's Child secure. John hopes you find the kind of peace this truth has brought to his life as you live out your life as a VICTOR!

ADDITIONAL RESOURCES

Join the conversation about Victor Living. Like our Facebook page and share your victor living stories. Post your thoughts at:

www.facebook.com/VictorLivingNow

Please be sure to use the hashtag #victorlivingnow for photos or stories you choose to share. Follow us on Instagram @victorlivingnow.

Please visit www.victorliving.com. There you will find additional resources to help you join the victor living conversation. Thanks for going on the journey with us!

Feel free to email the author directly at johnhovis@victorliving.com.

www.ingramcontent.com/pod-product-compliance
Lightning Source LLC
Chambersburg PA
CBHW061633040426
42446CB00010B/1402